UNDER THE HORNBEAMS

EMMA TARLO

UNDER THE HORNBEAMS

A True Story of Life in the Open

faber

First published in the UK and USA in 2024
by Faber & Faber Limited
The Bindery, 51 Hatton Garden
London EC1N 8HN

Typeset by Faber & Faber Limited
Printed and bound by CPI Group (UK) Ltd, Croydon, CR0 4YY

*This is a work of non-fiction. Individual names and potentially
identifying details have been altered in certain cases, and some
incidents and accounts are composites*

A CIP record for this book
is available from the British Library

ISBN 978–0–571–37980–4

MIX
Paper | Supporting
responsible forestry
FSC® C171272

Printed and bound in the UK on FSC® certified paper in line with our continuing
commitment to ethical business practices, sustainability and the environment.
For further information see faber.co.uk/environmental-policy

2 4 6 8 10 9 7 5 3 1

For Nick, Pascal, Bachi and Lizzie

Contents

1 Circulation

I am not sure where our story begins or at what moment it became a story. Was it built through springtime conversations in the long grass of the park, against the creeping tide of social distance? Or through standing in the mud under dripping trees in the persistent autumn rain? Did it grow out of the dreamy November fog or through sitting in reverent silence on moonlit winter nights, observed only by a passing fox? Was it about our daily sharing of these moments that seemed to expand space and stop time or about the brutal point of rupture when established routines were shattered? Perhaps it was all of these things.

'The Professor and the Tramp!' Nick announces one day, early in our acquaintance, as if suggesting a title for a West End play.

'I don't like labels,' I respond.

'You're right. You are Emma first and a professor later.'

'And you are a person first, not a tramp.'

The putative title may have had a good ring to it, but it obscured far more than it revealed. I think we both knew that even then. What linked us was not our distance but our connection. A connection we were forging in food, ideas and conversation under the open sky.

I suppose you could say it began with a meeting. An intro-duction of sorts. A friend who circuits Regent's Park with his dogs each morning had long ago mentioned that there were two men living under the trees in a secluded corner of the park. They had been living there for years, he said. They didn't consider themselves homeless but they didn't have any shelter either. This friend would often converse with the more extrovert of the two, Nick, and would sometimes drop off bananas, tangerines or slices of home-made bread.

'But presumably they've got a tent?' I asked, predictably.

'No.'

'So what do they do in the rain?'

'They stand under umbrellas.'

'But what about in winter? When it snows?' I persisted.

'They're there all year round. They stay in their sleeping bags when it's very cold and have tarpaulins to lie on.'

I admit I was intrigued by the idea of these two men living in the open air in one of London's Royal Parks, but not quite curious enough to go in search of them. Although my home was only a short stroll from the park, I had never strayed down the mud track leading to the quieter, wilder north-west edge that they inhabited, an area frequented mainly by joggers, dog walkers and birdwatchers, categories to which I did not belong.

I used the park mainly as a place of transit – a shortcut for getting to the tennis courts or the city centre, or to my favourite tranquil spot, a place known to locals as 'the Secret Garden', as if by calling it that it will continue to live up to the name. I was often on my bicycle when I crossed the park, which meant sticking to the main drag – the Broad Walk – lined with dignified acers, chestnut and plane trees that offered formality and grandeur. I had never come across these two men, Nick and Pascal, who were somehow living wild in one of the most cultivated parks of the capital.

Even so, sometimes, on stormy nights as I lie awake listening to the rain thrashing against my ill-fitting windows, I find myself thinking about them. Who are they? How are they managing right now? How did they come to be living this way?

Then lockdown is announced. Suddenly we are only permitted out of the house for one hour a day. Instead of nipping first thing to my local cafe or plunging into the Underground to get to the university where I teach, I find myself, like everyone else, localised and grounded. I develop a new routine of heading into the park or along the Regent's Canal as soon as I wake up, to enjoy the bright spring mornings before the crowds appear. Sometimes I am with my husband, Denis, but often I am alone. I begin to explore different areas of the park and become more attentive to its morphology and sounds. Two weeks in, at 7 a.m. on one of my daily walks, I bump into my friend – in so far as you can bump at a social distance – who is out with his dogs.

The dogs have no respect for the two-metre rule, and as they sniff and paw me I find myself asking: 'Those men you mentioned, who live under the trees . . . Where exactly are they?'

Without hesitation and before I have time to consider whether or not it is a good idea, he says, 'Come, I'll introduce you.'

I am led down a back route through a tangle of trees and long grasses, under a stream of faded Tibetan flags someone has left hanging in the tall branches, through a wooded passage, until we emerge in a leafy glen of chestnut and hornbeam trees vibrant with new leaf.

Lying flat on his back in a battered sleeping bag, so weathered that it looks more vegetable than mineral, is Pascal. His dark hair is wayward at the sides, his face thin, his brown eyes lively as they turn towards me. We are introduced and told we have French in common, but Pascal says he prefers to speak English. He has a pointed chin flanked by two six-inch dreadlocked spooks of beard hair which bob up and down as he speaks. He remains lying flat, his head just slightly raised in a position that to me looks uncomfortable. His voice is unusually quiet and hesitant, his expression friendly but shy. I feel excruciating embarrassment – as if we have barged straight into his bedroom and drawn back his private curtain of trees. I cannot wait to get away. He gestures to where we might find Nick, whose sleeping bag lies like an empty shell on the ground beside him.

We pass through a narrow passage of hawthorn and bramble. And there he is, seated on a bench in the sunshine, his legs elegantly crossed, cheeks flushed, long frizzled beard glowing silver and pale auburn in the morning light. He is reading *Private Eye*. He looks the epitome of good health and good humour, like a character from a Thomas Hardy novel without the gloom. Branches of hawthorn rigid with white blossom glow around his seat, creating a magnificent natural throne. If

4

Pascal is in his leafy private bedchamber, Nick is in his salon, ready to receive guests, or so it feels. I am introduced by my friend, but he is distracted by a phone call and wanders off. I find myself alone with Nick, wondering what we might talk about. Nick takes the lead.

'The other day your friend left us home-made bread with butter and jam, but I was busy in conversation, so the dogs and birds got to them first. Now, tell me, Emma: do you think that food was wasted?'

It is a playful question, but I can't help feeling it is also a challenge – a way of sussing me out. I can feel his laughing eyes fixed upon me. I hesitate.

'No,' I say. 'We all need to eat, whether birds, animals or humans.'

I get the impression he approves.

Soon he is asking me about the pandemic. He has noticed from his observations of behaviour in the park and through conversations with regulars that many people are extremely anxious and fearful but that everyone seems to be living it differently. How do I feel?

'Mostly relief,' I say, without hesitation now. 'Relief that my mother died just in time – before this whole thing started. Relief that she had a good death, if that makes sense.'

Nick's quizzical expression encourages me to go on.

'I didn't know what a "good death" was until then. But my sisters and I were able to be with her for the last twelve days of her life. We got her out of hospital and looked after her at home with the help of her carer. We could hold her hands, hug

5

her, feed her, accompany her to the end of her life. She died peacefully in her own bed and it all felt quite natural.'

I don't really know why I'm telling him all of this except that it is true and he seems like someone you would tell the truth to. And perhaps I also want our conversation to be real.

'We were able to give her a proper funeral just before Christmas,' I continue, 'one that she would have appreciated if she'd been there to see it. I just keep thinking how glad I am that she got out in time and didn't have to experience the horror of isolation that many old people are going through right now. She had Alzheimer's and wouldn't have understood what was going on. She would have felt abandoned and disoriented.'

'I'm very sorry about the loss of your mother,' Nick responds. 'You must still be grieving. But how wonderful that you could be with her. I wasn't there when my mother died, but I went to the funeral and I sat with her, beside the coffin, for some hours. I was able to thank her for all she'd done. It was important. People fear death,' he adds, 'but it really isn't something to be afraid of. It's a natural part of life, something we should embrace. I hope when the time comes I will greet death smiling.'

And so we talk about death and mothers and about the importance of being physically present. You could say that we had broken the ice except that there didn't seem to be much to break.

At some point in the conversation I ask how they are managing for food.

'We manage,' Nick says, not dismissively but as if such a question isn't particularly relevant. 'People are kind,' he adds. 'They bring us things. They get something out of it because they feel good about giving, and it's good for us as we get to eat the food.'

I like this comment, with its recognition of how givers are also receivers and receivers also givers: how this is not about needy victims and virtuous benefactors but about relationships of exchange. Here is someone who appears to have nothing in material terms but who seems to glow with an extraordinary sense of well-being. This is quite unlike the well-being advertised in management-speak, where it features as some goal that has to be worked at in one-hour lunchtime sessions but remains forever out of reach. Here is a genuine appreciator of life.

* * *

The next day, instead of continuing on my favourite path along the Regent's Canal, where I enjoy photographing the dancing reflections of trees in rippled water, I find myself coming off at what I later learn is Bridge 10. (I had never noticed before that the bridges had numbers.) I enter the park under the canopy of two tall plane trees hung with nubbly round fruit. There are paved footpaths here but instead I turn right along a mud track which takes me under giant twisted oak trees, past the bird sanctuary and along the narrow pathway of hawthorn and bramble. If my memory serves me right, this is the same path I took yesterday but in the opposite direction.

Coming out at the other side of this passage – 'a passage into a secret world', as Nick later describes it and as I come to live it – I am greeted by crab apple trees bowed down with abundant pink-white blossom and then a sense of space opening up. The long grass is laced with cow parsley at the edges, the tangle of trees to the far side create an impression of forest, and the generous copper beech glows purply-red in the distance. I feel as if I have wandered out of a London park into Alice's Wonderland.

Opposite the crab apple trees, secluded under a large chestnut and hornbeam, are Nick and Pascal's sleeping bags, one inhabited, one not. They are placed some way apart, with a few bagged possessions in between. At the time I assume this is their way of maintaining personal space, but I later learn that the distance is exactly two metres, in conformity with new government guidance on social distancing. I am walking past their domain. I'm not sure if we will converse again – and, if we do, what we will say – but I do glance in their direction half hoping, though not in any way expecting, that they will remember me and want to talk. Nick is bent over some tarpaulins, busy sorting through a small bundle of stuff, some of which has got wet in the unanticipated morning rain. He straightens his back and takes a few steps towards me.

'It's Emma, isn't it?'

Pascal remains in a horizontal position but gives me a small wave and a smile of recognition. I later come to realise that this is his usual position – lying flat, observing and from time to time waving at passers-by, and communicating the names of dogs and humans to Nick, whose eyesight is less sharp.

But on the rare occasions that he does stand up, Pascal cuts a distinctive figure, not only because he is tall and thin with striking features but also because his hair has matted into a thick felt which extends the full length of his back until it splits into a few thick locks tied together into a great knot just above the ankle. When he walks, taking long springy strides, the hair sways like a giant tail with a large boot on the end. Without the knot it would be sweeping the leaves. When he stands still it takes on the appearance of an extra leg.

'Pascal is rooting himself back into the ground,' Nick observes one day.

Pascal's explanation is simpler. 'It just started growing this way so I thought: why not leave it?'

'How long ago was that?' I ask.

'Ten years, I think. Perhaps more. Could be thirteen.'

Conversations with Pascal are sparse in words. Often wordless. When he does speak, his voice bears the slight trace of a French accent which is as gentle and discreet as the man himself. 'Quietist' is the word Nick uses to describe him.

By contrast, words flow liberally from Nick, whose voice has a lyrical, almost hypnotic quality and an accent I am never able to identify, although there are hints of Scouse in it. Discussions with him are fast-paced and intellectually challenging, full of unexpected twists and turns, and, above all, wide-ranging. On this, our second meeting, within the space of an hour – or maybe it is really three – we seem to hop effortlessly from Judaism, Christianity and the Bhagavad Gita to Theodor Adorno, Walter Benjamin and Marcel Proust, with a bit of Van Morrison in between. Am I familiar with the song 'In the Garden', he asks? It is one of his favourites. I tell him I will take a listen.

'I am not a religious man,' he tells me, 'but religions teach us imagination. They are all about awe.' This is a perspective I discuss in the anthropology lectures I am giving at the university and I share this fact with Nick. It is a view of religion that offers the possibility of both distance and appreciation – far more subtle and enriching than the dismissive inflexibility of new atheist perspectives.

Our conversation bounds seamlessly from the nature of religious experience to the perils of conspiracy theories, the limits and potential of robots, the tyranny of the class system and the importance of connecting with humans and with nature.

'Here we get the sun as it rises in the east, moves overhead during the day and sets here in the west, and these trees offer protection in the rain,' he says, explaining their choice of location. 'Returning to the awe we experienced when we were very young. That is what is important.'

I am aware that the government has recently announced an 'Everyone In' policy which includes providing accommodation to rough sleepers, who have been identified as particularly vulnerable during the pandemic. Hotels, hostels and student halls of residence are all being co-opted for this purpose and homeless charities are perceiving it as a watershed moment. I sense that Nick and Pascal might not find such offers appealing and ask if anyone has been round trying to get them into accommodation since the lockdown started.

'They've been round a few times,' Nick says. 'But I think they get it. I'm not homeless: this is my home!'

He points to the branches of the hornbeam under which we are standing, its leaves still glistening in the aftermath of the morning rain. On one of the lower branches sits a robin, listening and, from time to time, joining our conversation. It seems to be saying: Why should anyone want to leave this place?

As we speak, I am conscious that at home I have a large vat of spicy butternut squash soup simmering. Like many people newly confined to their homes, I am spending more and more time in the kitchen cooking things I wouldn't normally make. There is a cold nip in the air and I can't help thinking that, if I were outside, what I would really relish would be a mug of hot soup.

'I'm going home to have some soup for lunch that I've left cooking. I'd be happy to bring some down later if you'd like?' I suggest.

'That sounds good,' Nick says. Pascal nods.

As soon as I make this offer I realise that I don't have anything to put the soup in and explain as much. Pascal starts rummaging in a bag behind him and produces two flasks.

'Are those Jim's?' Nick asks.

'This one is but not this,' says Pascal, distinguishing between what look to me like two identical aluminium flasks. He selects the one that is not Jim's and hands it to me. Later I learn that Jim has two flasks that they plant in an allotted spot down by the canal every night and which he duly fills in the early hours with hot coffee or boiling water. Jim is employed as the canal sweeper. He is a small man of Caribbean origin who often looks preoccupied and rarely replies when I say hello to him on my early-morning walks along the towpath. With Nick and Pascal he sometimes converses and sometimes maintains silence. But this man has been faithfully filling up flasks for Nick and Pascal for several years. No one seems to know how many.

'Whenever you have time. It's greatly appreciated,' Nick says politely as Pascal hands me the flask.

And so I find myself walking home with one of the few objects they possess. This feels strange. I am struck by the trust it implies and also by the responsibility. I place it in my kitchen sink and give it a rapid but thorough wash. It is only as I do so that I remember that in these Covid times we aren't supposed to be touching each other's things. Cafes that are still open for takeaways are no longer willing to fill their customers' reusable cups and have retreated back to single-use paper and plastics. Whole articles in the press are devoted to how long the virus can survive on different materials. Metal seems to come out particularly badly. We are advised not to touch doorknobs and to slather our hands in gel whenever we return home. Some people have even taken to wearing plastic gloves for walking in the park. This probably isn't the time to be handling the flasks of strangers.

On the other hand, living as they do under the trees, Nick and Pascal seem unlikely to have been exposed to Covid. The risk is all in the other direction. What if I am carrying the virus unknowingly? What if I pass it to them via the flask? But it seems too late for such reservations. Now that I have taken it home it is my duty to return it filled. Nonetheless its presence, sitting expectantly by the kitchen sink, feels vaguely subversive.

I glance at it as I sit down to eat bread and soup with my husband and son. Denis, who is French and also an anthropologist, usually works in Paris on weekdays, but he managed to escape to London on the day the lockdown took effect there in order to be with his family. My son, Julius, would normally be about to return to university in Oxford, but there is little prospect of that in these strange times. And so the three of us are developing new habits – sitting together eating lunch in the middle of the working day when we would ordinarily be dispersed. I have adorned the soup with roasted salted squash seeds and fragments of crispy bacon, which make it look like a dish that might be served in a restaurant. Shall I take these accoutrements to the park too, I wonder? I decide against it. It seems pretentious.

As we enjoy our meal I tell Denis and Julius about my meeting with Nick and Pascal. They listen with surprise and interest and approve of the idea of sharing the soup.

It is a few hours before I return to the park with the flask newly filled and two slices of home-made apricot and almond cake wrapped in silver foil. Pascal is alone.

'That was quick!' he comments with a smile.

At the time I think that perhaps he is being sarcastic, that perhaps they expected me to return straight away. Later I realise that when people say they will bring some food down to the park it often does not appear until several days or weeks later. Sometimes months or even years.

Pascal takes the flask with a friendly nod. As he half sits up to receive it we exchange a few words, then I head home. And perhaps that is where the story really begins – with my participation in the movement of flasks in and out of the park, a movement that pre-dates me but in which I become intimately involved. The flask acts as a passport into their world, a currency of sorts.

* * *

'I've come bearing gifts,' Bachi announces the first time I meet him. It must be my fifth or sixth visit. Bachi is ambling towards Nick and Pascal, trailing behind his much-loved dog, Lizzie – a Ridgeback–Staffy cross, I'm told. She makes an immediate beeline for Nick.

'Ah, Lizzie!' he exclaims, welcoming her with gestures of affection. Lizzie wags her tail. The pleasure is clearly mutual.

It is the first time I have visited Nick and Pascal's grove in the late afternoon. It is the end of a warm but overcast day and the air is thick with the scent of cow parsley. The tall white flowers of the chestnut tree glow like magic lanterns, reminding me of an outdoor production of *A Midsummer Night's Dream* I saw as a child. I offer some date and walnut slice still warm from the tin – a recipe my best friend's mother used to greet us with when we were kids emerging freezing and hungry from an unheated outdoor swimming pool. Nick tells me they really enjoyed the soup the other day and thanks me for the cake.

'Bless your heart,' he says warmly. 'I could live off nuts and honey, olive oil and bread.'

It is clear as soon as Lizzie and Bachi appear that they are regular visitors. Later I come to learn that Bachi does a weekly online shop for Nick and Pascal, consulting them on its contents in advance. In summer it contains plenty of fruit, yoghurt, bread and cereal bars; in winter it includes instant porridge and Pot Noodles. I also learn that Bachi and Lizzie stop by every evening. Giving food and flasks of freshly boiled water is part of Bachi's relationship with Nick and Pascal, but it is clearly only one aspect. Hanging out with them in the fading light, discussing the latest political shenanigans, reminiscing about songs and films, sharing personal news and, above all, playing with Lizzie are all other factors that draw them together.

Lizzie comes towards me and wags her tail.

'She can't really see you properly: she's lost eighty per cent of her eyesight,' Bachi explains. 'She used to be used as bait in fighting. When I got her she was terrified of other dogs and wary of humans, but now she's friends with every dog in the park,' he says proudly. 'But this is where she is most relaxed – with Nick and Pascal.'

As I pat Lizzie, I confess to Bachi that I am more of a cat person than a dog person. But she seems to accept me in spite of this, judging by her tail movements and the way she is licking my hand.

Bachi remains standing some way off at the fringes of the overhanging trees. He is scrupulous about maintaining social distance. He places his bag of food on the ground for Nick and Pascal to collect rather than handing it directly to them. He is volunteering for the NHS, delivering medical supplies and pieces of equipment across London at different times of the day and night at this critical moment when Covid cases are rising and hospitals are finding it difficult to cope.

'The NHS saved my leg,' he tells me, 'so this is my way of giving something in return.'

Six months ago, Bachi was knocked down by a cyclist who was riding illegally on one of the side paths of the park. He had been worried for Lizzie, owing to her blindness, so to protect her he got run over in her place. It was a gesture that cost him dearly. He spent several months in a wheelchair, endured numerous operations and now has three metal plates in his leg and a permanent limp. But Lizzie was protected. That mattered more. To know this story is to begin to understand the strength of Bachi's love of Lizzie.

Bachi exudes kindness, quick wit and good humour – a combination that reminds me of my father – but he also exudes a strong sense of privacy and guardedness. He looks to be somewhere in his late forties or early fifties, with Indian features, sharp eyes, spectacles and grey-black hair. Tonight he gets out his iPhone – as I learn he often does – and plays us (at a distance) a 2016 cover version of 'The Sound of Silence' that he says he likes. The lions of London Zoo roar persistently from their corner of the park. Are they, like me, pining for the original version?

Nick listens very attentively until the song comes to an end.

'I always liked the Paul Simon version myself,' he concludes, 'but I suppose that's what I'm familiar with. You'd have to listen to this a few times to get used to it. But, then again, it's not just about who was singing but how you related to the music at the time when you heard it. It's linked to a certain moment of your life.'

Proust's madeleines immediately spring to mind but so too does the teenage excitement of feeling in love with Paul Simon – the short dark one rather than the tall slim blond one my best friend was attracted to.

Nick produces a large fancy tray of Persian pistachio nut sweets.

'Would you like one of these?' he asks. 'They were given to me by Mariam. She's a very nice Iranian woman who sometimes comes down. Someone gave them to her but she didn't want them so she brought them here. They were a bit dry but I left them out in the sun during the day and it's softened them up. They're quite nice.'

Bachi immediately turns his head. 'It would kill me if I ate one of those – literally. I'm seriously allergic to nuts, which is particularly lethal when attending Indian weddings!'

Having lived in India in the 1980s, and attended many weddings there, I sympathise with the awkwardness of this predicament. Nick is now holding the tray out in front of me. I hesitate, then take one – not because I want to eat it particularly but because I want to accept his hospitality and I sense he will recognise that.

'Have you listened to Van Morrison's "In the Garden" yet?' Nick asks me.

'Yes, I listened to it in the bath several times,' I tell him. 'I like it.'

'Good,' he concludes. 'And that's a good, relaxing place to listen.'

And so we casually pass the early evening together – Nick, Pascal, Lizzie, Bachi and me. It feels as if Nick and Pascal are hosting an impromptu soirée in a spacious and magnificently decorated living room filled with glistening light and birdsong. We talk music, dogs, foxes and trees. Nick recalls how he once saw a kestrel plunge feet first through the hornbeam, and describes how he and Pascal used to feed the foxes until there were five of them lined up expectantly every morning – then they decided maybe it wasn't such a good idea. 'I once woke up to find my hand warm and wet and then realised it was inside a fox's mouth,' he tells us.

As we chat, Lizzie moves about between us, sometimes receiving treats from Bachi, getting petted by Nick or licking Pascal's face and my hands. Pascal as ever remains lying flat. The whole scene feels curiously idyllic if somewhat clandestine at a time when opportunities for casual socialising have been curtailed. At seven forty Bachi announces he has to head back to be home in time to clap for the NHS. So our soirée comes to an abrupt end, except that it is really only just another beginning.

* * *

Entering Nick and Pascal's world is not about doing good but about the unspoken pleasure of simply being there. It is a pleasure magnified by the peculiarity of the times. Not just the magnificence of the unfurling spring but also the suffocating nature of lockdown, which seems to reverse the normal order of things. Suddenly a house feels like a restrictive device, the walls a straitjacket of bricks and mortar, the windows something to gaze through at a world that is becoming increasingly difficult to access. Lockdown means feeling locked up. Being outside, the opposite.

But when you do get outside for your allotted hour it often feels more like being let out on parole. My sister, incarcerated in a first-floor flat in Brighton without outdoor space, finds herself moved on by the police for sitting in a deserted spot reading a book. The benches of Regent's Park are physically cordoned off with ropes to prevent unnecessary lingering. Suddenly our participation in the outside world has become conditional on our being able to demonstrate that we are taking exercise and keeping fit rather than relaxing or simply enjoying the beauty of the day. Just at the very moment when people are tuning in anew to the appeal of birdsong and the delights of cherry blossom, they are told to get their trainers on and move along.

I find myself feeling guilty for stopping for a few seconds on the canal path to record birdsong or take photographs of the hawthorn blossom, half expecting someone to tell me that such loitering is unnecessary, forbidden. Under such conditions people are marching determinedly around the park at an unnatural pace; many have donned sports clothes and taken up jogging, others can be seen contorting their bodies into curious workouts, while the volume of cyclists whizzing around the Inner and Outer Circles has swelled to a swarm.

We may know this is all for the collective good, but that does not stop it feeling like a form of denial. We find ourselves deprived of the very fabric of our social life. The population has divided into those on the 'front line', hurled into a frenzy of physical interaction, and those pushed further and further into the interiority of their rooms, spending days contained not only by the four walls of their homes but also by the parameters of their computers. I am one of the latter.

The distance I have always strived to preserve between the type of work I do in my office at the university and what I do at home has collapsed. The university has come crashing into every room of my house without any respect for the notion of a working day. I find myself entrapped in a variety of digital formats – Microsoft Teams, Zoom and Skype meetings during the day, WhatsApps, text messages and emergency phone calls before and after the boundary of what that 'working day' might once have been.

At the university there is much that needs doing and all of it seems to need doing now, if not yesterday. Students are desperately in need of support; many of their assignments have to be redesigned; deadlines and modes of assessment have to be not only altered but passed through Kafkaesque layers of official approval; unfamiliar technologies need to be mastered and new techniques of teaching invented overnight – and all of this against a turbulent background of government cuts, uncertain recruitment figures, a spiralling deficit, unpopular restructuring initiatives from senior management and proposals for industrial action from the college union of which I am a member.

The more oppressive and constricting all of this feels, the more visiting Nick and Pascal feels like an escape. I can't help recognising a certain freedom in their way of life, in spite of the inevitable discipline and hardship it entails. Their day unfolds under a pink-rippled sky, serenaded by blackbirds, robins, magpies and crows, whose impromptu chorus mingles with the sounds of the other non-human inhabitants of the park – the familiar roar of the lions, the squawk of the hyacinth macaws and the distinctive call of the white-cheeked gibbons warming up their vocal cords before performing an extravagant fluted duet. Unlike these incarcerated creatures, Nick and Pascal are able to move about. As the sun rises they emerge from under the shelter of the branches of hornbeam and chestnut, stretching out their tarpaulins in the open to evaporate the morning dew from their sleeping bags and catch the sun on their faces and hands. As darkness descends they position their bedding back under the trees, watching the moon rise and listening to the gradual diminution of birdsong. To spend time with them is to enter a space apart, a meeting point where animals, plants, birds and humans converge and get on with the basic act of living, far removed from the digital warfare of work.

Some mornings Nick can be seen far off – a distant figure strolling in pensive mood, his head bent forward, his arms hanging loose from his shoulders, his voluminous beard catching the morning sunlight. Sometimes he is simply walking and thinking; at other times he is collecting litter using a metal stick with a pincered end – ideal for gathering up loo paper, which has begun to litter the more secluded corners of the park following the closure of the toilet facilities during lockdown. Dressed in mossy greens and greys, he blends in with the grasses and bramble. (Later, when I know him better, I take a photograph of him on his morning stroll. When I show it to him he inspects it closely, then concludes: 'Hmm. Ape!')

Nick tells me that he loves all the seasons, even when the weather is at its most extreme. 'When we had an incredible storm here, branches were coming down from the trees and this whole paddock glowed the most amazing antique gold. I was scared of the storm but attracted to it also. Its energy. Its rawness. So I went out and stood in the middle of it. If I ever begin to feel sorry for myself, I just think of the fox out in all weathers. We have a lot to learn from animals.'

Pleasure in being part of the animal kingdom is something Nick and Pascal share. They make sure that the natural bowl formed by the contorted roots of the hornbeam tree is always filled with water for passing dogs. Whatever they eat, they share with the birds. The robins are so familiar with them that it is not uncommon to see them perching on top of Pascal's boots or on a flask lid. From there they take their chances, flying between the two men to get their breakfast and sometimes even stopping off on their sleeping bags, relaxed in their calm presence. The magpies, jays and crows are a little more wary but nonetheless hang around, knowing where food might be forthcoming. Squirrels and tiny brown field mice are also regular companions. They rely on Nick and Pascal without being dependent on them, just as Nick and Pascal appear to rely on other humans without ever asking for food or being unduly perturbed if it doesn't appear.

But while there is a certain freedom to Nick and Pascal's existence in the park, this doesn't mean it is without structure. The more I visit at different times of day, the more I realise that their life has a rhythm. Nick rises early, around 5 a.m., to complete what he calls his 'ablutions'. He and Pascal often watch the breaking dawn as the sun rises like an orange fireball from behind the BT Tower in the distance, until it shines golden yellow from above the shimmering copper beech directly opposite. Nick collects the flasks of coffee and hot water from down by the canal. Pascal often goes to a building known as The Hub, which has sports and washing facilities, to collect supplies of cold water. Nick usually takes his morning stroll and collects rubbish, which he deposits in the park bins. By 8 a.m. they are installed back in their sleeping bags, breakfasting in the morning sun, with crows and robins hovering beside them. In Nick's case, his breakfast is accompanied by a slim hand-rolled cigarette.

After this, Nick often goes to what I call his study: a hornbeam tree set further back and not visible to passers-by. I first see him there one day when I come to deliver some bananas and collect the empty flask, ready to fill it with chicken soup still cooking on the hob at home. At first I think Pascal is alone amongst the cow parsley and alkanet but he gestures to a tree further into the undergrowth. And there is Nick, facing away from the park, his back against the trunk of the tree. His lower half is tucked into his sage-green sleeping bag and his top half is wrapped in a colourful hand-knitted stripy blanket. On his nose he wears reading specs. He looks part caterpillar, part human, like a giant insect out of Roald Dahl's *James and the Giant Peach*. On either side of him are piles of books and papers, and he is concentrated on the act of reading. I hesitate, not wanting to disturb him, but he welcomes me to join him and indicates a log where I can sit if I'm not rushing off. I am. But I don't.

'What are you reading?' I ask.

'*Germany: Memories of a Nation* by Neil MacGregor,' he replies. 'It's brilliant!'

The book is battered and damp but its pages are annotated with densely written comments and underlinings in blue biro. It is clear that Nick's reading is simultaneously an act of think-ing and of writing. I am struck by his thirst and enthusiasm to engage with the details of this weighty volume. He shows me some geometric drawings he is making in coloured biros, telling me they are about conceptions of time. Pages and pages of complex configurations. He is working on one inspired by Albrecht Dürer's *Melencolia*, with the angel fallen to the earth.

'I didn't learn anything at school,' he tells me. 'I failed all my exams. My mind was on other things.' I don't ask what those other things were but sense they are significant. 'I'm not an educated man, but I make sure that I'm not wilfully ignorant.'

The evidence of this is all around him. We talk about how education might take different forms and I say a bit about my work as an anthropologist, how it is really about taking an interest in people and their lives.

'Anthropology is about questioning the embedded assumptions that have become so familiar that they take on an aura of normality,' I tell him. 'If we pay attention to different ways of living it helps us question those norms. You may not have had a formal training but you are questioning those norms through how you live and you are constantly observing people here and interacting with them. I think in many ways you are an anthropologist of the park.'

Nick thinks this over. As far as I can tell he doesn't disagree. I make a mental note to give him a copy of one of the books I have written. I am aware of how pompous and alienating the term 'anthropologist' might sound and I want to demystify both it and myself.

When I return with chicken soup that evening, Lizzie and Bachi greet me warmly. I can sense something of a ritual beginning to form.

But patterns can also be broken.

The day after, it rains solidly all day and night and into the following morning. Sitting at home working long hours, I wonder about my friends in the park. It is a different kind of wondering than before, for now it is replete with detail. Where exactly do they lodge their sleeping bags to keep them dry? Do they manage to get any rest? What trees do they shelter under? What has happened to Nick's books and his amazing makeshift study? And then a new thought enters my head. Surely they could do with something more substantial than soup after a day and night of relentless rain?

I go to the kitchen cupboard and find a jar of dried lentils which I put to soak and then on to boil. I soon find myself frying onions, crushing garlic, grinding coriander and other spices, adding ginger and tomatoes and throwing the whole lot together into the pot of simmering lentils.

But how will I carry it to the park? A dislike of plastic means that I don't have any Tupperware and the dhal is too thick to put in the flask, which is still with Nick and Pascal in the park in any case.

'Didn't we bring one of those tiffin boxes back from India?' Denis asks.

In India tiffin boxes are a staple means of transporting food back and forth between homes, restaurant kitchens and work-places. Do we have one? If so, I certainly haven't used it since we returned from Delhi, where we lived for three years in the 1990s. I go into the spare room and start rooting around under the bed – a last resort for objects that have come to attain that ambiguous status between treasure and junk. Lo and behold, a tiffin box emerges, powdered with two decades of dust.

In Mumbai an intricate system exists whereby some 200,000 tiffin boxes – many of them filled with home-cooked food – are distributed on a daily basis to individual workers across the city. An ingenious array of coloured markings and symbols ensures that the same tiffins are returned empty to the right households at the end of the day. Distributing these containers of care and affection back and forth are some five thousand men known as dabbawalas who travel by bicycle or train. Why not extend this admirable tradition to Regent's Park?

My tiffin box conforms to the most classic model, consisting of three stainless-steel containers slotted vertically together and held tightly in place with an interlocking steel frame. It may not have been used for twenty-three years but by the time I wash it, it looks brand new. I fill the bottom two containers with piping-hot dhal and the top compartment with rhubarb crumble to be shared.

As soon as it stops raining, around midday, I head for the park, hanging the tiffin on the handlebar of my bicycle to keep it upright. The Outer Circle is awash with puddles. I lock my bike at the entrance opposite Bridge 10, under dripping trees, and follow the usual pathway. The air is filled with birdsong. It is as if all the birds of Regent's Park are compensating for the fact that they have not been able to sing for the last twenty-four hours. I can't help sharing their excitement. Everywhere water is dripping from saturated branches and leaves. But when I take the secret passage and arrive at the usual place, nobody is there.

I hang around with the tiffin, wondering if I should just leave it on the ground. Then Pascal suddenly appears from under the trees looking waif-like, his hair bestrewn with wet white petals that have blown down from the chestnut tree. He looks happy and whimsical wandering amongst the chirping birds and dripping trees.

'How was your night?' I ask.

'Ha! Wet!' he replies. 'It happens! We were standing up all night, so Nick is getting some rest now.'

He points to the ground, and there, camouflaged beneath the hornbeam that is usually his study, is Nick, curled up fast asleep in his sleeping bag.

I hand Pascal the tiffin. 'There's hot dhal in there if you want something hot, and a dessert in the top compartment,' I tell him.

Pascal takes the tiffin with an appreciative nod and hands me back the now-empty flask, which I take home.

The next day the two vessels swap places. The flask returns to the park filled with leek and potato soup, and Nick hands me the empty tiffin, a few wet leaves adhering to its underside.

'That dhal was delicious,' he says. 'It was good of you to bring it down in this weather. It's very much appreciated. And this – what a great invention!' he says, pointing to the tiffin. 'It brings back memories of India, that does. Take the best of multiculturalism. That's what we've always done in this country, and that's where we're heading for now.'

I put the empty tiffin in my bicycle basket and pedal home, sensing that something is happening. Their things are becoming my things; my things are becoming their things. Or perhaps all these things aren't anybody's things. The point about them is that they have entered into circulation, linking Nick and Pascal's world to mine and my world to theirs.

2 Food

'This food reminds me of the sort of thing my mother used to cook – wholesome,' Nick tells me one early afternoon in May when I nip into the park between meetings. Today I have brought a dish of steaming braised white cabbage and bacon, which I have just enjoyed for my own lunch. It is a bright, breezy day and the cow parsley is blindingly effervescent in the dappled sunlight. I am immediately transported into a luxurious world of natural crochet and lace which stretches into the distance under the trees. The acrimonious Teams meeting from which I emerged fifteen minutes earlier is already shrinking into insignificance. It is a mere flicker.

'My digestive system is working better since you started bringing us home-cooked food,' Nick continues. 'My clothes even feel like they're fitting better. And look at Pascal. I was worried he was getting thin of late but I could swear his face is filling out since you came along!'

If bringing food to the park is beginning to make a small difference to the lives of Nick and Pascal, the difference it is making to my own life is more extreme. It is not that it has changed my world view but that it is quietly altering my daily patterns of existence. But then what is our life if not our everyday patterns of behaviour? And surely food plays an important part in this. For food is about not just what we eat but also the social circumstances of its preparation and enjoyment.

As children we learn to eat from and with our families, developing collective tastes as well as individual preferences. In my own family Indian food happened to play an important role. It was not that anyone in the family was Indian but that my parents had conducted their courtship in 1950s London, principally in Indian restaurants. Coming from very different backgrounds – my mother from an obscure Protestant sect and my father from an Irish Jewish family whose origins could be traced back to Poland and Bessarabia – they shared little obvious common ground, whether in food, politics or religion. When shared taste is not inherited, it has to be created. In my parents' case, this was done through the medium of Madras chicken curry.

So significant was Madras chicken curry to their relationship and the building of a family that, throughout my childhood, every Friday evening was devoted to its preparation and eating. This may sound banal but it was very unusual in the small, entirely white Worcestershire town where I was brought up; my parents' making of chicken curry on a Friday night marked us out as different, if not mildly bohemian. It was a dish that wasn't served to guests since it was thought they couldn't cope with the heat. And they couldn't.

My sisters and I were also excluded from the meal when we were small owing to its spiciness, which in those days came direct from a tin of Bolst's Curry Powder: Hot. (These were the days before the British middle classes learned their spices and rediscovered the romance and toil of the pestle and mortar.) Since this was the only meal my parents ate without us, and the only one that was consumed in the dining room rather than the kitchen, chicken curry became some sort of passage to adulthood. Consequently everything about it – the crackle of the spices in the pan, the colours, the aroma, the novelty of the poppadoms as they inflated in the hot oil – was appealing even if the actual taste remained something of an impediment. I was determined to take up residence around the dining room table as a curry eater, and by the time I was nine or so I had managed it (*before* my older sister!). I had learned to like chicken curry and soon looked forward to it as my favourite meal of the week. It was never simply food.

Sometimes when I look back at my life trajectory I wonder if perhaps it was this multisensory experience of the weekly chicken curry ritual that drew me to India – first as a tourist and then as an anthropologist – beckoning me to explore something beyond my own provincial backyard. And our little corner of Worcestershire *was* provincial.

In the late 1980s, when I was conducting research for a PhD, I lived for over a year in a small village in Saurashtra, Gujarat, where amongst the many things my hosts taught me was how to cook a range of local staple dishes – khuddi, khichdi, bajra no rotlo, dhokla and, for special occasions, shrikhand. They enjoyed demonstrating how to make these dishes and laughed encouragingly at my laborious attempts to write them down in Gujarati script. They took pleasure in the fact that I would carry what many Indian townspeople regarded as 'village tastes' back to my home country. On my return I often cooked these dishes for friends and family, who enjoyed tasting foods you couldn't get in most Indian restaurants. For them this was a novelty; for me it was about memory and connection. These were the days when such a gesture was seen as cultural appreciation rather than cultural appropriation.

In our family, Indian food bound us together. Now that both of my parents are dead, chicken curry has taken on a memorial function. If my sisters and I meet up on a Friday evening, this is what we will cook.

When I got married, my cooking patterns changed. Having been raised in France, Denis was more inclined towards meat. It was not that he made a fuss, but for him a meal didn't feel like a meal without meat or fish. Since he was not keen on rice and since making Indian food with all the appropriate spices was time-consuming, I tended to cook Indian food less and less. Having a child altered my cooking patterns once again. At one stage the only green vegetable Julius would eat was beans, so we had beans with almost every meal. The food I bought and cooked during this period was oriented towards finding or creating dishes that might satisfy all three of us. This wasn't always easy but we succeeded in building certain tastes in common as well as maintaining and developing personal preferences.

But in October 2018, Denis was away working in India for three months and Julius had left London to go to university. Suddenly I was alone in the house and found myself confronted by the novel question of what *I* wanted to eat. I found it curiously difficult to answer. I was so used to purchasing and preparing food to suit our collective desires that I had forgotten what my individual ones were. I no longer needed to do a big shop, so instead would randomly enter the shops I passed on the way home from work. I would find myself standing in the aisles eyeing up the various options. Did I want to eat fish? What about some sushi? Or would I rather have a vegetarian dish, and, if so, what? Could I be bothered to spend time on cooking if it was just for me?

With the social element gone, I was left with just my own unidentifiable preferences to satisfy. In some ways it was gloriously freeing. I could eat at whatever time of day I pleased and never had to worry if there was enough food in the house. I knew I could always make do with pasta without anyone saying, 'Not pasta!' I vacillated between grazing on idiosyncratic choices some weeks and on others cooking a large casserole that would feed me every day without my having to think. When work was stressful the latter technique was effective, although by the time I got to the fifth day I was generally very bored of the dish, even if I did embellish it with added elements. It took *not* cooking for others to make me realise just how social cooking was.

* * *

Fast-forward eighteen months and a new phenomenon is affecting my cooking habits: news of a global pandemic and talk of a lockdown – a double whammy which sends people rushing to supermarkets to stockpile food. Being slow on the uptake and not prone to panic, by the time our family gets to a supermarket there is nothing edible left to buy. We wander up and down the empty aisles in amazement, wondering if we have accidentally walked into a dystopian futuristic film. The only fresh food in the entire store is a single packet of mince. We decide we might as well buy it. It is several months before I go to a supermarket again. Instead I find myself queuing at distance outside various small, relatively local shops that I can access on foot or on my bicycle. No longer a futuristic film but a backwards plunge into a street scene from communist Russia. Shopping has become time-consuming, but then again I am in the house more than ever before and so devote more time to cooking. I am back cooking for three, with my husband and son sometimes taking charge with varying degrees of enthusiasm.

When Nick and Pascal enter my life and consciousness a few weeks into lockdown, my shopping and cooking habits radically transform once more. Now when I shop I am thinking not of three people but of five. In my head I am trying to conjure up dishes that will be equally suitable for serving at home and taking to the park. That rules out certain foods – roasted joints, fish, chops – and makes other types of food more desirable: large casseroles, pulses, curries, stuffed vegetables. Most of these foods require fairly lengthy preparation and benefit from slow cooking. So instead of starting to cook the evening meal just an hour before eating it, I often begin in the morning, putting pulses on the stove at 8 a.m. before starting work at my computer. I then find myself tending to dishes at different times of day, adding fried onions and assorted vegetables when passing through the kitchen at lunchtime and only completing the dish in the evening. I decide it makes sense to make large quantities that will last at least two days and to alternate these with other dishes in between to offer variety. This requires cooking what feels like industrial quantities. In effect, within the space of a year and a half I have gone from cooking meals for one to preparing meals that can serve ten: Nick, Pascal, Denis, Julius and myself – twice! And since I like to keep two dishes on the go at any given time, this often means that on my hob I have food enough for twenty. Large pots and pans that were given as wedding presents and have seldom been used owing to their size now become my daily utensils.

This also means purchasing large amounts of raw ingredients, so my quantity of shopping shoots up. I am aware that I must be spending more on food than usual but this is offset by the fact that we are no longer going to cafes, pubs or restaurants. Whereas in the past we might pop out to eat, now it is the food from our table that is going out to be eaten. I console myself that at least some part of us is keeping mobile. It all seems to make sense in the crazy new logic of the times.

But it is not just my ways of shopping and cooking that change; it is also my attitude to time and my movements. The food can't get to the park unless I take it there. To walk to Nick and Pascal's location takes nearly half an hour, but cycling doesn't take more than ten minutes, so that becomes my preferred method. But I can't be cycling and eating at the same time. With each dish I cook I have to decide who is going to eat it first. Will Nick and Pascal get it fresh from the pan while we get the heated-up version – not always the most popular way round with my family when it delays our supper – or vice versa? This varies according to the dish. Then there is the question of when to deliver it. My working days are stuffed with online meetings, and other university work is spilling over into the evenings. In normal times, when my work was located at the university, there was never any question of my popping out in the middle of the day. In fact, when at work, I generally used to pick up just a sandwich or soup for lunch, which I ate at my computer or from time to time with a colleague who was as rushed as I was. But surely we are entitled to a notional lunch hour? And besides, when I travelled to work the journey took over an hour in each direction. So in theory there must be three hours of extra time available, even if it certainly doesn't feel that way.

Given that I am now working from home and that work now seems to adhere to every room in the house, I decide that it is within my rights to hop onto my bike in the middle of the day from time to time to deliver food to Nick and Pascal and have a quick chat, which is rarely ever that quick. These little trips break up the day and give me energy to cope with diving back on screen on my return. But my preferred slot for going to the park is the early evening, when in theory I can put work behind me (or at least that part of it that requires real-time digital interaction).

These evening visits offer an extraordinary sense of release. It is as if I have literally been let out of my computer and all the compressed tensions that have pulsated through it during the day – the said and the unsaid, the raising and lowering of digital hands, the side comments in the chat, the secret WhatsApp messaging that accompanies digital meetings, further dividing people who are officially logged on together. The very act of getting on my bicycle feels like an incredible act of freedom. The process of pedalling the same familiar route, locking my bike under the trees at the entrance opposite Bridge 10 and taking the 'passage into a secret world' is immediately uplifting. The sound of the birds at twilight, the sight of buttercups, pink campion, columbine and blackberry in flower in the fading light, the solidity of the oak trees and the rustle of the feathery hornbeam branches in the evening breeze all remind me that the university is just a small dot in the wider universe.

As April gives way to May, I begin to spend at least every other early evening in the park with Nick, Pascal, Bachi and Lizzie. My husband is usually still at his computer at this time and my son involved with his own stuff, so this becomes my time away from the confines of both work and home. Nick is always welcoming and soon suggests that I bring a folding chair so that I have somewhere to sit. I don't want to sit up on a chair when Nick and Pascal are down on the ground. However, in my study at home I have a treasured ancient three-legged milking stool; it's very low and the seat is a slice of tree trunk, shiny and worn to a curve by generations of seated bottoms. I decide to carry this to the park. Nick appreciates the grain of the wood and the good craftsmanship. A love of well-made objects is something we share. After I use it for the first time he offers to keep it safe with his stuff, tucked away under a tarpaulin just behind where he lays his head. I hesitate, not wanting the stool to get damaged in the rain. As if reading my mind, Nick produces a plastic carrier bag. 'I will make sure it is stored in this to protect it,' he says. And he does. When strong rains come later in the year my stool is stuffed deeper into the compact mound of Nick's affairs, which is known in street parlance as his 'skipper'. Never once do I find it wet.

The movement of the stool from my home to the park is significant. It means that a part of me has taken up residence in the park. It signals that I am welcome not just for my food but for my presence and conversation. That matters.

Usually when I arrive in the evenings, to my right I see Pascal lying in his sleeping bag under a chestnut tree, amusing himself by feeding birds and field mice or by simply being. To my left, sitting at a distance in the open amongst the long grasses that give this part of the park an ethereal look and feel, are Nick and Bachi, with Lizzie trotting contentedly between them. Bachi is sitting on a colourful stripy rug, large enough to accommodate himself and Lizzie. He always carries with him a bag containing Lizzie's water, toys and treats. A good two metres away sits Nick, half lying, half sitting in a lounging position that he manages to make look comfortable. His chosen spot is just in front of a bushel of flowering vetch, the blooms of which turn from pale green to mauve and deep purple before fading almost to white as the summer progresses. Sitting on a khaki-coloured jacket and wearing a grey jumper and trousers, Nick looks as if he has grown out of the ground, his beard just another form of vegetation. While Bachi always carries lots of equipment with him, Nick has only his red woollen hat, which contains his tobacco and roll-up papers and a lighter.

Usually I stop off and say hello to Pascal first and leave him the tiffin, with a brief explanation of what it contains. Sometimes he eats his portion straight away while it is still hot; other times he keeps it for the next day. Later I learn that both he and Nick time their eating with great care to be in control of the rhythm of their digestive systems and synchronise their bowel movements with the opening and closing of the park facilities.

After brief exchanges with Pascal I go over and join Nick and Bachi, forming the third prong of a triangle. If the grass is dry I sit directly on it, but if it is damp I unearth my wooden stool from Nick's skipper. Lizzie welcomes me into the formation and continually traces the space between us. Often we throw her toy between us as she pants her way from Nick to Bachi, from Bachi to Nick, from Nick to me, from me to Bachi or Nick and so forth. And so we are bound together by the invisible threads of her movements.

During the day, most of the problems I am dealing with feel intractable. Bureaucratic constraints are immovable; the uncertainty produced by Covid is expanding rather than contracting; tensions over racial justice, already at boiling point at the university long before George Floyd's brutal murder, are accelerating; the question of whether and how we are going to deliver teaching online next year hangs over us like a noose.

As the exam season arrives, new problems rear their heads. The college has announced it cannot guarantee teaching contracts for assistant lecturers the following year owing to the uncertainty of recruitment figures – an effect of Covid. Most of the assistant lecturers are our PhD students, with whom we normally have good relations. Many of them go on a wildcat strike over the precarity of short-term contracts, which are blighting universities up and down the country. I sympathise with their cause but find their methods painful. They decide to withhold the exam grades of the undergraduates whose work they have been marking. As the deadline for results approaches, stress levels rise. The striking PhD students want the department to pay them out of support for their cause. When we suggest we can pay them only when they release the grades, they feel let down; some are outraged. The union comes out on their side, as does the *Guardian*. Staff are divided over how we should respond, which results in what feels like a never-ending series of highly charged Zoom meetings. Then, when results day finally arrives and the undergraduates discover that they do not have any results, it is their turn to feel enraged. Why have we betrayed them when they have had such a difficult year, punctuated by two spates of industrial action and the pandemic? Their consternation is understandable, for without their grades final-year students cannot graduate and first- and second-year students cannot progress to the next year of their studies. The number of emergency telephone and WhatsApp calls before breakfast is increasing and the stress of fragmented loyalties feels overwhelming.

What a contrast it feels to be able to do something straight-forward – to chop up vegetables and put them in a pan, watch them steam, sizzle or roast, flavour them, assist in their transformation into a meal, apportion the food into the tif-fin compartments, cycle it to the park and give it to people who are pleased to receive it. This simple act stabilises me. It restores my faith in humanity and my confidence in my role in it. It reminds me that human interaction can feel positive and that simple actions can be fulfilling. However frustrated and desperate I feel at work, here is a place where what I do makes sense. The simple lessons of food.

Food has other things to teach me about redistribution. Before the pandemic, on those days when I was working from home, I would begin my day in a cafe. I needed a bit of outside before going inside. This is where I would do things like read a PhD student's chapter, edit a piece of writing or rework a book review. Since lockdown started, cafes have become places that can only serve takeaways. My dislike of paper cups makes this offer unappealing and I feel bereft of the outside perch from which to start my working day. So, for the first time in my life, I find myself purchasing a flask – two flasks, in fact. A big one for Nick and Pascal and a small one for me which has capacity for two and a half mugs of coffee. To breathe outside before opening my laptop in the morning is becoming as essential as taking refuge in the park in the evening. I take to setting out early with a flask of coffee and an old blue tin mug that Julius used to use for camping.

One morning, as I am walking across the bottom of Prim-rose Hill, I see a man called James sitting on a bench. I barely know him but have seen him around the local area for years, decades even. We usually just acknowledge each other with a smile of recognition but this time we get talking, asking each other how we are managing in these strange new times. James gestures for me to join him on the bench, which I do, taking up residence at the opposite end to where he is sitting. Some way into the conversation he opens a bag containing six or seven loaves of bread. 'Have some bread,' he says. 'Really. Please take some. It's good bread, but there's much too much for me. I was given it.' My mind immediately goes to Nick and Pascal. 'Thanks,' I say. 'I have some friends who live outside who would appreciate this.' I take a couple of loaves but he insists I take more. He tells me the bread was given to him by Germano from the local cafe. Apparently there is often bread that gets left over these days.

When the weekend arrives I pop into the cafe, purchase some croissants and then ask casually if by any chance they ever have any bread left over at the end of the day. I explain that I often take food to some men who are living outside under the trees. I can't bring myself to use the word 'homeless' as it doesn't feel right, but when Germano uses it I don't contradict him.

Germano's eyes brighten. 'We often have lots of loaves left over these days. It's really difficult to anticipate numbers at the moment. I used to have this great machine for making breadcrumbs so nothing ever went to waste but that machine is broken and I can't find a replacement anywhere. I hate letting good bread go to waste but I end up having to throw it away. Come!' He leads me to a back room for staff only and opens a black bin liner. It contains two sourdough loaves and several baguettes – some plain, others topped with sesame or poppy seeds. 'Can you take all of these?'

I get the distinct impression that he'd prefer me to take all of the loaves rather than pick and choose. So I take them. He is pleased to know the bread will not be wasted and I am pleased to have some good-quality baguettes to offer. Does Pascal, like my husband, miss decent French baguettes since coming to London, I wonder, or do years of living in the street and park mean that he has ceased to discriminate? Five baguettes seem too many to consume in one go so I keep one plus a small loaf for my family and take the other four and a large loaf to Nick and Pascal. I feel like I am going from dabbawala to a character from a Hovis advert, cycling around with bread overflowing from my wicker basket.

Doing the bread round adds a new layer of complexity to my movements. It means stopping off at the cafe every day, buying something for myself as this seems only courteous, and then politely enquiring if there is any leftover bread. Sometimes everything has been sold, but more often than not it hasn't, or Germano will tell me to pop back the next morning or later on that evening. These timings are restrictive, and the ritual of locking and unlocking my bicycle every time I stop off to enquire is tedious. But these small inconveniences are well worth it for the bounty of good bread they yield, which Nick in particular appreciates. Soon Bachi has cancelled his weekly order of sliced bread from the supermarket. Instead there is a regular flow of wholemeal, sourdough, brown and white loaves, buns and assorted baguettes, some fancy, some plain.

One morning I arrive at the cafe after a two-day absence. Germano beckons me to the storeroom. 'Please take all of this,' he says, handing me an entire bin liner full of bread. 'I've been keeping it for you.' It contains over twenty loaves, a selection of rolls and what feels like a bombardment of baguettes. 'It will all go in the bin if you don't take it,' he says as a means of persuasion. It works, although this time the bread won't fit into my bicycle basket. The quantity is intimidating. I even have difficulty dragging the bin liner home by hand. I feel I should go cycling around the borough distributing bread to anyone who wants it, only I don't have the time to do it on a working day. I text Bachi about the dilemma.

'I've got a big freezer at home,' he texts back. 'I can take 12 baguettes for freezing and then bring them to the park when Nick and Pascal's bread supplies are running low.'

I accept the offer. Soon Bachi has parked his polished black Jeep Wrangler outside my house for bread collection. My cats edge away as they see Lizzie's head poking out of the car window. I manage to stuff a few loaves into my tiny freezer for future use. Meanwhile I decide it is time I learned to make bread and butter pudding. The pudding is a success, the only problem being that it does not absorb anything like as much bread as I had hoped!

So Nick and Pascal – by dint of simply being there – have changed not only what I buy, what I cook, how much I cook and when I cook it, but also the topography of my day, which is now restructured around bread collection, food preparation and distribution, threaded between my professional duties.

And just as food is never simply food, so bread is not simply bread. 'Panis', the Latin word for bread, is an integral component of the word 'companion'. Companionship is about sharing, breaking bread together and accompanying one another. And with companionship comes conversation.

'It's about talking and walking *with* instead of simply standing facing each other,' Nick suggests. 'What is conversation?' he asks rhetorically. 'It's just the exchange of data. That's all it is. But some exchanges are more meaningful than others.'

Nick is all too aware of how meaningful exchanges can often be derailed or skewed when you are living in the street and belong to what he refers to as 'the apparently homeless'.

One evening, as I cross the leafy threshold of our hidden world, following the bold lead of a hopping crow, I hear the reverberating words 'God bless you!' coming from the secret grove. A woman, slight in stature, is rising off her knees, her face illuminated with a beatific smile. She has left Nick and Pascal some food and is clearly on a mission of mercy which seems to begin with 'feeding the poor'.

'She's a Christian,' Nick says, raising his eyebrows knowingly, as if that is all there is to be said. 'She left us this, which is kind of her. She means well. She said I reminded her of *Jesus*!'

'Well, I suppose that's kind of flattering,' I suggest, glancing at Pascal, who seems to find the analogy hilarious.

This woman with a mission turns up every few days for a couple of weeks or so. I often see her as she is returning from her visits. Once our paths cross directly as I am passing under the oak trees leading to the secret passage. I see her eyes register the tiffin box I am carrying and the direction in which I am heading. She smiles as if in solidarity. But after about three weeks she has disappeared. 'I think she had some emotional problems,' Nick explains. 'Maybe she was trying to absolve herself of something. She seemed to be almost tearful at times. At any rate I guess she's done what she needed to do as we haven't seen her in a while. I've noticed that over the years. When people are going through some sort of trauma they often feel the need to give things. You wouldn't believe how many attempts have been made to save us,' he continues, looking at Pascal, who laughs and nods in concurrence. 'When we were at Lincoln's Inn we'd get people trying to save us almost every day. I'd just tell them we'd already been saved many times!'

'And how did you respond?' I ask Pascal, trying to drag him into the conversation more directly. He just raises his eyebrows. 'You try me!' he says very quietly. And that is all.

'The Danish Church were round here the other day,' Nick continues. 'I told the vicar, "I'm happy to discuss absolutely any topic you like. Except religion." I'm not sure he really appreciated that.'

One blustery morning when I go to the park early, just after the gibbons have performed their acrobatic concert and while the grass is still damp with dew, I see a copy of *The Watchtower* open on Nick's sleeping bag.

'The Jehovah's Witness woman has been round,' he explains. 'She said a few prayers over us about the last days and gave us *this.'* He points to the pamphlet, which is entitled *The Search for Truth.* 'I've tried reading some of it out loud to Pascal but he instantly fell asleep.' Pascal grins. 'I didn't argue with her,' Nick continues, 'I just talked to her about Schumpeter's theory of creative destruction. I never dismiss people who are religious because I think for my mother religion was probably the only thing that kept her going. I've known too many people for whom it was important. Some sort of lifeline, I suppose. Our friend Pete found religion in Dartmoor. He'd been a gangmaster, that sort of thing, and was locked up for ten years. He wanted to mend his ways for the sake of his son. He became a born-again Christian and now lives in a caravan in Cornwall. He usually comes to stay with us for a few days around September. You should meet him. He sleeps down by the canal when he comes. I guess when you spend ten years in Dartmoor you have to find God!'

The Jehovah's Witness woman has apparently been coming to the park for years. 'You might not see her for a year or two and then she'll just turn up,' Nick tells me. 'Once she brought us a whole roast chicken; another time it was a leg of lamb cooked with rosemary. This time it was chicken pieces.'

Christians are not alone in trying to save Nick and Pascal through a combination of food and proselytisation. Amongst the enlightening literature they have received is the Hare Krishna version of the Bhagavad Gita, about which Nick is disparaging, preferring what he calls the 'proper version', which he tells me he has read from cover to cover both forwards and backwards. They have also received a copy of the Koran and a series of booklets about Islam from a kind and well-meaning young man who is working on a building site nearby. In this case the religious literature is accompanied by donations of clothing rather than food. The books all come directly from the Regent's Park Mosque and are part of its outreach literature. One is an Islam-made-simple book targeted at potential converts. Nick always receives such offerings with courtesy, and his natural curiosity means that he at least skims their pages. But he is not ripe for conversion, and Pascal even less so. He seems to regard religion as some sort of amusing human folly.

'Why would God be up there when he could be down here?' Nick asks. 'As far as I'm concerned, *this* is God with a capital G.' He points to his immediate environment, gesturing to the magnificence of the trees, the grasses and the sky, the appreciation of which he knows I share.

One day when I arrive in the park Nick and Pascal both have tall white polystyrene cups with lids beside their sleeping bags. It is food from the Hare Krishna distribution centre which a man has cycled over to them. 'We won't eat it,' Nick said. 'I don't trust it. I've learned my lesson. I was so ill I was hanging from the trees the last time I ate one of their meals! You have to be very careful to stay healthy in the street. You can't afford to take risks with food. We often used to get their handouts years ago, but then the quality went right downhill. You'd see all the homeless in Lincoln's Inn leaving it on their paper plates it was so bad. I don't think it was fresh.'

When I suggest, no doubt inappropriately, that it seems a waste to throw it away given that some guy has taken the trouble to deliver it, Nick says bluntly, 'If you want it, you have it!' I peer at the yellow slop in the polystyrene cup and do not feel tempted either by the food or the Krishna consciousness it embodies. I decline the offer, even if as our relationship develops I often do find myself accepting small gifts of food from Nick and Pascal when supplies from various donors exceed what they need or desire or when they simply want to enjoy the pleasure of sharing. It is part of a system of redistribution and exchange that we slip into.

Food, being not just food, often comes with expectations and projections. Years of living in the street and later the park have taught Nick and Pascal that. Accepting gifts of food from others can be a risky business – whether in terms of preserving good health or in terms of the types of exchanges it opens up. When Bachi and I offer food it comes without what Nick calls 'an agenda'. We are not trying to save or convert them or entice them into a shelter. We have no desire to change their way of life. I like to think they sense this, and perhaps that is why our offerings enable the type of exchange of data that Nick calls meaningful – his definition of good conversation.

3 Convergence

'I think of the park as a theatre,' Nick says one evening. 'You are here now and our conversation is real, but most of the people in the park are just actors playing parts. That's how I see it.'

We are sitting together in our socially distanced triangle – Nick, Bachi and me, with Lizzie bounding between us, enabling certain topics of conversation and protecting or distracting us from others. There is nothing planned in this geometric arrangement in the long grass and yet it has a habit of re-forming every evening that I manage to make it to the park. I know that, long before I turned up, Nick and Bachi would sit opposite each other to converse and play with Lizzie. Pascal's natural preference for quiet means that only once in the three years of Bachi's evening visits has he left his sleeping bag to join them. But this does not stop Nick regularly asking Pascal if he'd like to join the conversation. It is a rendezvous without boundaries, somehow managing to be simultaneously regular and spontaneous. When I start appearing on those late-spring and early-summer evenings, I am generously incorporated into this impromptu and convivial ritual without question or hesitation. Thinking back, it is probably Lizzie who decides this.

'Convergence' is the word that springs to mind when I think of those long summer evenings in the park. Occasionally other

people who know Nick and Pascal from earlier times pass by –
sometimes a friend forged through shared experiences in the
street or someone who has been conversing with them over
the years and has decided to drop off some food that evening;
sometimes someone in need of company and grounding. From
time to time these individuals join us in the long grass, temporarily stretching our socially distanced triangle into a wide
lozenge, but more often than not it is just the three of us with
Lizzie, our connector. Pascal's presence under the trees, choosing the music of birdsong and the company of field mice over
human conversation, is a reminder that there are other ways
of engaging with the world.

The fact that at first Bachi and I know almost nothing about
each other is irrelevant. We have converged in time and space
and both want to be here, which is enough. We share the fact
that we enjoy Nick's company and the beauty of this small
patch of wilderness in the park, with its unrelenting greenness
and ever-changing skies. We have both found ways of bringing
food – he through his weekly online shop and me by extending
my home cooking into the park. And the three of us get along
without effort, letting the conversation duck and dive freely.

'You can travel round and round the world but if you come
back with the same attitudes as before, what's the point?' Nick
asks rhetorically one evening. 'I've learned that you can sit
still in one place and the world comes to you.' Our evening
gatherings seem to confirm this.

Bachi rarely speaks about his personal life unless it concerns
Lizzie, which much of it does. After several months of meeting

up, I venture to ask him how he first got to know Nick and Pascal. He tells me he had been looking for a quiet place where Lizzie could relax. The trauma of her fighting past had made her so nervous and aggressive that the rescue home had been about to have her put down. When Bachi said he wanted to adopt her, the staff at the home had initially refused, saying she was too disturbed and violent to become a pet. Bachi had asked if he could spend some time alone with her. He sat quietly with his back to her and gained her confidence by waiting for her to make the first approach. In effect he lulled her into trusting him with his gentle and unthreatening manner, and within two hours had succeeded in convincing the home to let him adopt her. That was four years ago. They have been inseparable ever since.

'I won't go anywhere without Lizzie,' he makes clear. 'I only accept an invitation if she is invited too. She comes with me on all my NHS deliveries and the nurses and hospital staff have all fallen in love with her.'

Bachi first spotted Nick and Pascal when he found himself sheltering under the hornbeam trees during an unexpected rainstorm, and he made a mental note of the spot. Lizzie needed quiet time and the presence of gentle and unthreatening people. Nick and Pascal seemed to fit the bill. But it wasn't quite as simple as that: Bachi also needed quiet time and the company of gentle people with whom he could relax. He has severe ADHD – something he is quite open about – which makes it extremely difficult for him to switch off. But there was something about this part of the park, off the beaten track, something about the tranquillity of the evening light and the calming presence of Nick and Pascal, who were always there whatever the weather, that made relaxation possible.

'I saw Nick and Pascal under the trees and thought they might not mind if I sat not too far off,' he tells me. 'So I didn't sit with them but was near enough for them to see me and for interaction to be possible. I would sit in the long grass near their space and play with Lizzie, and sometimes Nick would appear and interact with her, and we began to exchange a few words. Then I started thinking that if I brought them some useful bits and pieces, then maybe they wouldn't mind my staying here whenever I wanted somewhere quiet to sit with Lizzie.'

'This is your space,' Bachi told Nick eventually. 'I don't want to intrude. But I do want to bring some value to my presence in your space.' Apparently Nick had been suspicious initially, worrying that Bachi might have an agenda, but Lizzie with her endearing doggish ways had eased the situation.

'With Lizzie it became an easy space to be in. Nick was gentle and played with her, and Lizzie was drawn to him. Then after a while Nick would sit down to join us in the grass and have a smoke and we would chat about anything, really. If the conversation got heavy, we could always play with Lizzie. She would keep it light.'

'Lizzie is my shield,' Bachi adds, not telling me why he needs a shield.

'I love that man,' Nick tells me. It is a purely platonic declaration. It is about trust and appreciation of the consistency of Bachi's undemanding support and good company over the years. 'Trust is the most difficult thing to develop in the street,' Nick adds. 'I have hobo paranoia but that's not clinical. It's based on experience. In the street you can't trust anyone.'

But why did Bachi want to be approached by animals and humans whom others might reject or overlook? The answer seems to lie in his own past.

'Nick reminded me of someone,' Bachi tells me much later, 'someone I knew when I was living in the street.'

My mind flashes back to a comment Nick once made that I didn't fully understand at the time: 'Bachi knows about the street because he's lived it.' This comment took me by surprise because the Bachi I was getting to know bit by bit and indirectly through our collective evening conversations was clearly prosperous, even if he was discreet by nature and totally unpretentious in his manner. He drove a Jeep, lived in a hi-tech designer glass building in Camden Town and had spent two decades of his life working as a trader for J. P. Morgan. He seemed to have unlimited knowledge of sports cars and a past that included leading fast-paced adventure tours in different locations around the world. That much I had come to know. Sitting together in the long grass, Nick speculated about whether it was the ADHD that had enabled Bachi to work as a trader. He was referring to the rapidity and restlessness associated with the condition. By the time I met Bachi it was over ten years since he had left J. P. Morgan and about the same amount of time since he had been diagnosed with ADHD. This was the Bachi I was becoming familiar with – the witty, post-trader, dog-adoring, NHS-volunteering, fidgety, clever, thoughtful and affable Bachi. But he clearly had another past.

The person Nick reminded Bachi of was Paul. Paul was a man living in the street who took Bachi under his wing when he turned up at Waterloo Bridge aged eighteen with nothing more than £60 in his pocket and a determination never to see his parents again – a decision he has stuck to ever since. Bachi chose Waterloo because this was where he used to hang out with fellow skateboarders, working the underpass beside the National Theatre. I have strong memories of walking along-side that underpass when heading to and from the theatre as a student, always feeling slightly threatened by the unrestrained masculine energy of the skateboarders and the grating sounds that vibrated from the dark graffiti-covered concrete. Was Bachi amongst the skaters when I walked past, I now wonder?

Whilst hanging out skateboarding, the young Bachi noticed the groups of people living a makeshift life under the bridge in what used to be called the Bullring area, also known as Cardboard City at the time. A few years later, in the name of regeneration, the area would be cleared of rough sleepers and a new IMAX cinema built over the space where they had once lived. But when Bachi arrived at Waterloo Bridge in the mid-1980s there were up to two hundred people eking out a life in the area. So this was where he headed, with no plan other than to get away from his family for good.

'I was lucky,' Bachi recalls. 'I got in with a good group of people on the street who supported each other. Paul was the one who held us together. He was a bit like Nick in lots of ways. He was gentle and kind and people naturally gathered around him. We formed a little community of five or six people and we shared whatever we had. We were protected from the crueller aspects of the street thanks to Paul.'

'Have you kept in touch with any of the people you knew from that time?' I ask.

'Only really Paul. Sadly he's dead now. I kept in touch with him to the end. He never wanted to leave his life in the street. He did not accept any offers of help from me except occasional gifts of food. There was also a girl. Her name was Zenia. She left the group after a while. I don't know where she went. Years later I was stuck in traffic driving over Vauxhall Bridge in a sports car when she started cleaning my windows. She didn't recognise me until I said something. We chatted a bit, then I had to drive on. I said, "Paul taught us something, and you are part of that. If you ever need anything, I'm here. Just let me know." But she never took me up on it. I used to drive that way deliberately quite often so that I could pay her five pounds for cleaning my windows, but that was the only contact we had.

'I have a very strong protective streak that I learned from Paul,' Bachi adds. 'When he died in 2014 it affected me a lot. If it wasn't for him, my life could have taken a very different direction. A very different direction,' he repeats with feeling.

Nick and Pascal connect Bachi to something in his past that is worth retaining and reliving – the humanity and conviviality he learned not from his family but in the street. From this experience he also learned to respect a certain way of living, even if he himself now lives in a very different way. I see this in Bachi's interactions not just with Nick and Pascal but with others who sometimes tentatively join our gathering. There is Matt, bottle permanently in hand, shabbily dressed, skinny and shaky on his feet and noticeably suspicious of Bachi and me for our apparent middle-classness. 'What are you doing hanging out with them?' he asks Nick accusingly when he thinks we are out of earshot, as if merely by talking to us Nick is becoming a class traitor. Matt is not homeless, it turns out. He has accepted council accommodation but, unlike Nick and Pascal, he exudes an air of destitution. He has known Nick and Pascal for many years from their Camden Town days, when they were all living in the street and getting handouts from the same places. He turns up a few times to our evening encounters, always edgy, bottle in hand, often angry and swearing. He generally remains standing up, hovering on the edge of our triangle and wandering about, as if to sit down would be an act of complicity he is unwilling to make. But he also seems reluctant to walk away, not wanting to miss the conversation, which he seems to find interesting in spite of himself. Bachi is always welcoming to Matt. He introduces Lizzie and invites him to sit and join us in a casual and unthreatening way. He seems to understand Matt's awkwardness, and rather than try to break through it, he works with it.

Then there is Jan, a little sparrow of a woman who is small and humble in her manner but who exudes good old-fashioned kindness to her core. 'Oh, I don't like to think of 'em being 'ere on their own at night,' she says, addressing me and Bachi. I get the impression she thinks we are a couple. 'It's so spooky! Anyway, I thought I'd just pop round on my way back from the supermarket.' She turns back to Nick and starts lifting items out of a large bag. 'I picked up these pasties – thought they'd fill you up for tonight anyway – oh, and I saw this giant chocolate brownie on offer. And here's some loo paper. Might come in handy.'

'Pascal will certainly appreciate the chocolate,' Nick replies, thanking her for her kindness, catching up on her news and enquiring after her son, about whom he has clearly had prior conversations. Jan never sits down to join us. She isn't the sort of person who would want to interfere but she seems to enjoy a passing chat. Bachi is always friendly and affable with her, jollying along the conversation, introducing Lizzie and keeping things light and convivial.

And then there is Keert, a sombre, thickset man of Estonian origin who is prone to depression and anxiety. He first met Nick and Pascal in the Rose Garden of Regent's Park about a decade ago, when he had been evicted from his flat and found himself provisionally homeless for a few weeks. The experience was a terrible shock for him, and Nick and Pascal advised him about how to handle the situation and what to do for food and shelter. Keert has never forgotten this, and although he now lives in a council flat in Ilford he frequently crosses the city, travelling to Regent's Park by bus, partly to imbibe the peace and quiet of the place but also to spend time with Nick and Pascal and unburden himself of his frustrations. The pandemic has exacerbated his feelings of anxiety and the park seems to function as an outlet where he can openly express his fears, including his suicidal fantasies and imaginings. Bachi always tries to encourage Keert to relax, trying to use Lizzie as a way of welcoming him into the group, and Keert sometimes tentatively joins us sitting in the long grass, although he later admits to me that he is not too keen on dogs. Bachi clearly has the capacity to mix with all sorts of people and put them at ease.

So there is Bachi the wealthy trader and Bachi the runaway homeless boy on the streets of London, Bachi the lover and saver of dogs (Lizzie is his fourth rescue) and Bachi the man who can mix with anyone. There is also Bachi before and after his diagnosis of ADHD. Fragments of these different Bachis surface during our evening conversations in the long grass, even though Bachi is by nature a noticeably private person who prefers attention to be focused on Lizzie rather than on himself.

'With my ADHD I'm not going to impose myself on anyone,' he declares one evening when we are talking about relationships. A pandemonium of parakeets is passing overhead – a shrieking green flash of feathers circulating between the crab apple trees, the chestnut and the copper beech. The sky is streaked pink with small puffy clouds, illuminated like candyfloss.

Bachi has been married twice, it turns out, and is now determined to stick to canine company. Lizzie originally entered his life as part of an attempt to repair his relationship with his second wife and to provide them with a common focus, given their mutual love of dogs. But now Lizzie is his sole cohabitant.

'It's the innocence of Lizzie that Bachi loves,' Nick observes one morning when we are drinking coffee under the hornbeam tree. 'And Lizzie *is* a very special dog. The way she comes up to you and looks straight into your face with her dark, half-blind eyes. I love that! Nonetheless I hope one day Bachi will have another relationship with his own species.'

'My ADHD tablets are basically a form of speed that helps me focus and calms me down,' Bachi explains one evening, referring to medication that increases the level of neurotransmitters in the brain. 'I used to do lots of high-risk stuff – skydiving, white-water rafting, mountaineering, driving fast cars, that kind of thing. I was always into extremes. That was the ADHD.'

'But how did you realise you had ADHD?' I ask. 'It's not necessarily something people identify in themselves.' I happen to have some insight into this topic from an anthropology student at my university who wrote his PhD thesis on the convoluted process whereby people seek recognition as adult ADHD sufferers. Until recently it was thought that only children suffer from ADHD. Getting a diagnosis as an adult required producing a complex body of evidence and developing new ways of interpreting difficult childhood experiences that had been understood differently at the time. There were ADHD support groups where people gathered to share their experiences and help each other through the bureaucratic hurdles of attaining recognition as well as coping with the diagnosis and medication. Most of the participants had found themselves being written off as unruly and disruptive when growing up and many had experienced relationship problems. Most had found it helpful to be given a new lens through which to understand their lives retrospectively.

'It was when I'd left the bank,' Bachi replies. 'I was climbing up the walls. I was very difficult to be with – unliveable with, really, I admit. My partner at the time persuaded me to go and see some mental health professionals. I booked in with the NHS but also booked appointments with three private doctors. They gave me a mass of tests, questionnaires et cetera, which were all different but they all came to the same conclusion: I had really high-level ADHD. One doctor even said he couldn't understand how I'd been able to function, given the level.'

'Was it a relief to have a diagnosis or was it disconcerting?' I ask, remembering my student's thesis.

'At first it was a relief, yes. It really was. Everything suddenly made sense – the huge adrenaline rush of banking, my endlessly flinging myself into dangerous situations, my impatience, my tendency to rush into leadership roles, my difficulties with concentrating at school, my whole childhood. But later I found it quite disturbing and confusing. I had difficulty locating who I was. If everything I'd done to date was ADHD-related, then who was I in all of that? What was the ADHD and what was me? How could I distinguish between the two? It made me question who I am. I started out on a very low dosage of medication but now I'm on a very high dosage.'

The Bachi I am getting to know, whose days revolve around walking Lizzie in the park, responding to the NHS Covid app and sitting down to chat with Nick and myself in the evenings, is a sedated Bachi who no longer does a whole range of high-risk activities that used to be second nature to him. 'Don't you ever miss the highs of the extreme activities you used to pursue?' I ask, realising that it is not only the medication but also the recent cycling accident that has slowed him down. With three metal plates in his legs and the lingering post-operation pain and stiffness, many of the things he used to do would be difficult, if not impossible.

'They weren't highs. They were just a way of helping me feel calm,' Bachi specifies.

'I can understand that,' Nick says contemplatively.

'It was the ADHD that meant I had to do all that stuff. Now I've learned to be more patient. I've learned a lot from Lizzie in that respect. When I had an IQ test I came out with an absurdly high score of a hundred and eighty-five, which is really on the autistic spectrum,' Bachi continues. 'It's associated with low empathy.'

'I wouldn't say you lack empathy,' Nick interjects.

'Well, maybe it's more that I act before I have time to process the empathy,' Bachi clarifies before turning to Lizzie, feeding her some home-cooked chicken breast from a toy which requires her to extract the food with her teeth.

And for the next twenty minutes it is Lizzie time. We throw one of her toys between us, enjoying her attempts to wrestle it from us; Bachi presents her with a ball that she proceeds to chew; and Nick stands up and whirls a string toy between his legs and around his body with playful laughter. Eventually Lizzie begins to tire and Bachi rolls up his stripy rug, puts on her harness and walks with her out of the park just as darkness is descending.

On another evening Nick and I are talking about books when Bachi comments, 'I can't get through the first page of a book myself. Ever since I left J. P. Morgan I haven't been able to read at all.'

'Is the ADHD something you feel you've got through or do you feel you are recovering?' Nick asks.

Bachi looks into space. 'I've always wished I could just be normal,' he says wistfully.

'What is normal?' I chirp in. 'And who draws the line between what is normal and what's not? And what makes normality so special anyway?' It seems a question worth asking of my companions, given that our very convergence in the park seems to question certain norms. 'There's a great book by the French philosopher Michel Foucault,' I go on, 'that looks at how ideas of madness and normality shift over time. I won't recommend it to you, Bachi, if you say you can't sit down to read the first page of a book, since it's not exactly a light read, especially being translated from the French. But it's good on this topic.'

'Ah yes, Foucault,' Nick says. 'Someone gave me a book of Foucault's. I think it was Mariam. She's a lecturer at London University,' he says, turning to me. 'You should meet her. I think you'd get on. I really must read that book.'

'Being normal may be comfortable,' I continue, 'but I'm not sure that it's all that interesting.' Nick seems to be nodding in agreement.

Bachi has by this time turned back to Lizzie. It is time for her coloured plastic ball to be brought out. As he says, Lizzie is his shield. When his second wife used to raise her voice, Lizzie would stand in front of Bachi and growl, as if to protect him. From then on she slept beside him on his bed.

Bachi usually leaves the park earlier than I do, before darkness descends, owing to Lizzie's diminishing eyesight. This means that when summer gives way to autumn and the nights draw closer, he leaves the park earlier and earlier. He has constructed a special illuminated dog harness with two high-quality bicycle lights built into it to help her find her way along the footpath in the half-light.

One evening Nick tells me that Bachi came down early without Lizzie and stayed just a few minutes. He had left Lizzie in his apartment as she seemed disoriented and unsteady on her feet. She was undergoing medical investigations. It is difficult to imagine Bachi coming to the park without Lizzie, as they are so intrinsically interlinked. I decide to give him a call when I get home. I find Bachi in a contemplative mood when I ring. He updates me about Lizzie's health situation. She has had a shaking episode and lost her balance a couple of times. He is sure it is not just her increasing level of blindness or arthritis. She seems lethargic and is off her food. He is taking her to the vet for multiple tests. She is resting on his lap as we speak.

It is unusual for us to speak on the phone or indeed converse alone. Somehow the conversation roves on to Bachi's past and I find myself asking him how he made the spectacular leap from living under Waterloo Bridge without either money or qualifications to becoming a trader at J. P. Morgan. It doesn't seem an obvious move.

'How long were you living in the street and how did you manage to work your way off it?' I ask, possibly too directly, but I am curious.

'I spent about eighteen months in the street,' Bachi tells me. 'I knew I had to do something to get myself out of the situation. We used to wrap ourselves up in the free newspapers to keep ourselves warm at night. One day I was reading the newspaper I was lying under and I noticed an advert for a job. It was to sort cheques for Midland Bank, working nights and paid cash in hand, no questions asked. I presented myself for the job and got it. I managed to earn some money working nights. I shared half of my earnings with the group, buying things people needed. But I saved the other half and after three or four months I had enough money to get myself a place to shelter. From there, I started applying for every job I could find. Manufacturers Hanover Trust took me on because four people had just resigned and they were badly in need of staff. I worked as a runner initially, moving about doing odd jobs for them, and from there I got into trading. It was just a case of being in the right place at the right time.'

'And having certain skills,' I suggest.

'The only skill was that I was interested and I learned over and above what I needed for my job. Being a runner meant hanging around a lot and that meant I observed how things worked and picked things up, and people noticed that. By 1992 I was in the trading room and by 1993 I was a trader. Once I became a trader there was a man named Geoff who took me under his wing. I've always been fortunate to meet people who helped me and showed me the ropes, a bit like Paul did on the street. Geoff taught me good values, such as: look after your customers and you'll find they come back to you and you develop relationships of trust that last. That was very, very unusual in trading. Most people are just in it for all they can get. Manufacturers Hanover Trust later merged into J. P. Morgan. I stayed there till 2010. I had no degree, no A-levels, no experience and no subtlety. I wasn't scared of speaking out to people above me. I didn't care.'

'Your life seems full of quite extreme situations!' I exclaim, to which Bachi replies, 'All I've ever done is firefight. I had to fight to get off the street, to get into trading, to overcome serious illness. I've never been able to just sit down and breathe. But that is exactly what I can do in the park with Lizzie, hanging out with Nick and Pascal.'

I understand what Bachi is talking about because I feel it too – the calm of the park, the relief of having a space to relax in, the conviviality of our casual evening encounters under the open sky and the pleasure of talking about life with people whose experiences and perspectives widen our understanding of the world.

And I notice that we are not alone. There are others who linger in the park, enjoying its calming qualities – an old man

I frequently spot under an umbrella in the rain who seems to be just standing there absorbing the atmosphere when most people have hurried home, a young woman I sometimes see resting motionless on a bench and a middle-aged man who often sits for hours cross-legged under the copper beech. People who, in spite of the command to keep moving, have stopped to imbibe the peace and solace of the park.

4 Meeting

'I've always wanted to live on my own,' Nick tells me one morning when I am visiting with a flask of black coffee for us to share. I am surprised by his comment, given that he and Pascal live side by side in such close proximity. I assume it must be a reference to his love of independence and self-sufficiency.

Chance would have it that Nick and I have identical tin mugs, royal blue on the outside, white on the inside – mine from fifteen years ago when my son used to go on school trips, Nick's a gift from a walker in the park. The flask contains enough for both of us to fill our mugs and have a top-up. Pascal declines the offer of coffee, finding it too bitter without milk. He makes himself a cup of tea with the water Jim brought this morning, adding plenty of sugar from his supplies. Later I will sometimes bring him a small jar of milk or, better still, a flask of hot chocolate, but that is in the cold winter months.

Sharing my morning coffee with Nick has become a substitute for going to the local cafe, now fully closed owing to Covid restrictions. To sit here with my new companions, observing the sun climbing in the morning sky until the point where it illuminates us on the dewy grass, feels like an extraordinary privilege – a taste of enchantment before the beginning of the working day.

I woke early this morning with the dawn chorus, watching the streaks of pink intensify in the sky before sunrise from the comfortable vantage point of my bed. I stayed lying there, with the window and curtains open, until I heard the distant elongated cry of the gibbons warming up their voices in preparation for their daily duet. Before meeting Nick and Pascal, I had never noticed that I could hear the gibbons from my bed, or at least never registered what that strange piping sound was. Experiencing the park at different moments of the day has made me more attentive to shifts in atmosphere, sound and light. It is as if the outside has become more present inside, my home more porous to what lies beyond its walls. Now, whenever I hear the cry of the gibbons, I picture them swinging on their long black arms, tilting their white-cheeked faces upwards and releasing undulating waves of sound into the morning sky from an improbable range of acrobatic poses. This is better than any alarm clock, not least because it is my call to the park.

When I arrived today, Nick and Pascal had already breakfasted. Now, as we sip our hot drinks, they are seated in their sleeping bags, their faces glowing in the morning sun. Three crows have arranged themselves at different levels in a nearby tree, flying down from time to time to peck at fragments of cornflakes. Squirrels are chasing each other up and down trees, weaving in and out of the undergrowth, their tails flashing in the distilled morning light. A plump pigeon wanders cautiously up to Pascal's ear as if wanting to whisper something in it. Pascal turns slowly towards it with an amused smile. His calmness and receptivity is such that the pigeon doesn't move. Blackcaps, thrushes and robins are our other companions. Everything feels fresh and alive.

The intensity of the light and multiplicity of sounds transport me back to early mornings in small towns in India. I picture the frenetic feeding of birds that takes place at sunrise, can hear the distant temple bells and see the mingling of animals, birds and humans, all channelling the energy of the morning sun in unison.

'Potency, I call it,' Nick says after we have sat there in silence for a while. It is indeed as if we are recharging ourselves directly through the sun's rays.

'How long have you been living in the park?' I ask eventually.

'It's quite a while now.' Nick arranges small tufts of tobacco onto a paper as he speaks. 'What is it, Pasc – four years?'

'Five,' Pascal utters.

'Five years. It's thanks to the park manager that we're here,' Nick continues. 'It's been a real privilege. Before that we were sleeping down by the canal and we were lugging our stuff back and forth.'

'And how long have you been living together?' I ask tentatively, taking note of Nick's declaration that he has always wanted to live alone.

Nick turns to Pascal. 'Fourteen, fifteen years?'

'Sixteen.'

Though he speaks little and is often barely audible when he does, Pascal is the keeper of dates and times. It is as if he carries the scaffold of their collective memory while Nick, less hinged to chronology, carries the richness of detail.

'I didn't want to carry on living my life in chronological time, having to do things by this time and that,' Nick explains. 'I preferred to stop time, rewind, get back to the centre, to use it as a compass. In India people go through different phases in their lives – marriage, children, family – and then in old age they rid themselves of possessions and go to the forest. I thought I'd go to the forest without doing all the other stuff first!' We both laugh. 'And I don't regret it. I've had a wonderful life and being here is phenomenal.'

'Sixteen years!' I exclaim, bringing us back to Pascal's intervention. 'That's a long time. Did you ever envisage you'd end up living together so long when you first met?'

Nick takes a puff of his neatly rolled cigarette. 'I was walking through the Strand at the time. There was an Eritrean guy I knew. He came up to me and said, "I've met someone living in the street who is different from the others. He thinks just the same way as you do. I want to introduce you." And we found Pascal in the place where they had facilities for homeless people to do their ablutions – loos, water, that sort of thing. He introduced us there. Of course, no two people think exactly alike,' Nick adds, 'but it's a pragmatic arrangement. You learn to live alongside each other.'

'A pretty good arrangement if it's lasted that long,' I suggest.

'An arrangement without an arrangement,' Pascal specifies.

Pascal makes his observation quietly. His dark eyes sparkle with a combination of shyness and perspicacity. He may not say much but there is never any doubt about his participation in the conversation.

And Pascal has summarised the situation well. It is an arrangement that works because it has come about through shared practice rather than planning or respect for social convention or obligation. Something in their lives has made it make more sense to live alongside each other than not. And it has gone on continuing to make sense for nineteen years (at the time of writing). This does not mean that their relationship is entirely devoid of complications. Occasionally they might sleep under separate trees for a few consecutive nights. Like any long-term cohabitation it requires adaptation and a willingness to elevate the good times over the bad.

'Remember how you thought I'd stolen thirty pounds and I told you to fuck off?' Nick says, turning to Pascal, remembering the early days of their relationship.

Pascal laughs, digesting the memory but saying nothing.

'They used to call you my shadow back on the street. You chose to keep silent. And no doubt you have your reasons. I've always said it's best to keep your own counsel.

'We used to lug our stuff around near Lincoln's Inn,' Nick continues. 'We would get handouts or collect food that had been chucked out. At Lincoln's Inn everyone used to turn to the wall to eat their food. They were scared that someone else might snatch it, that's the truth of the matter. But it wasn't just that. People in the street feel worthless or feel that people see them as worthless, so they don't want to interact. They don't want to see their image reflected back. And you quickly learn that you can't trust anyone in the street. You could find some decent stuff in the bins,' he continues, 'if you knew where to look. Pascal and I were good at it. He developed a liking for barbecued chicken and couscous that we'd find down the West End. Stuff left over from the restaurants. You had to be careful, of course, but I don't think you ever got ill, did you, Pasc?'

'Once,' Pascal interjects, 'on chocolate cake.'

'Oh, the chocolate cake from Patisserie Valerie!' Nick chuckles. 'Patisserie Valerie used to dump whole cakes in bags and chuck them in their bins at the end of the day. We used to raid those bins. Pascal has a sweet tooth. I'm more for savoury food and I'm wary of bacteria on sweet things, but Pascal was keener on that stuff and used to eat a lot of it. You probably ate the whole cake! I hear they might be closing them down now, Patisserie Valerie – corruption, that sort of thing.'

I am amused to hear them talk of Patisserie Valerie, with its pretensions to civility and grandeur and its overdecorated, cream-filled, fruit-topped cakes. It is a place that also holds very personal memories for me. Denis and I first went there straight after emerging from University College Hospital having seen the heartbeat of our son in embryo – a smudgy grey image on a scan. Until then all our trips to UCH had been for infertility investigations, unearthing a series of hitherto unknown abnormalities and potential impediments – polycystic ovaries, endometriosis, an inverted uterus, an incompatibility between his sperm and my fluids – none of which definitively signalled permanent infertility but all of which rendered pregnancy less and less likely, especially since I was by then over thirty-five, when fertility levels for women drop dramatically even without a list of unhelpful added factors of this kind. 'Unexplained infertility' was the label we had been given by the consultant and for me it came with a deep, low-level depression. Not the sort of depression that prevents you from being able to function at all but the sort that eats away at your capacity for enjoyment. The death of the future was what that indeterminate diagnosis meant to me.

Seeing a heartbeat on a scan no doubt feels miraculous for every first parent, but for us it had added magic and excitement. We were freed from daunting decisions about whether or not to pursue IVF and I was released instantaneously from the fug of depression, like a swimmer coming up to the surface to breathe after having spent four years underwater. In order not to leave any stone unturned I had eventually visited a Chinese acupuncturist in Camden Town, and within two weeks of inserting her needles she had announced that she thought I was pregnant from the look of my tongue. This seemed improbable but had subsequently been confirmed through two home pregnancy tests (why would I trust only one?), a blood test and now this scan. Patisserie Valerie, with its elegant painted interior and extravagant, brightly coloured cakes, represented a welcome transition out of the monochrome hospital environment with its invasive bodily intrusions. It represented a re-entry into an outside world full of promise.

Now, when I think back to that moment of eating my first pastry at Patisserie Valerie in the knowledge that there was a new heartbeat ticking healthily inside me, I wonder if maybe

Nick and Pascal were round the back, gathering yesterday's cakes out of the bins.

'There's the inside and the outside,' Nick comments, 'but I always seem to be on the threshold.'

'The threshold is often the most interesting place to be,' I suggest, aware that it is our meeting point.

Nick and Pascal's life together spills out in fragments scattered across a year's worth of conversations. To compose it into a single narrative is to give it a structure that goes against its very nature. It is less about things said than things lived and experienced in synchronicity – streets known, bins explored, ideas discussed, books read, food shared, friends and acquaintances developed, threats endured, storms weathered, suns and moons observed, memories forged in the act of living. They share the rhythms of a daily life that goes against the grain of societal norms, without the props of family, property or income; a life that combines both insecurity and freedom in equal measure, lived together in the open wherever that might be – in the street, under bridges, down by the canal and eventually in Regent's Park, where they have made their houseless home amongst the trees.

'I'm here as a sort of two-fingers-up, in a way,' Nick comments one day. 'I could live differently but I've always preferred being outdoors and I'm not that interested in possessions.' I have also heard him say quite simply, 'The park: it's heaven,' and, 'We come here for peace.'

'I knew early on, from fifteen or so, that I had to follow what I wanted,' Nick tells me. 'I've been homeless – or should

I say at home in the street – for over twenty years. When I met Pascal I was sleeping under Bridge 10 down by the canal and he was sleeping in one of the central parks on his own. That's not good. I was worried he had got in with the wrong people in the street. Pascal doesn't drink but he was hanging around with a man who kept trying to get him to drink. That's not right. I found out that man was living in a hostel that had a reputation. It was where they put people with alcohol and mental health problems. And there were people around who sometimes tried to recruit people off the street for porn films. He could have been vulnerable to that. So I said he could come along with me and we could watch out for each other's things and each other.'

Nick is often keen to emphasise this aspect: that their friendship is just a pragmatic arrangement and that they are not bound to one another.

'Relations in the street can be difficult. A lot of people are searching for family and get caught up in abusive situations. Some people think I'm a sort of street daddy for Pascal but that's not the case. We're just friends. We don't bother each other. We let each other be. We're not tied to each other in any way. The art of being together is to give the person the free-dom to be themselves without interference or coercion. That's von Humboldt for you. If I ever get a state pension, which I hope I do, I'll share it with Pascal, but that won't bond him to me. He is always free to go his own way and always has been.'

I think of the different faces of freedom and how that con-cept looks and feels to different people. Many people seeing

Nick and Pascal for the first time might assume that poverty and hunger constrain them from experiencing the luxury of anything we might want to call freedom. But people who engage with them through conversation and exchanges of food cannot help but be struck by how they embrace their way of life with a certain zest. And what is freedom if not the capacity to live life on your own terms?

I mention the book *A Free Man* by Aman Sethi, which recounts the life of Mohammed Ashraf, a poor man living in the streets of Delhi who earns a daily wage when he needs to by working as a labourer on building sites. He has no desire for accumulation and never earns more than what he needs for the next few days. Freedom, in Ashraf's view, is being able to tell your boss to 'fuck off'.

'It's important to be able to see beyond the mundane,' Nick responds, 'not to live your life on a conveyor belt, not to make life into a prison for yourself. I saw that when I used to work in factories.'

I am attentive to his comments. But I am not just thinking of factories. I am also thinking of how constricted and claustrophobic my own working life at the university has become. I used to value my job for the freedom it offered – freedom of thought, freedom of expression and freedom of how to manage time. But for some years now I have felt more and more tied to bureaucratic structures I don't believe in and constrained by ideological trends that seem to stifle the act of questioning. In short, I am aware of just how unfree I feel and how the conditions imposed by the pandemic may have exacerbated this sensation but are not at the root of it. Have I incarcerated myself without even noticing it by accepting one constraint too many? I do not idealise Nick and Pascal's way of life. I have no illusions about how demanding it is and am aware of the discipline it requires on a daily basis. I know I could never live this life, nor would I ever wish to, but I also recognise that there is a certain freedom in it and, in their case, contentment too. It is palpable not just to me but to others who engage with them.

'You're happy!' a woman exclaims almost accusingly as she passes Nick on the footpath towards the canal one morning. That is all she says. 'It's as if she can't imagine that anyone living in my situation could be happy,' he observes.

'You are Joy,' another woman declares, looking towards Pascal. 'And you, Wisdom,' she says to Nick. Strange announcements, perhaps, but not without pertinence.

One day, when I am strolling around the park with Nick, an elderly lady recognises him and calls out his name. She is delighted to see him. 'You're amazing,' she says with feeling. 'You are always so positive. It is so inspiring!'

'The homeless have been used as a negative example of what will happen to you if you don't follow society's delusions,' Nick comments, 'and there are some very real consequences if you don't, but I've also noticed you get a lot of creativity in the so-called oppressed group. You get a lot of suicide and drink problems too,' he adds, taking care not to glamorise homelessness, 'but there is creativity.'

One morning an elderly gentleman greets Nick warmly in the park while we are searching for mushrooms in the long grass. He has recently moved to Norfolk and hasn't seen Nick for a couple of years. 'How are you?' he calls out.

'How do I look?' Nick challenges with a broad smile, spreading his arms wide so that the man might inspect him from head to toe.

'You look very well,' the man admits.

Nick replies, 'I've come to the conclusion that if you have nothing, you actually have everything.'

'How so?'

'It brings out the best in people,' is Nick's answer.

'There must be a lot of solidarity in living together the way you and Pascal do,' I suggest one day when Nick has just insisted that their relationship is purely pragmatic.

'Yes, solidarity. That's exactly what it is. There have been occasions when people were being dismissive of me, and Pascal has broken his silence and told them, "You should listen to what he is saying." Pascal is a master of silence,' Nick continues. 'He's the enigma. I've learned quietude from him. There is a real discipline in that. But some people find it difficult. Once when there was a bad storm we were under the canal bridge and this Pakistani guy came under to take shelter. He was angry with the world. He was sounding off and kept turning to Pascal for his opinion – "Why won't you speak out?" That kind of thing. He wanted solidarity from another non-white person, but Pascal didn't say anything and the guy got very frustrated.'

I look at Pascal. I have never seen him in racialised terms and have no desire to interrogate him about his origins; there is something about his silence that invites you to respect his privacy. I know he is from Paris and that he prefers to speak English over French. I have even heard him say, with a hint of irony, 'You could call me an Anglophile' – but that is all I know and for the moment that is enough. It is only much later, when I come to the park one evening and mention that Julius and I have been watching the film *The Battle of Algiers*, that Pascal mentions that his family are from Algeria and that they are Berber. 'They're the sort of Jews of Algeria,' he adds for context.

Our discussion that evening is mostly about the film. I discover Pascal is something of a film buff. This might seem surprising given that he and Nick do not go to the cinema or have any access to devices on which to watch films. But Pascal used to work in a video shop before coming to England – so Nick tells me – and some years back the two of them would regularly hang out with a group of what he called his hobo friends at the South Bank, where they took shelter in the foyer of the Royal Festival Hall and watched old films on a DVD player that one of them had been given. Their knowledge of cinema is far more extensive than mine, even if most of the films they refer to date back over fifteen years. It is not uncommon for Nick to pepper the conversation with scenes from old films they have seen together. On such occasions he almost always turns to Pascal for titles, names of actors, directors, the year they saw the film. Pascal rarely fails to provide the details, and I often leave the park with a list of must-see film recommendations.

'You must watch *Withnail and I*,' Nick tells me. I, in my ignorance, am unfamiliar with the film. 'It's about out-of-work actors living in Camden Town. There's a scene in it towards the end when they're walking through Regent's Park. It's a comedy but it's worth seeing. Who's the main actor, Pasc?'

'Richard E. Grant,' Pascal answers, but that is all he contributes to the conversation. A few evenings later my son and I sit down to watch the film on iPlayer.

Pascal's capacity for silence intrigues me. It's as if by speaking less he can observe more. He is a very attentive listener and is always alert to small changes in his environment – a falling leaf, a hopeful squirrel, the hop of a nearby bird or hungry mouse. He interacts with these non-human presences with a mixture of pleasure and amusement and seems so at peace that he makes conversation feel unnecessary. When he does speak it often sounds as if he has not used his voice for a long time. Occasionally when I come to the park I find him alone. It takes me a while to settle into the silence and I often find myself beginning by sharing snippets of university life, which he seems to absorb with interest. Sometimes we also discuss the latest news, which he follows closely on his pocket radio. He is always better informed than I am about Trump's latest antics in the US, details of the ongoing Brexit gridlock, the most recent government announcements on social distancing or the extension of the furlough scheme. He is interested in what will happen when the scheme comes to an end. 'The universal minimum wage is not just a necessity,' he states emphatically, though very quietly, 'it's an inevitability.' He is concerned about how technology distances people from their surroundings and how it may eventually make us all redundant. I notice that he speaks more when Nick is not around.

One morning when I am delivering bread I find him alone in his usual position, lying flat and pillowless in his battered sleeping bag under the chestnut tree, a robin perched on one of the branches just above his head. The white chestnut flowers are no longer upright like torches. They have begun to droop as spring transitions to summer. The cow parsley is also beginning to fade and the hawthorn flowers are turning rusty on the tree. This is the moment when the long grasses and lustrous nettles in this corner of the park are splashed with colour in the form of pink campion, lady's bedstraw and golden buttercups. Pascal gives me a welcoming smile that encourages me to sit on a log near him. I find him more forthcoming than usual. When I comment on the robin perched above him, he replies, 'He's a regular and he likes to sit directly above my bed – which can be a bit of a problem! Nature is our teacher here,' he continues. 'You learn to be humble. It teaches you that. You adapt to whatever nature demands. When the conkers form we move our bedding to under the hornbeams so we don't get fired on. Last year – in August, I think – this chestnut tree was filled with parakeets. There must have been forty or so and they just devoured the tree. That wasn't a good time to be sitting under here, either from the noise perspective or the splashes. The pigeons can also be a problem.'

I look up at the trees, imagining the challenges posed by these different avian visitors.

'The weather has been really good these last few months,' Pascal observes, 'but last winter it was very wet. It rained every day for about six months.'

'How do you manage when it rains like that?' I ask.

'We just adapt as our ancestors must have done. But even we sometimes wonder how we can survive that much rain. We just stand up. It's all we can do.'

One evening, when I am delivering food later than usual, I find Pascal lying alone in the dark under a different tree than normal. He tells me Nick has gone to the canal to meet someone. I am struck by the vulnerability of their sleeping in the open without protection of any sort. The wind is up and the shadows of the trees are animating the night sky like dancing witches. I remember Nick once telling me how he was beaten up in a street near the edge of the park by a gang of youths using chains in an initiation ritual they called 'stroking'. He was left bruised and concussed for weeks. I ask Pascal if he is ever scared in the park at night.

'Scared of what?' he asks incredulously.

'I don't know. Humans? Animals?' I suggest.

He just laughs and says that the foxes have been coming very close at night recently and that one of them keeps stealing his socks.

'What about before you met Nick?' I ask. 'Were you ever anxious sleeping in the street when you first came to London?'

'No,' he replies. 'I used to sleep in St James's Park. They locked the park at night so I was on my own there. I'd seen that they had deckchairs for tourists. They used to charge people to sit in those chairs during the day.' He laughs at the idea of people having to pay to sit in a deckchair. 'I took one of the chairs and hid it behind some bushes. I'd get it out at night and sleep on it under the stars. In the morning I'd put the deckchair back in its hiding place and would go into town to get food. The security guards knew I was there. They saw me every morning but they never bothered me.'

There is something about the lightness and goodwill with which Nick and Pascal inhabit public space that seems to have encouraged park officials, social workers and the police to turn a blind eye and leave them in peace. To outsiders it might seem curious that they never build a shelter or erect a tent, but exposure to the elements is part of the challenge of their way of life. It is also their way of trying to respect the regulations of the Royal Parks, within reason. They are aware that Regent's Park is not an obvious place to take up residence and that their presence in the park is both ambiguous and precarious.

'Some people look down on us. All they see is an image of a homeless person, a loser,' Nick tells me one evening. 'They can't see beyond the image. But some people see us as guardians of the park. They say we offer security in the least populated areas. We have joggers and dog walkers telling us they are reassured by our presence.'

'I met someone the other day,' I say, 'who refers to you as "the philosopher under the tree".'

'I'm not a philosopher,' Nick insists, 'but I will listen to people, that's the thing, and I'm not afraid to give my opinion. You might think this is nature in the city but really it is the city in nature. Nature was here first and we are simply passing through. But I love the city and it has its uses. When I lose track of the date and time, I press one of the parking meters on the edge of the park and it brings me back to reality. And do you know how I judge the likelihood of rain? By looking at the level of cloud covering the top of the BT Tower. I use both nature and the city to orient myself.'

I try to imagine the space as a forest inhabited by wild animals and as a hunting ground used by Henry VIII, but everything around me has been planted and landscaped since. The city in nature.

'Michael Wood, the park manager, knows we're here. He's a good man,' Nick continues. 'I think he understands us. It is entirely thanks to him that we're here, and I am grateful for that. He came here once and he sliced his hand down on the ground with a thud and said, "There is a line between what is legal and what is not. It's a clear division." He was talking about the fact that we don't have the right to sleep in the park at night. But I said, "Nothing is ever that clear-cut. There is the yin and the yang and the line between them is curvy, not straight. You have a white dot in the black side and a black dot in the white side. But if you want us to leave the park, you only have to tell us and we'll leave."'

By not erecting a tent, building a structure or making a fire, Nick and Pascal keep their footprint in the park light. The materials of daily life – tarpaulins, sleeping bags, umbrellas, wellies and whatever food, clothes, books or supplies people give them – lack permanence. They are all transportable, even if they are rarely transported and have accumulated over the years, owing to the cult of giving that seems to have developed around them.

Their place under the trees may not take the form of a structure but it feels very much like home. I notice that when a man and woman stray into their territory one day, thinking that the path behind them might lead out of the park, the woman apologises with the words, 'Sorry to cross your backyard!' She has spontaneously sensed that this is not just their space but also their place. 'Don't forget to wipe your feet, will you?' Nick quips, raising laughter from everyone, given that we are all dressed in wellies and ankle-deep in squelchy mud. I too find myself using vocabulary infused with the idea of home. Once, when puddles obstruct me from arriving around the front, I find myself apologising for entering 'through the side entrance', to which Nick replies warmly, 'You are welcome to come in through the back door if you like!' Later I often do.

Nick has had a few interesting conversations with Michael Wood over the years and he seems to treasure these encounters. He remembers discussing G. K. Chesterton's definition of a stereotype with Wood's young son. 'Take one aspect of a person, blow it up and then take it to be the person' was how he summarised it. He also remembers talking about wildness and domesticity.

'Michael Wood told me that he once lost his dog, a beautiful grey lurcher, in the countryside. The dog had gone off following the scent of a fox and went missing for several hours. Michael was angry with the dog, but I don't think he should have blamed it and I said so, although I did add that I understand that you have to mediate between wildness and domestication. "That's right," Michael said, and he was looking straight at me as he said it!' Nick laughs heartily at the memory.

Another story he enjoys recounting is the time he and Pascal were lying in their sleeping bags one Christmas Day when snow was tumbling from the sky and only their faces were left visible under their snow-covered bags. The park was entirely empty. Then suddenly Michael appeared with a man who looked like he might be a relative. 'That man looked so surprised to see these two people buried up to their necks in snow! He chatted to us for a while, then he opened his wallet and gave fifteen pounds to Pascal with a smile. I've always wondered if they'd made a bet that day about whether or not we'd still be here.'

One evening Nick accompanies me over the bridge. He is on his way down to the towpath to plant the empty flasks for Jim and I am pushing my bicycle, preparing to cycle home. Just before we part I ask him something I have always been curious to know.

'What brought Pascal to London and to living in the street?'

There is a long pause, then Nick says, 'I don't know. You might find that surprising given that we've been sharing the same bit of plastic for sixteen years, but he's never told me.'

'Is that the longest you've ever lived with anyone?' I ask, to which he responds, 'It's certainly the longest I've ever been with a person I still don't know!'

5 Words

The sun is lowering in the west, illuminating leafy treetops in magnificent colours. Gold, turning pink. The long grasses are vibrating in the evening rays. Infinite shades of straw. Bees that have been hovering around the tantalising purple tassels of the flowering vetch are now retreating back to their hidden hives for the evening. Ants continue to weave their way between the grasses. Lizzie is doing her rounds, bounding between us, licking our hands and wagging her tail. Nick repeats something I have often heard him say: 'It's a real privilege being here.'

I understand Nick's sentiment as I watch the changing light and feel the tensions of work drain down my spine and disperse into the ground on which I sit. To be grounded in this way and simultaneously part of the expansive universe does indeed feel like an incredible privilege – all the more so when the world is in lockdown. I am also struck by how Nick's use of the term 'privilege' challenges conventional perceptions of homelessness, and how in the university environment I inhabit the word has very different associations.

But then words mean different things in different spaces. Sitting in the park on summer evenings like this, words, concepts and conversations somehow feel more open. It doesn't seem contradictory that a person perceived by the outside world as homeless should express a sense of privilege even if the two concepts – privilege and homelessness – are uncommon bedfellows. Nor does it feel impossible for me to experience a sense of privilege without it being attributed to my class, wealth or race. It reminds me just how restrictive words and concepts can become when their meanings get fixed and stuck in a groove through repetitive association and use.

Take 'homelessness'.

'I've never identified with the term "homeless",' Nick tells me, 'except as a category that the police might put on you.'

When I ask him what a home is, he replies quite simply, 'The world is my home.'

It is a statement that immediately renders the term 'homeless' inadequate, petty and parochial. When I try to describe Nick and Pascal's way of living to friends and acquaintances outside the park, I find myself up against this poverty of language and encounter a barrage of negative value judgements and stereotypes attached to the idea of living without a structure that conforms to our conceptions of a home.

'You mean tramps!' a friend states on the phone, crudely, as if I am somehow refusing to get to the point.

'Well, no. Not tramps. They're people who are living outside,' I specify. 'Under the trees,' I add, as if the trees will somehow make it better.

'Ah well, I suppose having a few pints under the trees is a good way of passing the time during lockdown!' another friend quips.

Who ever said anything about drink?

'They're not drinkers. That's not their thing at all,' I correct, irritated by the implicit suggestion of alcoholism.

'Do you mean *vagrants*?' the first acquaintance asks when I resist the words 'tramp' and 'homeless'.

Vagrant! Now that is not a word I was expecting to hear, with its pre-Dickensian associations. I am surprised to find it still in circulation and realise I am not entirely sure what it even means, although I'm aware of its connotations of criminality. When I get off the phone, I type the word into a search engine and am amused to be confronted by the following: 'Vagrant is a tool for building and managing virtual machine environments in a single workflow.' So the word 'vagrant' has clearly updated itself! Technology and commerce have brought it new meanings associated with the future, not the past. They are meanings barely comprehensible to me, and no doubt even less so to Nick and Pascal, who don't have anything to do with mobile phones or computers. But it doesn't take long to find the older meanings. The Merriam-Webster dictionary tells me a vagrant is 'one who has no established residence and wanders idly from place to place without lawful or visible means of support'. It offer the synonyms of 'vagabond' and 'tramp'. Meanwhile, freedictionary.com describes a vagabond as 'an idle wandering beggar or thief'.

What is clear from these descriptions is that the vagrant is defined through a series of binaries: idle versus active; unemployed versus employed; beggar versus earner; wanderer versus settler; criminal versus law-abiding citizen. The definition reminds me of Nick's earlier comment: 'The homeless have been used as a negative example of what will happen to you if you don't follow society's delusions.'

I decide to investigate the word 'vagabond' further with a certain trepidation. But, once again, I find that commerce has appropriated the term. I am confronted by a range of Vagabond Tara women's boots, followed by an image from a Japanese manga series. I look up the shoe company. It is Swedish. Skinny-legged models start striding around Berlin on my screen, wearing baseball caps, long coats and a variety of edgy, wedgy boots. Vagabond made cool. But again, it doesn't take long to find more of the older associations: 'beggar, bum, dodger, hobo, loiterer, malingerer, roamer, slacker, tramp, wayfarer'. The words 'disreputable', 'worthless' and 'shiftless' leap out of my screen.

I tap the word 'tramp' on my keyboard, hopeful that the associations will be a little less punitive. But I am disappoint-ed. Vocabulary.com says: 'If someone calls you a tramp, they either mean you're a slut or a hobo – each meaning comes from vagrant, or wanderer, and the low-life behaviors asso-ciated with vagrants.' With this new definition the negative connotations accumulate like layers of bitter toffee that can't be licked off. I seem to be going round in circles. Tramps are vagrants. Vagrants are vagabonds. Vagabonds are tramps. Is our vocabulary so lacking? Is it not possible to find a word which refers to living outside that isn't saturated with the stigma of uselessness and criminality?

'Of course, they can always throw the Vagrancy Act at you,' Nick comments one evening. 'We used to get that sometimes in the street.'

I look up the Vagrancy Act on the website of the charity Centrepoint and am shocked to learn that an act passed in 1824 – in the aftermath of the Napoleonic Wars, and originally designed to stop destitute returning soldiers from seeking alms through exposing their wounds and deformities – remains current to this day, with only minor amendments. It replaced a series of other acts which criminalised vagrancy, including the Vagabonds Acts of 1547 and 1572. The former legalised the enslavement and buying and selling of the so-called idle poor; the latter recommended whipping and ear-boring as punishments.

While the Vagrancy Act of today does not condone slavery, it does still criminalise homelessness. So while having a shelter might reasonably be considered a human right, not having one is apparently and unreasonably considered a crime, punishable with fines of up to £1,000. To regard the world as your home, as Nick does, is not permissible, it seems, unless accompanied by a physical structure.

When I ask Nick about terminology, he recounts a story: 'I remember, years ago, there were some kids trying to insult me and they were shouting, "You tramp! You tramp!" I turned to them as I walked past and said, "I'm not a tramp. I'm a hobo!"' Nick re-enacts the scene with a chuckle. 'A hobo is someone who is not working but might,' he specifies. 'A tramp these days is associated with drink and drugs and that kind of thing, which wasn't necessarily the case with the tramps of old, but they're a dying breed, at least according to some. A friend of mine was actually told that by a social worker: "We're just waiting for your generation to die out." In the street most people see themselves as victims,' he continues, 'but we're not, and some people find that disconcerting. When people look at us, what they see is a stereotype of a homeless person. But you have to go beyond the image.'

I think of all the work that goes into dismantling stereotypes and how they have an uncanny habit of reproducing themselves or taking on new guises as the meanings of words shift.

One evening, my spirits are low when I come to the park. Not even the smell of the summer grass or the distant thrum of a woodpecker can rouse me. The brutal murder of George Floyd in the US has unleashed a collective outpouring of protest against injustice. To witness this collective mobilisation inspires hope, even if the trigger for it is a grotesque reminder of the ongoing horrors of racism in its most crude and brutal form. I want to join the protests but fear of spreading Covid and infecting others has held me back. But many of my students – of all backgrounds – have been out protesting and I see their sense of empowerment as they feel the world shift under their feet. At the same time, in my own university department, what has emerged is not solidarity but division.

Despite the fact that every member of my department wholeheartedly condemns racial discrimination in all its forms, we are unable to formulate a collective statement to this effect. It is as if it has ignited a competition over whose version of anti-racism is most valid.

I find it difficult to believe that together we cannot find words with which to respond collectively to these events.

Words may not be enough but they are something, a starting point for acknowledgement and solidarity, and I have spent the last two days trying to help draft an email that everyone feels they can sign up to. But I have found myself deleting words almost as fast as I write them. The email is batted back and forth between colleagues for suggestions and amendments but is rejected at the last minute by a small group of various ethnicities and backgrounds who have put out an email in their own names. When I organise a Zoom meeting in an attempt to find common ground, I am told that no words are adequate in the face of the situation. At the same time the department stands accused of racism for its failure to speak out.

Increasingly I am finding that words seem to be failing me or letting me down. I realise that for most of my life I have experienced them as my friends, as the medium through which I can express ideas, explore the subtleties of the human condition, learn through attentive listening, converse and make connections. But of late I am finding words difficult to relate to. Their meanings seem to slip and slide out of my grasp. Words are morphing so rapidly that they are becoming instruments of alienation, sometimes barely recognisable, other times fraught with danger or treachery. The pandemic has exacerbated this process. Within the space of a few months it has given us a whole new vocabulary and set of associated concepts: 'social distancing', 'self-isolation', 'shielding', 'lockdown', 'quarantine', 'bubbles' and 'pods'. 'PPE' no longer refers to politics, philosophy and economics but to personal protective equipment. There is talk of 'Covid compliance', 'R numbers' and 'respiratory etiquette'. Conversations that once ended with 'Take care' now end with the words 'Stay safe.'

At the university, our vocabulary has been shifting for some years now in more or less subtle ways. Students have become reconceptualised as 'consumers', lecturers as 'service providers', the people with whom we engage in our research as 'stakeholders'. The language of business and innovation has penetrated every aspect of university life. We are encouraged to demonstrate the economic and social impact of our research, as if research is nothing more than a peculiarly indirect form of income generation or policy-making. I find myself trying to resist this alienating vocabulary but at the same time having to reproduce it in order to fulfil the requirements of my job. I am, after all, writing an impact case study about my own research and helping my department steer its way through the impending Research Excellence Framework, a national exercise which occurs every six years and determines a department's research ranking and its allocation of QR (quality-related research) funding.

But it is in teaching that words are proving the greatest challenge. Where once I felt I knew how to frame a subject with care and sensitivity, today every topic and the words associated with it seem fraught with peril as to whom they might upset and whether I even have the right to speak on the subject at all.

Social anthropology, the discipline to which I was attracted for its broad humanistic framework and its radical potential for challenging Eurocentric norms and stereotypes, has today become an object of extreme mistrust. Its problematic past, rooted and entangled in nineteenth-century colonialism, has come back to haunt it as an indelible accusation in the present. Like other anthropology departments up and down the country, we have embraced the project of decolonisation. Everyone agrees that this involves not simply critiquing anthropology's past (something most of us have been doing for a very long time) but also transforming its present and future, but none of us is quite sure what this means in real terms beyond encouraging greater diversity of practices and practitioners. Meanwhile, a prominent American anthropology journal carries an article and debate about the case for letting anthropology burn. Here, arguments are made that anthropology's problematic heritage, its foundations in whiteness and its assumption of a universal human subject make it no longer fit for purpose unless reconfigured as a form of radical activism oriented towards reparation and repair. The heat of these tensions is making quieter forms of anthropology difficult to teach. The new Covid-induced obligation to record lectures and upload them onto a scarily named software platform called Panopto makes the prospect of mobilising words into sentences and arguments even more daunting. Sometimes I wish I could take refuge in silence, but silence isn't an option for a lecturer.

Bachi and Nick are playing with Lizzie and talking about old advertisements and films. I am far away in my own world, just trying to sink my body into the ground and let the numerous stresses of the day drain away. I want to merge with the earth and enter a state of wordlessness, let the grass and the sky offer me some peace. But instead I find my mind awash with words deleted, aborted, unspoken, unspeakable. Inadequate words and impossible questions. The more they are suppressed, the more they seem to multiply in my head. Even my nights have become a whirlpool of unspoken words.

'How are you? You look subdued,' Nick comments eventually, turning his attention from Lizzie to me.

'I'm just a bit preoccupied. I've had a difficult two days at work,' I confess, not really wanting to extrapolate. I don't feel I have either the words or the energy. But Nick has sensed my mood and is attentive in a way that deserves a response. 'I've just spent two days trying to write a one-page email which can't be sent,' I explain. I find it exhausting and depressing. I am disappointed in how something of global importance can be converted into an opportunity for internal division.

Soon we are talking about the Black Lives Matter protests taking place in the city and around the world.

'I think they're a good thing, these protests,' Nick comments. 'Black people are showing they won't put up with stuff any longer. They've been shat on for centuries. It's like lancing a boil of society.'

I agree with his sentiment even if I wouldn't have phrased it that way.

'But I hope they don't import the race language and politics from America because this society is different and has a different history,' he continues. I agree with that analysis too, although I recognise that the nuances of these different problematic histories are often swept under the carpet in the current public debate. But Bachi is less aligned with the language of the protests. 'All lives matter,' he states. 'Period.'

The words hang heavily in the air.

It is impossible not to be aware of the recent history of this phrase and how it has been co-opted as a slogan by Donald Trump and the far right in the US, Britain and elsewhere. I am conscious of how it has been used to undermine, deflate and derail the Black Lives Matter movement, to a point where many regard it as quite simply unsayable. Of course, the words, if taken at face value, are not in themselves offensive. The very notion of human rights depends upon them. It is precisely because all lives matter that it is so necessary to insist that Black lives matter at this particular moment, since they have so often been treated as if they do not. Has the far right's strategic use of the phrase distorted and perverted its meaning to such an extent that it cannot be used? Or are we, by accepting this, conceding to the far right's power to redefine our vocabulary and its meaning? My head is awhirl with such contemplations. These days I have lost confidence in my own judgement of words. Or is it simply that the words have lost their innocence?

'I mean *all* lives, human and non-human,' Bachi continues, no doubt sensing my unease, 'and that includes Lizzie's.' And Bachi certainly means what he says. What better proof of it than the fact that he was willing to fling himself in front of a speeding bicycle, risking his own life in an attempt to save hers?

I look around me at Lizzie and at the squirrels and the

crows, the insects in the long grass, the purple vetch and leafy hornbeam trees, and hold on to this expansive idea of 'all lives' that the park makes possible. This moment of tranquillity is, however, soon cut short by Matt arriving on the scene, beer can in hand, angry at the retraction or revision of various films and comedies he enjoyed in his youth. 'It's bullshit,' he rails. 'White lives matter too. They should listen to Gandhi. He promoted tolerance and peace for everyone.'

Matt's intervention shakes me out of my state of wordlessness.

'Well, Gandhi's role in history is also being reconsidered today,' I point out. 'Some people see him as racist and misogynistic. His statue has been pulled down in Johannesburg and some are calling for its removal in Leicester.'

'What's the sense in that?' Matt asks with anger and incredulity.

'Gandhi did little to help Black South Africans in their struggle against colonialism and apartheid even though he lived in South Africa for over twenty years. He also reproduced some of the negative racial stereotypes of his day.'

'He was for everyone,' Matt interjects, pacing around our triangle impatiently.

'I agree with you that he was an exceptional man who was trying to bring about a more equal society. He was a leading figure in the struggle against colonial rule in India, and there are people all over the world who continue to be inspired by his ideas about non-violence and ecology. Martin Luther King thought him one of the greatest men in world history, but that doesn't mean he was without fault. Like all of us, he was a product of his times.'

I can see that Matt is not convinced. He remains sceptical at the idea that anyone can legitimately question Gandhi's image and I am left wondering about the basis of his attachment to Gandhi. Is it Gandhi's contestation of authority that appeals to him, or the way he broke down social barriers? Or is it how Gandhi brought dignity to the act of living in poverty?

Matt's resentment of Black Lives Matter seems more clearly explicable than his devotion to Gandhi. To him the movement feels like it excludes him and effaces his own very real experiences of marginalisation and social exclusion as a white working-class man living on the breadline.

'What bugs me is how they're meddling with TV shows like *Little Britain* and *Fawlty Towers*. They're even calling for *Gone with the Wind* to be taken off air,' he adds incredulously.

'Well, there's a control-of-language thing going on,' Bachi interjects. 'You hear the N-word used in films made by Black people, but no one else can use the term.'

'Well, that's totally understandable,' I leap in. 'If people choose to appropriate a term that has been used as an insult against them, it means something very different to the original use. It becomes a choice, not an imposition.'

Nick nods. 'Some people call me "tramp" or "hobo",' he says, 'so sometimes I'll appropriate those terms. People are sick of being looked down on and stereotyped. I remember when we were at Lincoln's Inn and there was a distribution of blankets, and there was this foreign journalist trying to take photos and people really objected. They didn't want to be seen that way.'

Nick's experience of being at the receiving end of negative stereotypes and his highly developed sense of empathy make him receptive to the oppression of others, and he has been witness to how Black people in particular are often targeted by the police.

'I used to hang out in the street with some Jamaican lads and the police wouldn't leave them alone. The lads didn't want to have to answer all their endless questions, and the police kept saying, "If you haven't got anything to hide, then speak!" And of course what they were suggesting was that if they didn't speak, then they must have stuff to hide, so they were obviously guilty. I remember saying to the policeman, "Well, they've still got a right to privacy." Have you ever had people treat you in a particular way because of your background or skin colour?' Nick asks, turning to Bachi and choosing his words with care.

'Yes,' Bachi replies, 'especially around 9/11. As a dark-skinned bearded man with a rucksack, I was stopped by the police several times, and you could feel the hostility from people around you. I stopped using the Underground altogether at that time. I was afraid. There were other times too. I once had my nose broken in a racist attack,' he adds.

But Bachi also makes it clear that he is not interested in trying to define his life or the world around him through the lenses of race and racism. The ups and downs of his life have been too unique and varied to be slotted into that framework.

I realise that if some of my more activist colleagues or

students overheard our conversation this evening we would be dismissed point blank as racist – Bachi for saying 'all lives matter', Nick for intervening on behalf of his Jamaican friends, Matt for saying 'white lives matter' and me for failing to take this as an opportunity to condemn and re-educate everyone assembled. But I am too aware of our different positionalities and experiences. This is not the place for a lecture about the concepts of white privilege and white ignorance, which anyway feel limited for comprehending the social complexities of our small gathering in the park, never mind the wider world we humans, animals and plants cohabit.

'I like to keep myself in a position of perpetual doubt,' Nick says one evening when we are once again nestled at a distance in the long grass. 'It allows me the possibility of being wrong.' I savour his comment. It breathes openness, and here under the evening sky we seem able to put that openness into practice, to listen attentively to each other's opinions, to harbour the possibility of being wrong at a time when so much public debate is about entrenched positions and moral certitude. When I think of all the research I have conducted over the years, I recognise how doubt and the position of not knowing and reserving judgement have been keys to learning and have enabled me to become aware of complexities I would otherwise have missed. Whether critiquing colonialism or state violence in India, challenging Eurocentric stereotypes of Muslims in Britain or exposing the inequalities embedded in the global trade in human hair, my research has always been speculative and open-ended. It developed in an explorative way, learning from the ground up, leaving room for recognising ambiguities and opening up new questions as it went along.

I am aware that the space for speculative research of this kind is contracting as external funding initiatives have become increasingly oriented towards income generation or problem-solving agendas in which the problems are predefined, the categories uncontested and the results and impacts pre-anticipated, functioning as justification for the funding. It is an external agenda that is fundamentally anti-imagination and ultimately against any research that is not results-driven. Meanwhile, within the university, the space for freedom of thought is contracting for other reasons. A unidimensional reading of history and the building of defences against poten-tial accusations are shaping what can and can't be taught and shutting down conversations in disturbing ways.

One evening I log on to a Zoom workshop on decolonising the institution. I listen to people of colour recounting their experiences of discrimination in universities and museums. Their pain and frustration is palpable. They speak of the lack of opportunities for promotion and of the tokenism of diversity and inclusion agendas. 'It is time for white people in positions of power to step aside and leave space for Black people,' I hear one woman say. 'But, of course, they won't because they just want to cling to their power and privilege and prevent us from getting promoted.'

Listening to her arguments, I feel myself caught in an increasingly familiar double bind. I want to support the strug-gle for social and economic justice and the battle against racial discrimination both within and outside the institution, but I am finding the public debate about race increasingly stifling and restrictive. I worry that it is regressive and reductive in how it reinforces the idea of race more than interrogating its ideological foundations. At the same time I recognise the long-lasting injustice that histories of slavery and colonialism have produced and the need to address the very real structural and material disadvantages they have left in their wake. You don't have to look very far to see how few Black academics and curators there are in top positions in British universities and museums.

I am aware that in the eyes of the speaker I no doubt correspond to the stereotype of the privileged white professor jealously guarding her position of power. But I also know that I have never been attracted to power and that I am much more interested in encouraging and collaborating with students and colleagues of colour than holding them back. As I listen, a new train of thought enters my mind as quiet as a whisper. What if I were to do what the woman in the Zoom meeting suggests that people 'like me' would never do? What if I decided to step down from my position and role, 'leaving space', as she puts it? Surely this would bring about a more concrete difference than any attempt I can make as a white professor to decolonise anthropology in a context where my very whiteness is conceptualised as key to the problem?

I have been feeling so stressed, constricted and worn down by university politics and workload over the last two years that the idea of stepping aside is not unappealing. It might give me the time and space to put into practice a quieter form of critically engaged anthropology. I am already working with a local museum to create a travelling exhibition about hair, based in part on my earlier research. The exhibition involves collaborating with artists, designers, hairdressers and curators from a range of different backgrounds, and with local community groups in London. We are already beginning to have new conversations, explore different hair heritages, redress absences in historical narratives, showcase different talents and highlight hair-related discrimination. It is an opportunity to put decolonial anthropology into practice, and it feels more productive and exciting than the recriminatory debates happening in the university. But to leave my job, my profession, my salary, my security, the university where I have been employed for the last seventeen years and where I have learned so much? The thought seems almost unimaginable. But the seed of the idea has been planted.

'I'm contemplating leaving my job,' I tell Nick tentatively one morning when I have come to the park early, my heart fluttering briefly at the sight of two jays teetering on the branches overhead. He is in his makeshift study under the hornbeam tree, surrounded by books and papers. He gestures for me to sit on a log beside him.

We are both watching the swooping movements of the jays, the blue of their wings flashing in the distilled morning light. 'I think you should stick at it,' he says slowly after a moment. 'These are interesting times.'

'That's true,' I say, 'but I'm not sure I can cope with the stress of the times any more. I'm not sure I've got the stamina.'

'What would you do if you left?' he asks.

'Write,' I say, and he nods his head.

I don't stay long. I need to cycle home for a Zoom meeting with a young administrative colleague with whom I work closely.

'How are you?' she asks brightly. It is an innocent question but it is fatal. Instead of words, an uncontrollable stream of tears flows down my cheeks. And once the tears begin, they will not stop.

'Get a grip,' I keep telling myself. 'This is so unprofessional.' But it doesn't make any difference. I am not just weeping, I am in convulsions, so much so that I can barely even apologise. But I know her too well and respect her too much to simply bow out. I owe her at least some explanation. 'It's just stress,' I hear myself mumble unconvincingly.

Stress! Now there is a heavy-weight-bearing word. What a multitude of diverse experiences are compressed between the S's that seal it at both ends. But although it may be difficult to define, it is not difficult to recognise. As staff we are devoting a lot of time attending to the stresses and needs of our students, but our own stress has few outlets. It is restricted to circulation through illicit texts, WhatsApp messages and late-night or early-morning phone calls, and in my case conversations in the park – the backstage of communications. Front of stage we are on screen, trying to manage the ever-moving bureaucratic quagmire of the pandemic; trying to work out how to deliver teaching virtually; trying to liaise with disaffected PhD students over the marking boycott, while simultaneously supporting their opposition to precarious short-term contracts; trying to decolonise the curriculum; and attending workshops on 'racial reckoning'. How can I explain the pressure-cooker effect of all this to the young woman on the screen in front of me?

Stress. A senior colleague WhatsApps me in a Zoom meeting to say she is too choked up to speak. Stress. A professor re-records the same lecture four times out of fear she might have said something that might offend someone. Stress. A colleague turns to a psychotherapist to develop techniques for handling the hostility she feels at work. Stress. Another colleague buys herself an amulet as protection. Stress. A colleague offers money to a charity as penance for giving essay feedback that a student deems offensive. Stress. An early-evening text message from a senior colleague reads: 'Just managed to get through an entire day without breaking down even once!' It ends with a string of smiling emoji faces in dark glasses. Stress.

Being a professor is undoubtedly a privilege but it is one that I am finding increasingly difficult to cope with at a very basic human level. I tell two colleagues about my embarrassing breakdown over Zoom, and they tell me I should take some time off for stress. I am not the sort of person who ever takes sick leave but I recognise that I can barely function, so I obey.

Doctors' surgeries are closed owing to the pandemic, so I am offered a telephone consultation. I find myself speaking, or at least trying to speak, to a pleasant young GP. For the first five minutes I can only weep but eventually I become more coherent. He says he will sign me off work for two weeks. 'No, just one,' I hear myself snort pathetically. 'I don't want more than one.' I am thinking of all the people I will let down and the massive backlog of work that will await me on my return. 'Well, we can review the situation again after one week,' he says kindly. I hear him asking questions designed to find out if I am likely to self-harm. I don't blame him, given what I know I sound like, but I reassure him that I don't have any desire to harm myself and have never had a suicidal thought in my life. 'I just need to extract myself from the day-to-day tensions of my working environment and I need some space to decide whether or not to quit my job,' I tell him. 'I can't make that sort of decision when I'm in this state.' He agrees.

He tries to quiz me about why work is so stressful, and I don't know what to say, except that I am surrounded by staff and students in a state of moral outrage, that my department and discipline stand accused of racism, that the accusation is structural not personal but that it is difficult to separate the personal from the structural when you are part of the structure. I also tell him that the discrepancy between these public accusations and the private phone calls from students of colour thanking me for all my support for them and their projects is doing my head in. I feel I have entered an Orwellian world of double-speak in which words have become traps, and that the pressure of being encapsulated in a virtual environment all day long is suffocating. He sounds a bit taken aback. Just hearing his reaction reminds me that the atmosphere at work is far from healthy.

And so I am granted a week. A week of recovery. The next morning I head to the park. I tell Nick and Pascal that I am going away for a few days as I contemplate whether or not to leave my job. It is early July and the travel restrictions have just been lifted. I drive off to Cornwall. Julius kindly offers to come with me for the first two days, probably anxious that I might crash the car if I drive alone, given the state of tension he has seen me in of late. But as soon as I am away from work my stress begins to evaporate. I walk on the cliffs. I swim in the sea, letting the cold water lap at my skin. I think. I breathe. I reconnect to that other meaning of 'privilege' – the sheer pleasure of being alive in this extraordinary universe, a pleasure that reconnects me to Nick and Pascal in the park. And as the world opens out, the tensions of the university contract, feel less significant, almost fictional.

A friend and ex-colleague comes to join me for a few days. She does not guide me in my decision-making. She just hears me out. I draw up a list of pros and cons about staying or leaving. Reasons for staying: I still have faith in the emancipatory potential of anthropology; I find teaching rewarding; I want to be able to support students and colleagues at a time that is difficult for everyone. Reasons for leaving: a desire to write and think creatively; a desire to escape the politics and bureaucracy of the institution; a desire to recover freedom of expression; and the realisation that I can access my pension early and that, even if this is not enough to live on, I will somehow find a way of getting by. Nick and Pascal have taught me that security, however important, is not the only thing in life.

The week fulfils its restorative function. I return to London refreshed and resolute. I have gone back and forth over the arguments and decided to carry on for three more years. That way I can support my student who has just been awarded the BAME student bursary and who is relying on me to supervise her PhD. I can also support the new head of department in her role at this undeniably difficult time. Three years will take me to the age of sixty, which seems a more reasonable age for retirement than fifty-seven. It all makes sense.

The phone rings. A friend and colleague asks me what I have decided, and I tell her I have decided to stick it out for three more years. But instead of simply accepting my response, she asks in the point-blank tone of a lawyer: 'Can you take me through your reasoning?' So I spout out my various reasons, and she comes back with a rejoinder.

'I don't think those reasons are sufficient,' she says. 'All your reasons are about other people. You haven't given me a single reason why *you* want to stay. What will *you* get out of it?'

'What? Me personally? If I take away my feelings of duty?' Somehow I haven't ever thought like this before.

'Yes, you personally,' she insists.

There is a prolonged silence. Then I hear myself say, 'I can't think of a single reason. I'm *desperate* to get out!'

The words are clear and uncompromising, and I am grateful to this colleague and friend for enabling me to find them. She reassures me that I should be able to get the right to continue supervising PhD students written into my voluntary severance contract. And as for being an anthropologist, there is probably more scope for creative anthropology outside the university than within it right now. She makes it clear that she thinks my leaving will be a loss to the department but that for me it will probably be a gain.

When I get to the park that evening I feel as if I have been away for several months, even though it is only seven days. But the purple knapweed and yellow lady's bedstraw help bridge the gap between the Cornish cliffs and Regent's Park. I am amazed at the speed with which the blackberries have ripened and watch three women harvesting them into Tupperware boxes as I approach the secret passage.

The first person I see is Bachi, lying on the grass in his usual spot with Lizzie. I sit down opposite and tell him I have made the decision to leave my job. He approves wholeheartedly. 'I wouldn't have lasted five minutes in your environment,' he says.

A few moments later Nick joins us and takes up residence in front of the purple vetch. He is warm and welcoming, and I feel a sense of peace and pleasure at resuming our connection in the park. I may have been away for only a week but I have missed our gatherings and our casual chatter on long summer evenings. We share news of Cornwall and the park and we play with Lizzie, who pads between us. Eventually I turn to Nick and say, 'I know you won't approve but I've decided to leave my job.'

He doesn't react as I expect. 'Once you told me that you wanted to write more books, I understood it,' he says. There is kindness in his voice. Nick has read my book about the global trade in human hair from cover to cover and often brings up topics from it in conversation. He intuitively gets what anthropology is about. 'You are just a human being fascinated in other humans, and so you should be and so am I,' he says with an accepting smile. 'We are *Homo sapiens sapiens* – and we're a wonderful species!'

On the day of my fifty-seventh birthday I apply for voluntary severance, knowing that I won't hear the outcome until September and will have to work out my notice until December. Nonetheless I live the application process as an act of rebirth. A privilege. The privilege of being able to embrace freedom, which is surely the greatest privilege of them all and which I share with two men who might appear the opposite of privileged, but who understand the meaning of the term in its broadest sense.

6 Rain

We know more is on its way. Bachi has been consulting his weather app and the forecast is constant rain, scheduled to last for several consecutive days and nights. When I make my way to Nick and Pascal this morning, squelching quietly along a soft path of leaf-lacquered mud, I find that Nick has already shifted his tarpaulin and sleeping bag to under the study tree in anticipation. He is checking through his possessions to see what needs drying from the night.

'The tree doesn't protect you, but it gives you time,' he explains. 'It takes ten minutes for the rain to drip through these branches, so you have ten minutes to get organised.'

It is the first day of October and the hornbeam is still thick with leaves, deep green on the lower branches, a little lighter on the higher ones and tinged with gold tips on the upper branches which fan towards the sky. A temporary umbrella.

It has rained most of the night. The ground is already soggy and the grass laden with droplets. I have come to deliver a flask of freshly boiled water and hot buttered toast and honey – aware that it won't be as hot as I wish by the time I have cycled it to the park. It is wrapped in several layers of silver foil and served under an old Indian copper dish in the form of a dome, which still bears the imprint of the hammer that knocked it into shape perhaps a century ago. The first time I delivered food under that dome, Nick lifted the lid and pinged his finger against the edge, then held it to his ear before passing it to me and Pascal to catch the vibration. The deep gong-like sound with its long resonant echo delighted us and we took turns to ping it and pass it round. I was conscious that this dish had been sitting inanimate on a shelf in my house for over twenty years, during which time I had never once thought of listening to what it might wish to express. Now, whenever I pass it at home, I release its sacred sound, which transports me to a Buddhist monastery I visited many years ago in the mythically named town of Shangri-La on the China–Tibet border.

I have watched Nick get organised for rain before. He is by nature neat and meticulous, arranging his things with care and preparing to wrap them in tarpaulins lined with plastic in such a way that nothing will get wet. A respect for material things is something we share.

'If you don't keep things dry, they deteriorate very quickly,' he comments. 'You've only got to look at Pascal's sleeping bag!' Pascal raises his eyebrows and we all chuckle.

Pascal's sleeping bag has indeed deteriorated further since I first encountered it. Its external surface has taken on a mushroomy quality in the damp autumn weather. Its innards have burst their banks and are exploding out of the side seams, which can no longer hold them in place, leaving an unnatural luminous fuzz of whiteness against the leaf-strewn grass. But Pascal is fond of that sleeping bag, which appeared mysteriously in the night along with a box of chocolates two Christmases ago, and although he has other sleeping bags given by well-wishers he always keeps this one as his external crust.

Pascal's attitude to rain is quite different from Nick's. He likes to take his chances and tends to remain lying down until he has the physical confirmation that if he stays put he will get saturated. At that point he takes action, folding up his already swollen bedding under a tarpaulin and unearthing his woollen hat, which he only wears when it rains. Sometimes his more laissez-faire approach pays off: the predicted rain does not arrive and he has not had the hassle of moving and reorganising his affairs. But other times he gets caught out and eventually joins Nick standing under the trees – damp but not particularly concerned.

'It's not good to stay lying down in the rain. It gets to your chest,' Nick says. 'Keeping yourself dry is important. The skin is the largest organ we have and we have to respect it. If you want to live this life, you need to look after your health.' I am not sure if these comments are intended for Pascal or me or both. Maybe neither.

The forecast is grim but Nick and Pascal are no newcomers to the vagaries of the weather. I remember one night back in late August, when the wind was howling so loudly that I found myself incapable of sleep. At four o'clock in the morning I gave up trying and switched on my bedside lamp. It wasn't just the vibrato of my rattling windows and the wolf-like cry of the wind that were keeping me awake; it was the thought of Nick and Pascal outside in the storm while I was comfortably snuggled under two Indian quilts, with a purring cat at the end of my bed. The contrast felt unbearable. Inhuman. I fantasised about driving to the park and inviting them into my house for the night. But, when I thought about it, I wasn't at all sure they would want to spend the night in my home, given their stated preference for being outdoors. Nor was it clear where they would sleep if they did come. The spare room was piled high with debris from an exhibition, which made the double bed totally inaccessible. And even if it were accessible, would they want to share a double bed? I turned to my mobile to get information about what they might be up against. There was a yellow weather warning that had been in place since 9 a.m. and was predicted to last twenty-four hours.

It was true that when I had visited the park earlier that day the wind had been excessive. The outer layer of Pascal's sleeping bag was flapping uncontrollably, exposing its entire anatomy, and Nick's beard and my hair were taking flight, making rapid changes of direction with the sudden gusts. Dry leaves were spinning off the ground, forming swirls which flung themselves into our faces as we talked. And the branches of the hornbeam tree were caught in a spectacular dance, as if operating on a giant spring. One minute its branches were sweeping to the ground, the next they were rising into the air as if ready to take off. I had never seen a tree in such a state of animation and was entranced by how it could be in perpetual motion yet grounded in one spot.

From time to time we gave up on our attempts to converse against the force of such winds and simply watched the tree with shared admiration. 'They used to make crossbows from the hornbeam,' Nick commented.

But that was in the daytime. Now it was night. The same wind that had felt exhilarating in the morning now felt threatening, hostile and relentless. How could anyone caught in its constant bombardment either lie, sit or stand?

I flicked the screen on my mobile and read:

Storm Francis will bring some very strong winds leading to disruption to travel and power supplies along with potential damage to trees. Injuries and dangers to life from flying debris are possible . . .

I tried to picture them in the park. How could they huddle under the trees for protection when the trees themselves were in danger of fragmenting? I imagined branches and twigs wrenched from their trunks and whirling about, lethal and invisible in the darkness. But surely standing or lying in the open grassland would be equally impossible? Images of King Lear sprang to mind. Were Nick and Pascal mad to remain outside in the storm? Or would the storm push them to the brink of madness? Was *I* mad not to go out and offer them shelter, even if they might turn it down? Or would such an offer be an act of madness? I spent the remainder of the night in a state of restlessness; even Zebedee the cat was agitated by the end of it.

But when I arrived in the park the following morning it became clear that the only madness had been my own inability to sleep. When I enquired about the winds of the night, Nick said with relish: 'It was wonderful! I was watching the hornbeam. It was breathing in and out like a giant lung inflating and deflating.' And that was the end of that.

But now that there are several days of rain ahead, this feels different. It is not a single night of drama but a persistent stretch of ceaseless rain during which it will be impossible to sleep at any point.

I leave the dome of toast, concerned that I might be getting in the way as they make use of the short period between one bout of rain and another. I cycle off to the Secret Garden. I am the only human there. Squirrels are bounding across the lawn, and a robin, with whom I have become intimately acquainted, perches first on the wooden bench beside me and eventual-ly on my blue tin mug, which is resting on the arm of the bench. Like Nick and Pascal's corner of the park, the Secret Garden already looks and feels to be at saturation point. The grass is pappy underfoot. Huge droplets of water hold their form at the base of the hosta leaves, which may have lost their spring and summer perfection but are still holding up, and the Japanese anemones glow a luminous white against the many hues of green. There is beauty and peace in this watery world awaiting the next deluge.

I am due to play tennis this evening but, needless to say, it is cancelled long in advance. The rain starts slowly around 10 a.m. but steadily gains force throughout the day. By the time we reach evening it is pounding hard. I am inside with my son and we cook ourselves a comforting meal of moules-frites for supper, which we eat by candlelight. It is cosy but I am conscious of Nick and Pascal outside in the storm. I am just about to switch off the lights downstairs and make my way up to bed when I find myself turning to Julius and asking if he is willing to accompany me to the park to deliver some hot food to Nick and Pascal. He has met them once or twice before, and I don't fancy venturing out alone in the dark and wet.

'What time is it?' he asks, surprised by my request.

'It's just gone eleven,' I reply. 'I know it's absurdly late but I'd really like them to have something hot in this ghastly weather.'

'Sure!' says Julius, totally unperturbed by the time and the rain. So I heat up some chicken soup and bread and butter pudding I prepared earlier in the day with them in mind, and fill some flasks with hot water.

We put on wellies and wrap ourselves in waterproofs, which prove hopelessly inadequate. To cycle is impossible in this combination of wind and rain so we trudge our way through the darkness along the flooded pathway at the bottom of Primrose Hill. The rain is almost horizontal and our cheeks are soon wet and glistening. When we reach the Outer Circle the gates to the park have been locked for some hours and in the darkness I find it difficult to tell which section of railings is closest to their grove. I call out their names into the rain and darkness, softly at first, then as loudly as I dare given that there is still some passing traffic on the road outside the park and I don't want to attract attention towards Nick and Pascal's presence inside. But the wind seems to lift my voice to nowhere.

'Perhaps they've taken shelter under one of the canal bridges, given the ferocity of the rain,' I suggest, having sometimes heard them discuss such an option, usually only to dismiss it.

'We can try looking there if you want,' Julius replies. So we plod warily down the slippery shadowed pathway towards the canal. It is pitch black and I can't help feeling scared, as if a stranger with a knife is about to leap out from behind the bushes and stab me – even though I know on a rational level that this is entirely ridiculous. Who on earth in their right mind would be hanging out in this weather, let alone with a knife? But there is something primal about the wetness and darkness and I feel a visceral reluctance to step into the unknown, exacerbated no doubt by the fact that I was once mugged in the dark on one of the canal bridges. I find myself imagining absurd scenarios in which Julius tries to defend me and gets wounded or even killed in the process, all because I had the absurd idea of trying to deliver home-made bread and butter pudding at midnight.

'Let's go home,' I suggest, feeling stupid for having dragged him out on this failed mission. But to his credit he doesn't complain and we chat merrily on the return journey, even if the bag of provisions weighs heavily on my aching shoulder. We both seem strangely refreshed and exhilarated when we cross the threshold of the house, as if we have shared something special by setting out in the turbulent night and feeling the full force of the rain. Julius is relatively dry on our return. I am drenched through even though he has kindly lent me his parka. 'I did tell you it's showerproof, not waterproof,' he reminds me.

That night I sleep well, but when I awake the rain is still pounding hard, now in direct vertical lines. I am taken back to the summer of 1989, when I was a PhD student living in Ahmedabad. I remember the breaking of the first monsoon after four consecutive years of drought. There was an atmosphere of elation in the streets as people rushed out to embrace the rain, which ran down their faces and glued their clothes to their bodies. But the ground had been hardened by the drought and was unable to absorb the water, so roads and pathways soon became rivers and streams. And while the rain was exciting and desperately needed, it also became debilitating. What I remember most was the complete inability to keep anything dry. Even my purse went mouldy.

I go down to the kitchen and reheat the food and fill fresh flasks of hot water. This time, given that the wind has died down, I decide to cycle. It is still raining hard so I put on a rarely used purple cycling cloak I picked up in a street market in Beijing when caught in a sudden storm. The cloak is longer at the front than at the back and can be slotted over the handlebars. I go steadily along the road, looking like a mobile purple tent, swishing through the puddles slowly so as not to cause too much splash. I dismount at one of the canal bridges, where cycling is forbidden, only to discover that it has become a bowl of shin-deep water. There is no one about so I cycle slowly through it to prevent my walking boots from filling up.

To my surprise, at the entrance of the park some very young children are hovering about dressed in football gear. I can almost see the goose pimples on their legs. They are accompanied by eager and harassed-looking parents who have risen early on a Saturday morning to bring them here. But the football coaches are standing at the gates telling everyone the park is completely flooded and there won't be any football training today. Already drenched, they turn heel and troop back in the direction of their cars and homes. I am amazed that these parents have taken the trouble to drag themselves and their children to the park in such extreme weather and wonder what this represents. Dedication, ambition or simply habit?

Once inside the park, there is no one about. I skid tentatively through the mud that leads to the passage to the secret world. But two lake-sized puddles have formed under the ancient oak trees, which makes progress difficult. Crows are wading through the water, looking like seabirds, and freshly fallen golden leaves are floating over the surface, lending a certain glory to the scene. I realise I am seeing double. The birds, the trees, the leaves are all turned upside down in reflections. Everything that rises above the surface is reproduced below it. I am struck by the beauty of this waterlogged universe even as I concentrate hard on trying not to slip over in the mud. I wish I had worn my wellies, though cycling in them has its challenges.

I am not sure if Nick and Pascal will be here, given my abortive attempt to reach them last night, but as soon as I splosh my way through the puddles of the secret passage, passing the shiny golden crab apples, which look psychedelic in this light, I hear voices from under the hornbeams. As I wend my way through the side entrance of their home I am greeted by a spectacular umbrella-scape reminiscent of Japanese woodblock prints. There are three dark-blue umbrellas propped up in the branches of the hornbeam, under which Nick and Pascal stand,

and two coloured ones propped up in other trees, under which hang carrier bags containing food and possessions. Yet more umbrellas are open on the ground, protecting their stored things, which are bound up in blue tarpaulins and held down by branches and logs. And with the umbrellas comes a magnificent thrumming of raindrops tapping at different levels and rates, creating a musical score that is somewhere between African drumming and Philip Glass.

Nick and Pascal seem to be in a jovial mood and both greet me with broad smiles.

'We were just talking about you!' Nick says. 'I was saying to Pasc, "I don't think she'll be coming down in this, do you?"'

'And what did you say?' I ask Pascal.

'I said I wasn't sure,' he says with a friendly shrug.

'Well, I don't like to be too predictable,' I reply. Nick opens me a large umbrella, which I readily accept as I hand over the food and flasks. 'This is a great set-up,' I say, admiring the simplicity and ingenuity of the arrangement and feeling welcomed into this secret hub of protection carved out of the otherwise rain-ravaged park.

'Well, our arms get tired if we have to hold umbrellas up twenty-four-seven. These are from Bachi, from when he used to run a company taking people on adventure tours in fast cars. He says we can have as many of them as we like. He swears they're indestructible, and they do seem to be pretty strong from my experience.'

I take in the slogan emblazoned in white on the rim of the navy umbrellas: 'Petrolhead Nirvana'. A relic of one of Bachi's surprising past lives! The navy shines black as bat wings as the rain slides down the sides.

'Did you manage to get any sleep at all?' I ask, almost certain of the answer.

'No, we've been standing all night, although we took it in turns to sit on a log for short intervals,' Nick says. 'It's interesting to see what happens to your mind in this situation. From time to time it just cuts out, even when you're in the middle of formulating a sentence. I like observing what happens. You can learn something from these experiences. There's a discipline in that.'

I tell them I tried to come down with food last night but that my voice seemed to get lost in the storm.

'Ah! That's amazing, 'cos I thought I heard my name but then I thought I must be imagining it,' Nick responds. 'There was a car that went past with music on and I thought the voice must have been from that. Then later I wondered if it might have been your voice. But the mind starts hallucinating a bit when you don't have any sleep, so it's difficult to know what's real and what's not. Bless your heart for thinking of us and coming down in this weather.'

'Bless your heart' isn't a phrase I hear very often. In fact Nick is the only person I know who uses it, but there is something warm and embracing about it, especially now in the persistent rain.

'We won't be able to keep everything dry in rain like this – it's just not possible,' Nick explains, looking anxiously towards his entombed skipper. 'The trunk of the hornbeam

draws water into the centre since all the branches slope directly towards it at different angles. It's good in a way as you don't
get too much water dripping down from the branches, but you
get great pools of water forming at the base. And it's hardly
stopped. How many hours is it now, Pasc?'

'Thirty-four,' Pascal replies precisely.

'The rain teaches you patience,' Nick adds. 'I love the rain.
And we need it.'

Their high spirits are infectious. They seem to be living the
situation as a challenge and are glowing from the experience,
even if Nick confesses to having stiff joints from all the standing. Both have rosy cheeks. Nick's beard is frizzled with the
humidity and Pascal's felted hair disappears under his puffer
jacket, then reappears, snaking down to his ankles. He seems to
have managed to keep it from dragging in the mud.

I suggest they might want to have the bread and butter pudding while it's still hot, or at least warm. But Nick says that
if he eats something solid like that he'll want to sleep, which
he can't do right now, so he smokes a rollie instead and then
spoons some soup out of the tiffin. Pascal also prefers to delay
eating.

The music of the rain is all about us. Water is gushing down
the hornbeam trunk, which glows the deep green of fairy
stories populated by hobgoblins and sprites. I am struck by how
everything is animated in the rain. The world in movement.

'Thirty-four hours isn't our record,' says Nick. 'Our record
is, what, forty hours? That was last year. Did you come down
to the park last autumn? Do you remember how it rained

every day for months and this whole area under the trees was a mudbath?'

'I certainly remember the floods,' I say. 'But I didn't see the park. For me that period is associated with the days leading up to my mother's death and with driving back and forth to a hospital in Worcester where she was in intensive care. She'd been rushed there with pneumonia and was hooked up to machines.'

'I'm sorry,' Nick replies. 'That must have been a shock, seeing her like that.'

'It was one of those moments when everything happens so quickly you don't have time for shock. I'd received a phone call saying she might not last the night. So I left London with just an overnight bag, but in fact she lived on for twelve days and I ended up having to nip down to the local shopping centre to buy socks and pants.'

Nick and Pascal laugh at this detail.

'My sisters and I stayed in my mum's house in Droitwich, along with her carer. The main road between Droitwich and Worcester was blocked with roadworks so we'd drive along the back routes, which were completely flooded several times a day. I remember swishing through great basins of water as if in a speedboat, hoping my car wouldn't pack up. That week we kept up a twenty-four-hour vigil at the hospital, sitting by her side in shifts day and night. Somehow the constant rain felt appropriate to the situation. Everything felt surreal. Eventually we got permission for her to come home to die, but even that was complicated by the rain.'

'How come?' Nick asks, so I carry on.

'The ambulance that was bringing her home got caught in a traffic jam trying to leave the hospital car park. It took fifty minutes just to get to the exit and that was before the seven-mile drive home, and the heating wasn't working in the ambulance. My mother was swaddled up like a baby and strapped onto a stretcher, so only her face was exposed. I think she was oblivious to the cold, dark and rain, but there was something about the combination of pneumonia, the defunct heating system and the raging storm that was disconcerting. And then the ambulance driver was worried about swerving through the floods. But we made it in the end.'

'Do you think she was aware that she was going home?' Nick asks.

'I think so, at some level, but the Alzheimer's meant it wasn't easy to tell. I remember thinking she looked at peace in that ambulance, and she was certainly very pleased when I told her in the hospital that we were going home. I travelled with her, so that was reassuring. I was freezing but she didn't look cold.'

I start flicking through my mobile phone and find a grainy picture of my mother bundled up inside the ambulance, looking like a Russian doll in the half-light, and another one of her at home, relaxed in her bed, surrounded by flowers, with my niece sitting beside her looking whimsical and playing the guitar. Nick studies both photos with intensity before passing them to Pascal. He notes that my mother looks at peace and that there is a serene atmosphere in her room. He is interested in death and what might pass through a person's mind at that moment. He asks if my mother was prepared for death. Again I say that it was difficult to judge but that we were all around her and accompanied her as best we could to the edge of life.

'She had her family with her,' Nick says. 'All three daughters. That's wonderful. That would have meant a lot to her.' He is right.

'So, for me, her death and the autumn rains last year blur into one another,' I conclude.

'It'll be pneumonia that gets us in the end, or some secondary infection,' Nick reflects absent-mindedly.

'Well, they do call it the old man's friend,' I say, trying to keep the mood light.

'Maybe I'll become one of those old men sitting on a park bench discussing death with passers-by. The only difference being that I'll be living on the bench!'

Nick laughs, and Pascal and I join in.

Our conversation changes tempo in sync with the rhythm of the rain. The raindrops, though still plump, have slowed down and their rhythmic beat is less frenetic and almost jaunty. More funk than blues. The water sliding down the hornbeam trunk has turned from a stream to a trickle. In all the time we have been here – perhaps two hours, maybe more; time has little meaning in our bubble – we have not seen a single person go by.

As the morning drips on, more and more watery memories flood our minds.

'I intend to return to the sea sometime,' Nick comments. 'I love the water. My mum used to take me swimming as a kid and I loved plunging in and sinking my body to the bottom like a submarine, then popping back up to the surface at the last minute. But once I nearly drowned. I stayed down too long and thought I wasn't going to make it back up. I can still remember that feeling of fighting to break for air. It was an incredible moment when my head broke through the surface of the water, still covered in a watery film. It felt like the moment of birth itself and I remember the amazing sensation of realising what it is to be alive.'

'We had a swimming teacher who used to put us through our paces,' I recall. 'The whole school was terrified of her. When I was ten she had us teaching the little reception kids, who were three or four years old; we'd have to bob them up and down in the water to the rhythm of "The Grand Old Duke of York", and when the teacher sang, "And when they were down, they were down," we had to sink the kids down so their heads were underwater. Most of them were in floods of tears when they came up and clinging so tightly to us with their arms and legs that we were virtually strangled. It was supposed to take away their fear of water, apparently!'

'Either that or put them off water for life,' Nick says. 'That sounds so cruel.'

'It was. The only advantage of her methods is that we all became expert swimmers. Once, when I must have been around eight years old, we did a sponsored swim and all the neighbours in the street had sponsored me per length, assuming that I wouldn't do more than two. But once I was in the water I got lost in the act of swimming and just carried on, length after length. I wasn't aware of either the time or the cold and couldn't see any reason to stop while my arms and legs were willing to carry on. At twenty lengths I was told that was the maximum possible so I got out, feeling quite proud of my newfound resilience. But I then had the embarrassment of having to collect the money. My mother made me explain to people that they weren't expected to pay per length as I'd swum much further than expected, but most people didn't want to appear mean so I raised a lot of money!'

Nick enjoys the story and asks how much, but it isn't the money that has stuck in my mind but the sensation of inhabiting water. I have carried that sensation into adulthood and love to swim in the sea, whatever the temperature or weather.

I notice that as we hang out under the hornbeam both Pascal and myself are jigging from leg to leg more or less in unison. When I comment on this, Nick laughs and says, 'That's the hobo dance! It's what you find yourself doing when your feet are cold and you've been standing up for too many hours. All the hobos do it.'

'I loved swimming in the sea,' Pascal comments. 'We always went to Algeria for our summer holidays and as a kid I spent all the time in the water. Once we had masks and the sights underwater were so amazing that I just stayed in the sea all day, and my family wondered where I was.'

'How long were you swimming?' I ask.

'Fourteen hours,' he replies. 'Apparently! That's what people said. I didn't notice anything. The time had just gone.'

It strikes me that all our tales of water are tales of endurance, of testing our limits and the boundaries of the elements in which we dwell. I had never noticed before how water distorts time.

I am just contemplating leaving when the rain suddenly ups its pace once more, so I stay put. Nick turns to Pascal. 'Are those shoes waterproof? Are you sure you're not getting cold? Why don't you wear your wellies?' There is kindness and concern in his voice – like the tone of a parent who doesn't want to sound controlling but who nonetheless wants to get their point across.

'I don't like wellies. These are a bit damp but they're fine,' Pascal replies, making it clear he is not going to accept suggestions and doesn't like the fuss.

The conversation turns to what they will do if it carries on raining for a third night.

'We could go down by the canal and sleep under one of the bridges, but it can get rough down there. We used to get kids pelting stones at us and Pascal is sensitive to smells. Petrol from the boats, and urine.'

'What about the bandstand?' I suggest. 'At least you'd have a raised surface where you could lie down.' Nick says it is too near the centre and too public, aware that the park is officially out of bounds at night. He suggests they could take shelter under the canopy of the cafe, which is nearer this end of the park and less conspicuous. Pascal makes it clear he is not interested in moving and would rather stay put.

'This park used to be open all night in the early days,' Nick recalls. 'You used to see these Polish lads washing in the fountain on the Broad Walk in the early mornings. They were returning from night shifts and they'd strip right down to their waists to wash, even in midwinter.'

The tempo of the rain has changed once more. The last outburst has ended almost as quickly as it began. Everything is still dripping madly but there is no longer any rain falling directly from the sky. It is the gibbons that alert us to this. We hear their plaintive cry through the trees. It is unusual to hear them in the middle of the day like this, their preferred time being the early morning.

'It's mournful in a way, that sound. I can't help finding it sad,' Nick comments.

'Yes, haunting,' I concur.

'They are calling out but there is nobody to hear them because they're in a zoo.'

We listen, wondering what they might be saying.

'They are a father and son, apparently,' I add.

'Where is the mother?' Nick asks.

It is a question I cannot answer. But I take the sound of the gibbons and the appearance of the crows as my cue to leave. It is 1 p.m. and I have been in the park all morning.

As I lumber off, Nick calls out loudly, 'Emma!' I turn around. 'You are walking just like a hobo! And, by the way, thanks!'

I stop to photograph the crab apple trees, which are bursting with small gleaming fruit, perfectly round. A few have fallen to the ground, pelted off prematurely by the rain. They look like Christmas-tree baubles accidentally wedged in mud.

The first dog walker has appeared in the park. When I get to the bridge I see joggers wondering how to cross the water in their trainers. The first cyclists have begun to do the rounds of the Outer Circle – all signs that the park is springing back to everyday life.

I feel as if I am emerging from another country.

7 Childhood

'My mother came up to me one day and asked me, "What is a cunt?" I told her, "You married one!"'

We are sitting in the open grass at twilight, talking about our childhoods. Bachi and Lizzie have already left, preferring to get home before the darkness descends, but Nick and I remain seated – he reclining in his usual spot in front of the purple vetch, me lying opposite at two metres' distance on a tarpaulin he has produced for me as the ground is damp. The light is fading and the clouds glow a luminous mauve. Crows are flying overhead, flapping their voluminous blue-black wings, which somehow look magnified in the half-light.

'I love this time of day,' Nick comments. 'It's my favourite, this and the early mornings when the park is empty of people. It's when we find peace.'

'Except when I come along with my chatter!' I interject.

'It's very welcome chatter. We have conversations – real conversations, I mean.'

We sit there for a moment absorbing the quiet of the evening and the slow progression of the colours across the sky.

'I couldn't understand as a child why my mother stayed with him. Later when I asked, "Why didn't you leave?" she said we would have been taken into care – my sister and me, not my brother, who was ten years older. She didn't want to lose us. So she kept quiet. That and she didn't want the neighbours to know what was going on. Respectability was very important to her.'

'People cared a lot about respectability in those days,' I say.

'There was a lot of silence in my family.'

'Sometimes silence is what enables families to go on,' I suggest, 'but silence can also be destructive, burdensome, especially on children.'

'I was shy as a child. I observed things. I'd be in the room next door. My mother would pretend nothing was happening but you could hear stuff going on. And you could see the swelling on her face. She'd come into the room and she wouldn't say a word. She'd just get out the ironing board and start ironing madly, with her jaw distorted into a fixed expression.'

Nick sits upright and mimics his mother pressing down on the ironing board, moving her arm back and forth in rapid jerky movements, her jaw set rigid. The performance lasts only a flash but is horribly evocative. What was going through her head at those moments, I wonder? Fear? Anger? Humiliation? The desire to simply blot everything out? The illusion that if she walled herself in silence she could hide what was going on from the children? I wonder how many other women have been forced to find stability in their ironing boards, rebalancing themselves through the solidity of domestic tools and tasks.

'Policemen's boots at the door. That's all you see when you're little: the shiny black boots and the trousers. But she sent them away. "It's nothing, Officer. Everything's fine here. It must be a mistake."'

What was going on in the agile mind of young Nick, who was making his deductions whilst imbibing the impossibility of being able to speak about what he was seeing, hearing and surmising? Was his sister, two years his senior, upstairs in her bedroom, perhaps? I try to picture the three of them, isolated by the compulsory silence yet hyper-attentive to the sounds and movements of the man who was eating away at any sense of security the home might offer.

'It's terrible how we internalise the idea that we must not tell,' I say, reminded of a traumatic incident from my own childhood. 'There wasn't any violence in my family and the small town where I grew up was very safe, or at least that was how it felt. But one day when I was seven I was walking to my friend's house when I got stopped by a man on a bicycle who said he was a doctor and that he needed to examine me urgently to see if I had a disease that lots of girls got. I knew immediately that something was ominous. But he was an adult and I was a child, and I didn't dare question his authority. I was trapped and paralysed.'

'I suppose this happened in the dark,' Nick comments.

'No. It was the middle of the day, in broad daylight in a residential street – but there was no one around. He ordered me to pull down my pants and then he started trying to stick his fingers inside me. I didn't really understand what he was doing. I wasn't familiar with my own anatomy but I knew that it hurt and it felt forbidden. I started to sob. He told me that I was a cry-baby and that I should grow up. When he'd finished fiddling he pulled my pants up and looked me very seriously in the eye. "Now, you mustn't tell any adults about this. You understand? If you tell anyone about this you are going to get into big trouble. BIG, BIG trouble. GOT IT?" I nodded and promised I wouldn't say anything. I can still remember the menacing intensity of his small green-grey eyes staring down at me. Then he sped off on his bicycle. I wiped my eyes and tried to compose myself before walking home.'

'What sort of age was he, this bloke?' Nick asks.

'Well, to me he was an adult. A man. But I think in reality he was about eighteen. But what I remember most about this incident is the terrible burden of the silence he placed on me and the sense of horror and shame that came with trying to keep this secret. As I plodded home my head was pounding with a single phrase: "I MUSTN'T tell anyone, MUSTN'T tell anyone. MUSTN'T." I was trying to will myself into silence. That seemed more important than anything else. But when I opened the kitchen door and tried to say hello to my mother, my voice came out in an unnatural squeak and then I burst into uncontrollable tears. So my mother immediately knew something was wrong. She coaxed an account out of me, then rang the police.'

'That's good. So she took action. That was the right thing to do.'

'Yes. And it made all the difference. It converted the painful burden of my terrible secret into something that felt more like an adventure story. A policewoman arrived at the door and I had to explain to her what had happened. I panicked for a moment when she asked me to demonstrate how far my pants were down as I thought she expected me to pull them down again. But she saw my panic and said I could just point to how far. When I described the man with his bag flung across his shoulder, she suspected he was a newspaper delivery boy and we drove down to the town centre – my mother, the policewoman, my sister and I – and crouched behind a statue opposite W. H. Smith in the hope that I might identify him. We watched various delivery boys returning and were just about to give up when I suddenly spotted him arriving late on his bicycle. He was arrested there and then. My last image of him was looking out of the back window of my mum's car into the police car behind. When he saw me he pulled a horrible face and stuck out his tongue.'

'So what happened to him? Was he sent to prison?'

'I think he just got a fine and was put on a different delivery round. But for me the fact that he was caught made all the difference. It restored order in my world. It showed me that terrible things could not be allowed to happen. I am convinced I would have been much more damaged by this episode if I had managed to keep silent. It was my tears that saved me.'

'I recognise that feeling of knowing something is wrong when you're a child but not knowing how to articulate it,' Nick says. 'It wasn't as bad as your story but once in a department store there was this man near the changing rooms who tried to touch me. I knew it was wrong. I fled to the safety of my mother's side but I didn't tell her anything. I wouldn't have known what to say. For me the real problem was at home,' he continues. 'My father was unpredictable and everything felt in constant flux, so your psyche was primed to expect the unexpected. You tended to start something but you couldn't finish it. And I couldn't concentrate at school. I wasn't interested. I wanted to get home. It wasn't that I preferred being at home to being at school but I was worried about what might be happening to my mother, even if he was supposed to be out at work in the day.'

I note how often Nick refers to his father as 'he', as if the word 'father' is something this man is unworthy of.

'What was his line of work?' I ask.

'I'm not really sure,' Nick says. 'That's strange, isn't it? He was an educated man, apparently – spoke Hebrew and Arabic, so I'm told, but I don't even know if that's true. He handed me a rifle once and taught me to shoot a bird. I buried it after. It felt wrong. That is the first and last time I have ever killed anything, to my knowledge. I consider all creatures to be sentient beings. His violence doesn't define me. I learned from it. I took it as an example of how not to be and went in search of something better. And I decided early on: Don't wallow in your misfortunes, but don't censure them either. His violence became a reference point. That's all. How can a man destroy his own family? How can he harm the woman who gave birth to you and brings you your toast in the morning? I needed to explore those questions. Walter Benjamin and other writers like Adorno accompanied me in my search for answers. I never show violence to animals or humans. I do sometimes experience anger but I consider it a weakness to be mastered.'

'Not many people are able to do that,' I suggest. 'A lot of people reproduce the violence they experience as kids in spite of themselves. You seem to have been able to convert cruelty into empathy and kindness. That's no mean feat.'

'That's because I observed my mother and how she behaved,' Nick replies simply. 'She fed me and protected me, literally. She was divine. I learned so much from her. She didn't tell you what to do but you picked things up. From her I learned that a butterfly is better off with its wings on than without them – that sort of thing. Cleave unto one another, it tells you in the Bible, but it's difficult to cleave onto the one who's holding the cleaver, who might just split you down the middle, sort of thing!'

We both burst out laughing at this disconcerting yet ingenious linguistic somersault even as we linger on the horror of the image.

'I'm standing in the way between him and my mother, fearing that I might be killed. It could be the end any minute.'

As Nick remembers his childhood fear he also tries to imagine what might have been going on in his mother's head.

'"Free. Free. I want to be free. Put anything sharp away. Find a way out. But – the children? Cling on to your vows. Cling to the Church. Cling to something."'

I think once again of the ironing board.

'Have you ever seen that film *Funny Games* by Michael Haneke?' Nick asks suddenly. I think he is changing the subject, but he isn't.

'No, I don't think I have.'

'Well, you may not want to. But that film felt so familiar to me when I saw it. There's this serial killer who ingratiates his way into a family by pretending to be nice and then slowly subjects its members to torture. I recognised so much of that film. He was sixty-three when he died and I just remember feeling glad that he was dead, glad for my mother. I didn't want to go to the funeral but my mother insisted, so I went for her sake. My brother started saying the sorts of things people feel obliged to say on such occasions. "He wasn't really all that bad!" – that sort of thing. And I just looked at him in disbelief.'

'When did you last see your brother?' I ask.

'I haven't had any contact with my family for over twenty years. I often used to sit under the dining room table as a child,' Nick remembers. 'I think that was where I felt most secure. One day I was under the table when I overheard my sister ask my mother, "Why do the men of the family always sit at the end of the table?" And I heard my mother answer, "Because they think they are the ones with the power."'

'Think' is the word that stands out here. Men may think they have the power, but his mother is clearly suggesting otherwise. She is inviting her children to recognise the difference between appearances and reality, or 'what passes for reality', as Nick specifies, retaining the idea that reality itself may be illusory. An early lesson in relativity and one he has retained for sixty-odd years.

'My mother once told me that she'd tried to abort me when she was pregnant because of his violence. So you can be killed before you are born! When she told me that, I just said, "Well, it must have been very difficult for you." Her eyes welled up and she put her arms around me. I was left wondering how she tried to do it. But years later she denied it. I heard her explain to a friend that abortion was murder and that she was against it on Christian grounds. When I reminded her of that earlier conversation she said, "I didn't ever tell you that." So what is the truth? How can you ever know?'

'Well, maybe she felt ashamed about having contemplated it and effaced the episode from her mind,' I suggest, wanting instinctively to defend his long-suffering mother, although in truth she does not need defending. Nick's memories of her are warm and loving, and his respect for her unflinching.

'She was in her eighties when she died. It's strange. I don't remember the exact date – neither the day nor the year – but I loved her to bits. She lived a quiet life after he'd gone. There weren't many people at her funeral. There were more at *his*.' Nick's voice rises with a certain disgust as he says this.

'Well, I guess there do tend to be fewer people at funerals for people who are old when they die,' I suggest. 'A lot of their friends have already gone by that stage.'

'That's true,' Nick says, and he pauses. 'I hadn't thought of that. Thank you for pointing that out.'

The evening is growing darker. I have not stayed this late in the park before. The trees have merged into obscurity and Nick has morphed into an indistinct bearded shape. A lone owl is hooting from a distant tree. Apart from Pascal, who must still be lying in the shadows of the hornbeams, we are alone. The park feels very different than in daylight, like a space apart. I realise the gates must already be locked but I find myself reluctant to move, not just because the nightfall is compellingly beautiful but also because the darkness seems to be making our conversation more intimate and focused. It is as if we are on an island where no one can disturb us. I have often heard Nick mention how distracted he was at school by his anxiety about his mother's safety, but tonight, under the purple-black sky, a new childhood episode emerges gradually, bit by bit.

'Education didn't seem relevant to me. I didn't listen to the teachers and I couldn't do exams. But there was one lady teacher I remember who got through to me a bit. She took some interest. She even gave me ten out of ten for an essay. She said it was really good.'

'Can you remember what you wrote about?' I ask, wanting retrospectively for a teacher to recognise his deep and roving intelligence.

'Well, I remember the assignment. It was to write an essay about a day at home. Ha! I don't know how old I was, but I must have been quite young. Still in shorts. Too young to be self-conscious. So I guess they were expecting nice stuff about playing football in the garden, that sort of thing, but that wasn't what I wrote. I described a day at home, since that was what they were asking us to do.' He chuckles as he recalls the incident and then his mind shoots off on a tangent and he is talking about US politics. It is at least twenty minutes before I encourage him back.

'So you wrote about your home life?'

'To me it was just a normal day I was describing, but not to the teacher, apparently.'

I picture the teacher settling down at her kitchen table to read a bunch of children's essays – making cakes with Mother, taking the dog for a walk, playing ball in the garden, until she comes across an essay that stops her in her tracks. What was Nick describing, I wonder? Was he recounting his observations from under the dining room table? Or was he describing one of the more dramatic stories that he has previously told me about? That iconic Christmas Day with blood on the carpet, when his brother retaliated and smashed his father's head through the window. The sister holding the carving knife for cutting the turkey. The sound of the doorbell ringing. The commotion of bundling the bleeding father into the back room. Nick opening the door to the neighbours with a smile and a 'Happy Christmas'. An episode from his childhood that has left an indelible and recurring imprint.

Whatever he wrote, it was clearly exceptional in some way – not only because he was congratulated for it but because three days later he found himself called to the headmaster's office. Once again Nick wanders away from the story. History and politics intervene. But I try to draw him back to the work of excavation.

'So you had to go to see the headmaster?' I say.

'Ah yes, so I was sitting on the bench outside his office, not knowing why I was there, when suddenly the door bursts open and out comes the headmaster and my parents with him! And they're all staring at me. My mum kneels down and takes my hands in hers and she just looks at me with burning eyes. And my father is stony and silent. Then the next day at home, when my mother wasn't looking, he came up behind me while I was eating my cornflakes. He grabbed the back of my head and rammed my face into the cereal bowl. He was a brutal man. I wanted to kill him.'

'You'd exposed him and he must have been furious, but it was probably a good thing that you did,' I suggest.

'I don't say any of this to feel sorry for myself. I've had a wonderful life. And it taught me to look for something better and experience other ways of living. I've lived in ashrams in India and on a kibbutz in Israel. I've seen better ways of doing things.'

Nick's childhood does not emerge in straight lines but in small fragments: shards of vivid memory spliced together, some good, some bad, sometimes triggered by an external prompt – the sound of a child crying, a dish of favourite food, a jumper someone is wearing. Our discussions of family stretch in fits and starts over the year. Sometimes as we chat under the hornbeams during the daytime happy memories bubble to the surface. He reminisces about the magic of going to the local fairground, which felt like the entire world from a child's perspective, with its candyfloss and goldfish you could take home in water-filled plastic bags. Then there was Aunt Joan with her bouffant hairstyle; picnic outings with his mother in the countryside on the Cheshire–Wirral border; trips to the seaside and the Liverpool docks. And there were some comfortable memories from within the home too, in spite of everything.

'I enjoyed helping my mother in the kitchen,' he recalls. 'She was a really good cook and her food was homely: pies, puddings, that sort of thing. She would boil up stock from the bones, just as you do in those soups. And I'd help with some of the smaller tasks. It was my responsibility to put just a little bit of cream in the mash! Remember that Angel Delight? You'd whisk it until the consistency transformed and you'd get this fine, sweet butterscotch powder rising out of the bowl and you could breathe it in.'

'Butterscotch was my favourite flavour,' I add. 'I didn't like any of the pink flavours. And do you remember the jelly cubes? I actually bought a box of them the other day. Hadn't seen them for decades. They only cost eighty pence even now!'

'Oh, the jelly! You had to tug at them to tear them apart and you couldn't help eating a cube or two 'cos it was like a chewy sweet.'

'I liked the pineapple flavour best, and the green one. I think it was lime.'

'Shelling peas – that was another task I often did,' Nick remembers. 'I used to enjoy that. You could run your finger through the pod and hoover up the contents in one go. I loved eating them raw and would pop them into my mouth when my mother wasn't looking.'

'I did that too! That was my favourite kitchen task!'

'Some of them were really sweet and juicy, and then you'd suddenly get one that felt and tasted like a stone.' We laugh at how we both assumed we were the only ones to commit these innocent childhood transgressions in the kitchen.

The atmospheres of our childhoods may have been very different but elements of the material backdrop were similar. We were brought up in the same era and both share a predilection for fine detail. One day, standing under a dripping tree in the drizzle, we enjoy diverting ourselves from the cold with memories of childhood pleasures: finding toys in the cereal packet, watching *Animal Magic* and *Blue Peter*. Nick talks about his collection of painted models of cars and aeroplanes, and I mention my collection of *Magic Roundabout* figures, which I confess I still have hidden away in a drawer somewhere.

'Ermintrude the cow! Florence! And the one with a moustache who bounced about on a spring?!' Nick recalls, laughing.

'Zebedee,' I say.

'Zebedee! Now it's coming back! Is that who you named your cat after, by any chance?'

'Yes!' I admit. 'Some people thought we chose Zebedee for its biblical connotations but really, for me, it evokes *The Magic Roundabout*!'

By the time Bachi joins us today, padding his way through the damp grass, Nick, Pascal and I are all standing huddled under an umbrella watching an episode of *The Clangers* on my mobile phone and enjoying imitating the sounds of those endearing knitted planetary figures who made actual words seem unnecessary. I can't help thinking Pascal must approve of that. It was my favourite programme as a small child, and Nick's too. We smile with affection at the familiar, if long-buried, sight of the Soup Dragon emerging from its hole. It is like re-encountering an old friend after several decades. And

Pascal smiles too, even though he is meeting the Soup Dragon for the first time.

'I'm afraid we've regressed to *The Clangers*,' I tell Bachi as he comes towards us.

'You mean *progressed*!' Nick corrects.

Like all childhoods, Nick's also contains its comic incidents, such as the time when the cat's tail caught fire and Nick's mother caught him whacking the much-loved pet. 'She thought I was being cruel to it until she realised I was putting out the fire!'

There are classic boyhood memories too of playing football with the local kids and hanging out in the youth club.

'I was coming out of Birkenhead and I'd cycle through this working-class area in the morning. I was from what you'd call a lower-bourgeois middle-class background, a mix of middle and working class, I suppose – not that class has any concrete reality, in my opinion. I would knock around with the kids from the housing estates because they were the only ones who'd talk to you. And it would be simple communication. "Hey, d'you wanna play football?" It was as simple as that. And I did.'

But threaded through these banal childhood experiences like a poisonous weed are the memories of bedwetting, of not daring to go to sleep at night, of waiting for his father when he didn't turn up for a promised trip to the cinema, or being dumped in front of a pint of beer in a pub while his father went off with his mates, and of his mother's silent suffering.

'Some people just aren't responsible enough to have children. I saw what drink does to a person's face, and not just his face either. He wanted me to go into the army. Thought I needed disciplining. I didn't need disciplining but I did challenge him. I was always the kid who asked the questions.' It is not difficult to imagine that. 'Perhaps he was conditioned,' Nick adds reflexively. 'He may have even tried to uncondition himself. You enter the labyrinth clutching a thread, but if the thread runs out before you get to the centre you find yourself backtracking until you've wound the thread back into a ball.' There is a hint of generosity in this phrase, suggesting that perhaps his father could not help himself. 'In later life he took to gardening,' Nick adds. 'Perhaps he found some peace in that. He may have been schizophrenic. Who knows? By the time he died I think he was living in his Daimler in the garage.'

Always countering the negative images of the father are the images of Nick's mother: stoical, practical, responsible, caring – looking after house and family, trying to understand and protect her son, trying to give him hope and aspirations.

'My mother was hoping to give me stability, so she sent me down to the MAYC, the Methodist Association Youth Club, where you could run around, play badminton – which incidentally I was good at. I was even a youth club leader since I knew how to follow instructions, that sort of thing. And it was she who first told me about Martin Luther King. She said there was this wonderful man who was going to solve the race problem – which is what they called it in those days. One day the youth club organised a coach trip to London from the Wirral. We went to Earls Court or one of those places to hear Cliff Richard talk about God. I was an adolescent at the time – maybe thirteen or fourteen years old. And they put up Martin Luther King's image and speech on a huge screen. I had already heard it before but hearing it here in this giant auditorium with all these people in London, I was really quite affected by the whole thing. His anti-violence message and the "love your neighbour" bit left a deep impression in my mind. So I was sitting there dreamily enamoured by the message when suddenly I felt a thwack on the back of my head, which made me come to from my contemplations. And then I realised that everyone else was standing up and clapping, and these two boys behind thought I was being irreverent 'cos I was still sitting down, so they'd clonked me on the head.' Nick laughs at the recollection. 'And I thought at the time: Well, Martin Luther King wouldn't approve of that! But it was formative to me, that experience, and hopefully I can say that every minute I have lived I have challenged myself.'

Sometimes when we exchange childhood memories Nick turns to Pascal and asks him about his own childhood. But Pascal remains characteristically enigmatic. We learn that he is the eldest of two brothers and that his brother is married with kids, but that is as much as he divulges. Even Nick's innocent question, 'Did your parents read to you when you were little?', is somehow shrugged off with such ambiguity that it is impossible to tell if the answer is yes or no.

But one morning when I arrive early in the park with a flask of coffee and a bag of mini pains au chocolat, I find Nick propped up against a different tree from normal, sitting in a patch of low sun, his beard gleaming. His expression is stern and concentrated, reminding me of the image of Great Agrippa from the *Struwwelpeter* stories. I see immediately that he is totally absorbed in his tiny pocket radio and will not want to be disturbed.

'It's about Dürer,' he explains. 'I'd quite like to hear it. Why don't you have a chat to Pascal?'

I take the polite hint and head off towards Pascal, not at all sure what we will have a chat about but certain that he will greet the pastries with enthusiasm and appreciate the jar of milk I have brought for his sweet tea. I find him in relaxed mood. To my surprise he sits bolt upright and, in his quiet way, seems quite open to conversation.

I ask him what he used to have for breakfast when growing up.

'Milky cocoa or sugary milk with just a hint of coffee, and pains au chocolat or sometimes cakes,' he tells me.

And gradually we get onto the subject of his family. His mother was a French teacher; his father an electrician who was very practical and could fix anything.

'I hated it,' he replies as soon as I ask about school, 'the fixed hours, the sitting in rows, the endless discipline. But I was good at it. I could do things quickly. I was the one in the family who was destined to have a successful future. But then, ironically, the situation got reversed!' He laughs but without any hint of bitterness or apparent regret. 'My brother works in an office. He's into computing, I think – like everyone else, it seems.

'I was good at maths. I didn't enjoy the subject at school but outside school I liked playing with maths quite a lot. I can't remember most of that stuff now,' he says, laughing again. 'And philosophy. I liked that but I was always accused of being "hors-sujet"!'

'Did you experience racism when you were growing up?' I ask, knowing that Paris has its racial tensions.

'You did get people getting all wound up sometimes. You'd get the French, Algerians and Berbers all calling each other names. That sort of thing is hard-wired. But I never got wound up about it. I found it amusing. It was just part of our daily interactions and I never saw it as malicious.'

We talk a bit about families and I ask if he would describe his as functional or dysfunctional. I am aware that the question is absurdly crude but his answer is delightfully sophisticated.

'Oh, functionally dysfunctional,' he says, 'like most families, I suppose.' Then he pauses and adds, 'You could relax. It wasn't a place where you couldn't relax like in Nick's case. It wasn't difficult in that sense.'

Later in our conversation Pascal makes a comment about his long matted hair.

'It's an irreverence for convention, in a way.'

'Do you think you've always had an irreverence for convention or is that something you developed over time?' I ask.

'Yes, always!' he answers without hesitation. 'I was born like that. I think it's innate.'

I ask when he last saw his father, and he says it must be at least ten years ago but that he has had contact over the phone occasionally since that time.

I do not want our conversation to feel like an interrogation so I ease off on the questions and start talking about an old Jewish man I heard interviewed on Radio 4 this morning. He was an Auschwitz survivor aged one hundred who has just written a book called *The Happiest Man on Earth*. His motto, I tell Pascal, is the three H's: Happiness, Hope and Health.

'Ah, Hope!' Pascal repeats with a smile. 'Hope is the fuel of humanity!'

I gather up my empty flask, glad to have shared the pains au chocolat with Pascal and a small lone field mouse who hovered beside him throughout the conversation, pecking at the occasional crumbs.

Bachi's childhood is no more accessible than Pascal's. He would rather focus on the present and future than on a past he cannot change. But his image of his parents is unforgivingly negative. His mother was tyrannical. School was constrictive. Holiday trips to visit relatives in India were spent mainly in bed with an upset stomach. His allergies and ADHD had gone unrecognised and he was blamed for being a difficult kid. The tiny glimpses of his childhood that emerge all seem to have a single message attached: *Get me out of here!*

School has let down all three of my companions. Education in the form they encountered it as children felt meaningless and irrelevant, like something that prevented them from learning and living. My own encounter with school was quite different. It was not that it was inspiring but rather that it gave me solid blocks I could build with in the future. Nick often refers to himself as uneducated, but nothing could be further from the truth. I know very few people as dedicated to learning as he, and a desire to carry on learning is something we share. Sometimes when I watch him read I am almost jealous of the way he engages with books so directly. He does not just read them; he writes all over them in blue biro, dialoguing with the contents as he goes along. They become not just thinking devices but archives and companions too.

Occasionally, triggered by particular conversations, I offer a new companion from the books on my shelves at home. Shortly after our long nostalgic conversation about food, I offer him a copy of Nigel Slater's childhood memoir, *Toast*. To give a book about food to someone who doesn't have access to a kitchen might seem perverse. But to me there is something in this book that seems to resonate with Nick's childhood – not just the careful attention to material details but also the sensitive perceptions of a boy out of kilter with the family in which he finds himself. A boy who has the capacity to stand outside and observe even as he is immersed in a situation beyond his control. 'It's quite dark,' Nick comments, 'but I really enjoyed it. He was quite unhappy in his childhood, although his family wasn't too bad.' We go on to discuss the details, and I find myself lying in bed rereading it a few days later, entranced by the combination of food and foreboding.

The other book I give him is *Fugitive Pieces* by the Canadian author Anne Michaels. Nick is immediately taken with the title. I have not read it for years but in my mind it is one of the wisest and most astute portraits of what it might be like to live in the aftermath of childhood violence. But it is also about the redemptive possibilities of relationships that do not conform to the conventional framework. Nick and Pascal's 'arrangement without an arrangement' springs to my mind as I pull it from the shelf, and I smile when I see Nick reading the book out loud to Pascal next time I come by.

8 Fruits

Summer is quietly transitioning into autumn. The days are getting shorter and there is a cool nip in the air as the evening descends. The hornbeams still retain their greenness but the horse chestnut leaves are crinkled and brown, prematurely aged by the invasion of tiny leaf-mining moths which leave unwelcome patterns on their surface. Many have already fallen to the ground. The edges of the park are fruiting with blackberries, mulberries, hawthorn, rosehip and chestnuts, and the squirrels are busy chasing each other up and down the trees and scurrying through the dry leaves in search of conkers, which peep like shiny brown eyes from their bursting prickly shells.

I have spent a lazy Sunday afternoon with Nick and Pascal and am just about to leave when Nick says, 'We were wondering, Emma, would you like this?' He unearths a slightly dishevelled-looking bottle of olive oil. It is opened but almost full. 'Someone brought it down but we don't really have any use for it here. We wondered if it would be any use to you? We've had it a while but I don't think it's gone off.'

'I think I should be able to use it,' I say, opening the bottle and giving the oil a tentative sniff. 'It doesn't smell rancid or anything.' The label bears the trace of tiny scratches that have no doubt been made by mice, and the outside of the bottle is splattered with dry mud even though it has been protected from the worst of the elements by being buried amongst their affairs.

'Oh, and while you're at it . . .' Nick continues, looking towards Pascal. Pascal rummages in a plastic bag and produces a fancy sealed pack of ibérico ham sliced into different cuts.

'That looks like good stuff,' I comment. 'Surely you might want to eat it?' I am not comfortable with the idea of taking food away from them.

'We won't. It's not the sort of thing we eat,' Nick tells me. They seem put off by the fact that it is smoked rather than cooked. 'We thought you might want it. And we'd like to give you something. You've been bringing stuff down so regularly and we really appreciate it.'

Put like that, the offer seems hard to refuse. But still, to eat the ham that someone has gifted to them feels inappropriate, so I suggest instead that I find a way of incorporating it into a cooked meal that they can enjoy. I stuff the ham into my bag along with some empty dishes and the olive oil, which Nick wraps carefully in a separate plastic carrier bag so that it will not spill.

I use the ham in dishes that will return at least in part to the park. Soon Jamie Oliver's braised white cabbage with bacon recipe – which has become something of a lunchtime favourite – is adapted to braised white cabbage with ibérico ham. And so the ham re-enters the park in a new cooked form, a gift regifted and returned, to be eaten by Nick and Pascal while the remainder is eaten by me and my family in the kitchen at home.

I enjoy the circularity. The oil makes a similar circuit over the next few weeks, leaking its way back to the park in a variety of hot dishes, and soon it is the fruits of the park themselves that are being recycled back to their place of origin.

It begins with mulberries. I have never noticed that there is a mulberry tree in Regent's Park before, but a friend points it out. It is a mature tree with ample twisted branches covered by lush foliage. Its elongated ruby-coloured berries are darker than raspberries but not as dark as blackberries. They grow on stems that are hidden under a veil of heavily veined leaves. Together we set about harvesting some of these tantalising fruits, carefully lifting the green leaves in order to access the sweet finds underneath and making sure that plenty remains for birds and other wildlife. It is much more difficult than we expect. Our hands and wrists soon stain bright red as we try to caress the soft fruits off their stubborn stems.

I'm not sure whether or not our activity is legal, but my bloodied hands certainly make me look and feel like a criminal. I try to reassure myself that I have read somewhere that foraging is permissible as long as it is for personal rather than commercial use. The fact that I will return the fruits to the park once cooked makes my forays seem harmless enough – nothing more than a benevolent form of temporary hijacking. Besides, if the birds of the park are entitled to the fruits, why not its human inhabitants?

Oddly enough it is a policeman who encouraged me to reason in this way. Years ago Denis and I went on an early-morning cycle ride which took us to the Secret Garden. To our surprise, shortly after we entered the garden we were followed in by a policeman in full uniform who started scrutinising the flower beds as if expecting to find evidence of criminal activity there. It was an incongruous sight at six o'clock in the morning in this blissfully peaceful garden, and after a while we couldn't resist asking him what he was looking for.

'I'm looking for evidence of guerrilla gardening,' he commented, looking slightly embarrassed.

'What's that?' we asked.

'It's when people plant flowers illegally in places they shouldn't be,' he told us, making it obvious that he had clearly suspected us of smuggling alien plants into the royal beds. My long hair, my husband's beard, the shabby bicycles, the early time of day all seemed to have conspired to mark us out as guerrilla suspects.

We carried on chatting to the policeman as he continued his rounds to the sound of blackbirds, robins and woodpeckers. In one of the flower beds, at the back, some ripe vine tomatoes were growing, adding a splash of vibrant red to the otherwise formal flower arrangement.

'Are you going to eat those?' the policeman asked, pointing at the tomatoes.

'Of course not,' we replied, shocked at the suggestion.

'Well, if you don't, nobody else will – they'll only go to waste!' he retorted, laughing. He went on to tell us that the policy of the Royal Parks was to remove plants before they died so that everything always looked perfect. This meant that policemen like himself loved having Regent's Park on their beat as they could recuperate the healthy uprooted flowers and shrubs and replant them for themselves. He was due to retire soon and was looking forward to developing his back garden. 'Some of the best gardens in London!' he said, referring to police backyards.

I have no idea of the veracity of what he told us. He may have been a bit of a bluffer. But his account has left an indelible image in my mind of London metropolitan policemen spending their Sunday afternoons tending to spectacular gardens stuffed with exotic floral rejects from Regent's Park. What began as the policeman suspecting us of guerrilla gardening ended with him encouraging us to eat the fruits of the park. Even so, we were resistant to the idea and left the tomatoes undisturbed in their decorative beds.

On my way back from the mulberry tree I pick a few blackberries to supplement the mulberries in anticipation of preparing a fruit crumble. I notice when I rinse the mulberries that a few small green caterpillars float to the surface and try to climb their way out of my sink. This is not the first time I have inadvertently carried wildlife from the park into my kitchen. A few days ago I noticed a small spider dangling off one of the flasks.

The next day, between meetings, I find myself looking up the history of the ancient art of foraging and come across the term 'usufruct', which translates quite literally from the Latin as 'use of the fruits'. Where the ancient principle of usufruct applies, the usufructaries – in this case foragers – have the right to enjoy the fruits of a public tree as long as the tree is not harmed and the use is for the public good. In the United States the term is indelibly associated with Thomas Jefferson, who in 1789 famously declared that 'the earth belongs in usufruct to the living'. In other words, it is for use rather than possession or exploitation. It strikes me that this notion aptly describes Nick and Pascal's way of living in the park, whereby they make use of the space whilst taking care to treat the environment with respect, including its trees, birds, foxes, mice and passing dogs and humans.

I add the mulberries and blackberries to some chopped cooking apple which is already simmering and watch the reds and purples diffuse across the surface, eventually dyeing the apple flesh a deep rich magenta. I make a crumble top in a separate bowl with butter, flour, sugar and oats, then sprinkle it onto the steaming fruit. When the dish emerges from the oven half an hour later the edges are burnished blackish red and tiny translucent ruby-coloured bubbles peep through the cracks of crumble. I take pleasure in the fact that the fruits are journeying from the park to my home and back again. I put foil over the dish to keep it warm and pour some cream into an old jam jar before cycling to the park with these treasures carefully balanced in my basket.

'That's beautiful,' Nick comments when he receives the earthenware dish with the crumble still warm and fragrant from the oven. 'And I'll keep that piece of foil too, if you don't mind.'

'Ah, blackberries!' Pascal comments. 'We have to watch out right now!' He points to the splatters of purple bird droppings that adorn their surroundings, reassuring me that the birds have eaten their fair share.

Next time I come to the park Nick comments on how he enjoyed the blend of sweetness and sharpness. I notice that he has made an aerial out of the aluminium foil and attached it to his small pocket radio. We share our perceptions of the latest news, having both listened to the *Today* programme this morning.

As September progresses, most of the fruit left behind on the blackberry bushes begins to look wizened and insects take over from birds and humans as their main consumers. We are approaching Michaelmas Day, after which it is said that the blackberries belong to the devil. According to mythology, this is the day when Lucifer was cast out of heaven, landing on a thorny blackberry bush and cursing the fruits by splattering them with his spit or urine, depending on which version of the story you encounter.

By now, avian attention in the park has shifted from the blackberry bushes to the crab apple trees, and it is the ring-necked parakeets that are the most enthusiastic takers, even if they have to contend with the occasional carrion crow. The parakeets have the advantage of numbers. Clustering together, they swoop through the sky, creating an improbably bright trail of luminous green before landing on the upper branches of the crab apple trees, which are bobbly with fruit. Their rau-cous high-pitched squawking fills the air until they settle down to the serious business of eating. Some dig their mighty beaks directly into the solid fruits; others elegantly pluck whole crab apples from the tree and decorously peck at them, using one claw to grip on to the branch and the other to hold the fruit.

The parakeets seem to be at their hungriest in the early morning when the autumn sunshine is strong and the crab apples gleam golden yellow against a clear blue sky. The neon green of their feathers and the impudent scarlet of their beaks and claws bring an unexpected tropical glow to the park. I cannot resist trying to capture this scene on my mobile each time I pass but am always disappointed by the results. It isn't just that parakeets make restless portrait sitters and that I don't have an adequate zoom lens on my camera. It is that nothing can beat the actual experience of being here, at the heart of this vibrant scene of fruity carnage taking place in an otherwise deserted corner of the park.

'It's a competition,' Nick comments jovially. 'The parakeets get the ones on top, the humans get the ones below and the ones in the middle are left to rot on the tree. They really ought to prune these trees, though. The fruits are so tightly packed that it's difficult for them to grow.'

The next day when I return to the park Nick presents me with a bag filled to the brim with perfectly formed crab apples, which I receive with thanks. As they roll out of the bag into my kitchen sink I can feel the magic of the park come to life in my kitchen. For months now I have been watching the slow and miraculous transformation of the trees, from the moment they glowed with fresh pink and white spring blossom to the point when tiny hard green fruits emerged and gradually transitioned into the rich golden baubles that now bob up and down in the water. I remove the odd leaf and stem and set about researching how to make crab apple jelly.

The arrival of the crab apples in my house gives me the opportunity to unearth my mother's preserving pan, which I rescued from the garage of the family home just two weeks ago. Ever since my mother's death, my sisters and I have been planning to clear the house but have been thwarted by restrictions on travel. We still have many decisions to make about what to keep and what to renounce, but one object that was non-negotiable was my mother's old-fashioned aluminium preserving pan. For more than fifty consecutive years she made her annual supply of marmalade in this pan. I still have vivid memories of returning home from school on winter days only to find the smell of simmering citrus fruit diffused throughout the entire house and to witness the strange sight of a nappy of pips and pith suspended from the handle of the pan. And I remember the excitement of seeing tall jars of hot gleaming marmalade appear on the kitchen table, even if at the time I did not like the taste. While my younger sister got my mother's elegant silver filigree marmalade pot, I got the preserving pan with its five decades' worth of stains. I had after all become my mother's chief marmalade assistant in the last few years of her life.

When I look up recipes for crab apple jelly on YouTube, I find myself transported into a variety of carefully curated kitchens – some intentionally rough-and-tumble, some conspicuously designer and others self-consciously rustic. Whatever the kitchen and whoever the cook, the basic principle is the same: fruit, water and alarming amounts of sugar. Soon my entire house is filled with the delightful aroma of crab apples bursting out of their skins as they simmer and explode in the boiling water. The next step is to mash them using my mother's old potato masher so that the pulp is loosed and crushed before being strained through a fine cloth (a fragment of an old Indian nightdress). I tie the cloth into a bundle containing the pectin-rich pips, cores and skin that will help the jelly set, then fix the bundle to the handle of the pan and leave it to dangle there all day, resisting the temptation to speed it up by punching and squeezing. Seeing the dangling cloth bundle and hearing the slow drip-drip takes me back to village kitchens in Gujarat where I often sat with women preparing shrikhand, a rich dessert made from yoghurt that is left to strain overnight until it forms a clay-like white ball which is later mixed with sugar and flavoured with saffron or cardamom. It is a popular Gujarati dish for special occasions and I have eaten it at many a wedding.

During the eight hours between suspending the fruity bundle and untying it, I am absorbed in my laptop. A new term has just begun. My letter of resignation has been accepted and I am working out my three months' notice, which will take me to mid-December. The knowledge that I am leaving frees me from the more stifling aspects of the job – bureaucracy, politics and planning – and enables me to concentrate on the part that really matters: teaching. Ever since the pandemic began we have been wrestling with how we will deliver courses virtually in the autumn term. Now, at last, instead of discussing it, we are actually doing it. It is with pleasure and excitement that I meet a new cohort of students who pop onto my screen like phantoms and seem as keen to engage with the course as I am, even if our interactions are restricted to 2D.

The sticky bundle has finally stopped dripping by the time I return to it in the early evening. When I open the cloth a perfect yellow ball of crab apple debris emerges, looking like a sculpture that Anish Kapoor might have created. I have difficulty throwing it away and can't resist photographing it first. It is time to boil the remaining liquid, tip in the sugar and let the concoction bubble and hiss. As I inhale the pungent fumes I remember with sadness how, on the last occasion we made marmalade together in the year of her death, my mother sat in her wheelchair in the fragrant steam-filled kitchen and said bewilderedly that she couldn't smell a thing.

Soon I am pouring the viscous liquid into three jars. On one label I write: 'The Return of the Crab Apples, October 2020'. Nick appreciates the inscription when I take it to the park the following morning, passing the parakeets, who are still busy breakfasting in the treetops. He insists we all sample the jelly immediately and we conclude that it is good – better, he tells me, than the last time someone made jam from those crab apples. I share pictures I have taken on my mobile of the different stages of jelly-making. As Nick scrolls through them he stops at the picture of the yellow ball of crab apple pulp.

'That's amazing,' he says. 'Scale it up and you've got a whole planet!'

Sharing images has become common practice. I share mine digitally and Nick shares his verbally, narrating the wonders of a particular dawn sky or the rhythm of the moving branches in the night.

'I don't have a camera,' he says, 'but I store certain images for you in my mind, as I know you'd love them.'

I play my video recording of the gibbons doing their singing and acrobatics routine and show my endless photographs of tree trunks, lichens, leaves and cloud formations.

'You don't need to see these,' I say. 'You're here all the time!'

'But I want to see them,' Nick replies. 'You have an eye and you notice things. When you're living here all the time you sometimes forget to look.'

Whenever I hand him my mobile to scroll through the images, he always passes it on to Pascal, who raises his eyebrows and sometimes poses a question or makes a reference to a film scene.

It is round about this time that I wander over to the other side of the park early one morning and stumble across a giant-sized pale-green door with a brass handle, standing upright and in the middle of the grass. It hangs in a frame and looks like the front door of a townhouse, only two or three times the size and without any house attached. Whichever side you look through it, you see grass, trees, pathways and a scattering of autumn leaves, and when you push it open and walk through you feel like a small child stepping into a secret world that adults can't see. It is a sculpture called *L'Âge d'Or* by Gavin Turk, which has been installed as part of the annual Frieze exhibition. Most years the presence of Frieze is something of a mixed blessing to park lovers. It means disrupted traffic, cumbersome marquees, high entrance fees, people tramping about and weeks of mud in the aftermath. But this year the main exhibition has gone online, leaving only the free outdoor sculpture component on view.

Perhaps it is because we are all unnaturally starved of material interactions in this time of closed galleries, theatres and museums, but this year's sculptures seem more vivid and meaningful than any I have seen before. Kalliopi Lemos's vast metal plait rising out of the grass and pointing to the sky reminds me of Pascal's matted hair and Nick's observation that Pascal is rooting himself back into the ground. But it is Gavin Turk's open door that speaks most directly to me, for it encapsulates my current state of being – half in, half out, no longer conscious or desirous of the distinction between inside and outside, park and home. I am reminded of Nick's earlier comment: 'There's the inside and the outside, but I always seem to be on the threshold.'

Next time I visit Nick and Pascal, I show them images of the sculptures. I'd like to suggest we visit them together but I feel shy to do so. I don't want to risk their being looked at strangely by people who might not expect to see them there, or to make them feel obliged to react in a particular way. I am aware that on the one occasion I have walked through the park with Pascal there was a man scurrying surreptitiously behind us, secretly photographing his hair, and that once his image even appeared on the front of the *Metro* newspaper, along with a sinister headline about migrants and terrorism. Perhaps I am fearful too that they might consider me pretentious if they see me recontextualised in the context of Frieze. And so, ironically, we share the sculptures through images on my screen even though they are just a short walk away at the other side of the park, reminding me that some thresholds are invisible.

Now that term has begun I often nip to the park straight after teaching sessions, when in normal times I would wind down with my colleagues or pop to the university canteen for lunch. Alternatively I arrive at the end of the working day when it is already half dark. This means I rarely spend time with Bachi and Lizzie these days, since they've usually left the park by the time I get there. Occasionally we cross paths as they are leaving and I see Lizzie rigged up with two bicycle lights to help her follow the path. 'Her eyesight is getting worse,' Bachi tells me on one such occasion. He has just come through the park gates and I am just about to enter them. First I lock my bicycle to the outside of the railings, not wanting it to get shut inside the park. Lizzie wags her tail and licks my hand in recognition, and I give her a friendly stroke. Nick has come out with them. He tells me he'll be back soon and hopes I'll still be there. But when he returns he seems surprised to see me sitting under the hornbeams with Pascal.

'I thought you'd gone,' he says. 'I couldn't see your bicycle. Did you bring it in?'

'No. I left it locked just outside,' I say.

'Yes, I saw where you locked it but I swear it's not there now, unless my eyesight's playing tricks in the dark.'

I find this hard to believe, partly because the bicycle isn't fancy but also because I have been using it so frequently to shuttle to and from the park that it feels like an extension of my arms and legs. But Nick is right. It has been lopped off the railings.

'Shall I walk back with you?' Nick offers, concerned about me walking home alone in the dark.

'No, it's alright,' I say, still unable to believe that my old green bicycle with its crumbling but capacious wicker basket, sturdy companion of the last five years, has disappeared out of my life just like that. On the way home, and for several days after, I find myself looking out for it, expecting to see it abandoned by a tree, locked outside a pub or floating in the canal, but it is gone.

I soon realise that without my bicycle I can no longer simply nip to the park and that delivering regular food is going to be difficult. Then I suddenly remember that I do have another bike at home – albeit not one that works – a rusty old orange bike that appeared mysteriously outside our house almost a year ago. I found it leaning there on the night I drove back just after my mother's death. There was a number on the side which I rang a few times to no avail. For a week I left it there, expecting someone to cycle off on it, but nobody did. I soon realised that the wheels were jammed. It didn't seem worth bothering the police about. So eventually, to get it out of the way, I dumped it on the flat roof extension at the back of the house, intending to take it to the recycling centre in Kentish Town someday. Needless to say, I forgot all about it. But now, with my own bicycle stolen, the orange bike that was no doubt also stolen at some stage in its life springs to mind. Perhaps I should get it revamped and use it? Perhaps I should simply see all of this as part of the inevitable redistribution of bicycles in London?

Reluctantly accepting that my much-loved green bicycle really has gone for good, I drive the orange one to a shop in Camden and get it repaired for £80. I decide this is now my bike – in usufruct, if not in ownership. If anyone ever turns up to reclaim it, it will be theirs, but of course they never do. Soon I am cycling to the park on it, but instead of locking it outside in the early evenings I wheel it in and prop it against a tree when visiting Nick and Pascal. It amuses me when several people comment on how well it matches my orange coat, as if this was an aesthetic choice. The bike was from the street; the coat I have been wearing for years and was from Oxfam. Everything was recycled.

A new dilemma arises at this time. Now when the park gates are locked, which is happening earlier and earlier with the coming of the autumn equinox and the changing of the clocks, it is not only me who is locked inside but my bicycle too.

'Come on, Pascal,' Nick says on such occasions, and Pascal rises out of his sleeping bag to assist. The three of us troop along a narrow mud path in the darkness to the edge of the park, taking care not to stab our eyes on the low-lying branches. First I leap over the railings – an art I have more or less perfected, although the purple bruises on the backs of my thighs seem to suggest otherwise – then Nick and Pascal carefully lift the bicycle over the railings and lower it so that I can reclaim it on the other side. Each time they do this I am aware of how easily their gesture could be misunderstood by passing strangers or, worse still, the police. But we are careful to make sure that we are never seen.

'Why don't you get your sleeping bag out and kip down here for the night?' Nick sometimes suggests. 'You could sleep a little way off or bring a friend down if you wanted security. You'd love waking up under the trees.' The offer is extremely appealing but I feel it would be awkward to explain to Denis and Julius. They are both very tolerant of my disappearing for hours and delaying supper, but I think they might find my sleeping in the park a bit much. I decide I'll wait until they are not at home before taking up the offer of joining Nick and Pascal for a night or two and experiencing first-hand the pleasure of watching the transition from night to day.

Often when I leave in the darkness I spot a fox silently winding its way in or out of the park or padding quietly through the moonlit streets before disappearing into somebody's garden. It cares little for boundaries and I feel an affinity with it. We are both connectors.

One damp morning in late October when I arrive in the park, Nick tells me he has something for me. He presents me with six mushrooms he has gathered from a corner of the park.

'Go over there,' he says. 'You'll see where they're growing.' I go to where he is pointing but at first see only dew-covered grass and fading, lightly frosted leaves, which are now more numerous on the ground than on the trees. Nick gets up and joins me, and suddenly I see them, their smooth round heads peeping through the grass like perfect secrets.

'Who says perfection doesn't exist?' Nick asks. 'Perfection is when you recognise the imperfection. Do you think they're edible?'

'I'm not sure,' I say. 'I could try looking it up.'

Back home I photograph the mushrooms and send images to a couple of friends who I think might know about such things, but they both text back saying they are unsure of how to identify them. My sister's partner reminds me that they were once very ill after eating some mushrooms they had foraged.

Anxious but not defeated, I turn to YouTube, where there are numerous helpful videos and websites which explain the ins and outs of identification. The key thing to establish is whether these are yellow stainers, which are deadly poisonous, or horse mushrooms, which are excellent on toast. I scratch a couple and leave them to see if they will stain ominously yellow in the next few minutes, but they don't. Nor do they smell suspicious. So I conclude that they must be horse mushrooms. I chop them up and start cooking them, adding butter and garlic. Everything looks and smells fine but I can't avoid the lingering anxiety that they could be poisonous. I have visions of giving them to Nick and Pascal to eat and returning to the park the next day to find them dead in their sleeping bags. I decide I cannot give them without taking on the traditional role of poison tester, so I tentatively nibble a couple of pieces. They taste delicious. I make toast, ladle the mushrooms on top, wrap the whole lot in foil and put the package under the dome-shaped copper dish for protection. I put some baked aubergine and rice in the tiffin for the main meal. The mushrooms on toast can be the starter, I think.

When I present them in the park, Pascal looks sceptical, but Nick says he will eat them in the morning.

'The toast will be cold by then,' I point out.

'Yes, but I want to try them out on the birds first,' he quips.

When I say I have tasted them, he says, 'Well, we can go out together!'

But that night as I lie in bed my imagination runs wild. I see Nick and Pascal, lying cold and stiff in their sleeping bags, being discovered by a passing dog walker who calls the police. There is an investigation. I confess. I say I fed them the mushrooms but I also plead, asking, 'Am I entirely culpable given that my intentions were good and that Nick had given me the mushrooms to cook?' Is this murder or manslaughter? I picture the headlines in the *Camden New Journal* and hear the testimony of people who knew Nick and Pascal. I am distraught about my actions and horrified that they are no longer of this world. I want to go to the funeral but will they let me if I am in custody?

By the time I get to the morning, I am exhausted. Work commitments mean it is lunchtime before I am able to head to the park. It is drizzly outside so I don my wellies and wade through the damp leaves that have accumulated overnight. As I take the muddy passageway into the secret grove, I can hear their voices and spot an umbrella in a tree.

'So, did you eat the mushrooms?' I ask, smiling.

Pascal says he didn't try them. Nick tells me, 'I tested them out on two crows. One took some morsels up into a tree and pecked away at them there; the other ignored them completely, so I wasn't sure what to make of that. I ate quite a lot but I got a bit of a headache, which could have been the mushrooms or might have just been psychological. So I didn't finish them. But they did taste good,' he adds diplomatically.

'Well, I'm just glad you're alive,' I confess. 'I was mentally attending your funeral in the night. There were lots of people there, by the way!'

'Covid!' quips Pascal, barely audibly. 'Don't forget Covid. No more than fifteen allowed at funerals!'

With death on our minds, the conversation turns to a friend of theirs who is anxious about the announcement of a second lockdown and has been talking of suicide once again.

The end of October is wet and windy but it is also beautiful. Each day the trees look different and the pavements and pathways are strewn with a new tapestry of colours. The sky is volatile, with thunderous grey clouds one minute and short-lived rainbows the next. When the sun does appear, everything glows magnificently in the wetness. A smell of cider oozes from the ground under the crab apple trees and the parakeets have moved on. Sometimes the leaves that drop take on the look of gold coins tumbling like manna from the sky. Those that fall onto the road are quickly pressed into red, orange, green and tan-coloured skeletons by the passing cars. Those swept off the pavements leave such perfect prints of their outlines that it is possible to identify the species of tree they are from.

I carry these autumn colours in and out of my kitchen in fruit and vegetable form. I make beetroot soup so rich in colour that it reminds me of the velvet curtains you used to see in theatres. 'Looks like blood,' Pascal declares when he sees it. I make spiced red cabbage with apple and raisins that glows the purple of bishops' robes and I enjoy mimicking the colours and forms of the leaves by stuffing stout round courgettes, different varieties of squash and red, yellow and green peppers with assorted fillings. All of these are divided between my kitchen and the park. And one day, when I open the copper dome I brought back from the park a few days earlier, a stack of autumn leaves spring out, seemingly delighted at having been released after days of incarceration. The sight makes me laugh out loud. 'I was just sending you a bit of the park,' Nick explains a few days later.

Both my kitchen and the street are alive with autumn, and sometimes more alive than I would want. One night I am awoken at 3 a.m. by a terrible screeching sound that sets my heart racing. At first I think it is a baby howling or a woman being attacked, then slowly it dawns on me that this must be the shriek of foxes mating. But when I draw the curtains what I see are two raging foxes either side of my car, competing, it seems, for prey. There must be an animal underneath, I think, and then it dawns on me that it could be one of my cats. I rush down the stairs in my night things and fling my front door open with trepidation, making as much noise as I can. The foxes back off reluctantly, disturbed by my human presence, and

I see a line of fluff dart into the house from under the car. It moves so fast that I cannot even identify what it is, but it turns out to be Fudge, Zebedee's feline sister. I have difficulty returning to sleep that night. The brutality of the sound of those excited foxes lingers with me through to the morning.

Meanwhile, inside my house other non-human presences are lurking. One evening when I open a low kitchen cupboard a huge rat springs out. It is as shocked by my presence as I am by its and we jump around each other in circles, much to the amusement of Julius, who is witness to the scene. The rat then disappears behind the fridge. When I empty the cupboard from which it sprang I find scraps of paper it has shredded amongst the droppings. We try to block up the cupboard from behind so that it can't get back in. I hope that given it found its way into the house it will find its way out again, but it doesn't seem to work like that. Every time I come down to the kitchen in the early morning I can hear it rustling about and making strange gnawing sounds behind the cupboards. The cats hear it too and stand by on high alert, their ears twitching with excitement, but they don't seem to intimidate the rat. One day I find that it has gnawed the buttons off the remote control for the TV and tried to carry the device into a hole in the wall. Pascal finds this hilarious when I tell him and we exchange jokes about the techno rat and enjoy watching a YouTube animation in which rats hold an illicit party during lockdown.

Our kitchen has also become home to an elusive slug that occasionally shows up in the bread bin and leaves a labyrinth of silvery trails across my chopping boards, much to my son's disgust. Is this an individual slug or a whole slime of slugs? I have no way of knowing. But whenever I pick up a chopping board or pan I find that new semi-transparent interlaced patterns have been created across its surface. I am no longer surprised by such discoveries, perhaps because metaphorically I have left the door open and expect the threshold to be crossed.

9 Loss

It is a bleak November morning. Thunderous slate-grey clouds scud across the sky. The wind is both relentless and unpredictable, throwing dead leaves and other debris into the air as it changes force and direction. From time to time the clouds burst and thick drops of rain pelt into my small mossy backyard, which is dark and dank at the best of times. Today it looks particularly barren through my kitchen window. The sound of the rat – or could it be rats? – gnawing away behind the cupboard fills me with a sense of foreboding. Are they breeding in there? I have tried to book an appointment with pest control, but with Covid infections on the rise they are short-staffed and booked up for weeks. The cats, though still fascinated by the noise and no doubt the odour, which is beyond the limits of my inferior human perception, do nothing more active than stare in frustration at the cupboard.

I am feeling nervous. For the first time since our getting to know each other we have made a formal arrangement. We will meet under the hornbeams at 3 p.m., assuming that the ashes arrive in time. Nick, Pascal, Bachi, me. Weather no barrier.

Today is Bachi's birthday and I am busy making him a cake. I had intended it as a surprise but when I asked Nick's advice about what sort of cake he thought Bachi might like, he reminded me of Bachi's allergies.

'He's so allergic to nuts that he won't even buy us peanuts in a packet, and he might be allergic to other things too. I think it's best to ask him directly,' Nick advised. So I phoned Bachi but the conversation was awkward.

'I'd like to make a cake for your birthday. Do you have any favourites?' I asked.

'Oh no. I wish I'd never mentioned my birthday!' Bachi replied with feeling. 'Really, please don't. I don't want anything. I don't want any fuss and I don't want to put anyone to trouble.'

'It isn't any trouble,' I insisted. 'I'd like to make you a cake. Just tell me the sort of cake you'd like.' I hadn't expected this to be so complicated. Bachi's resistance to the idea of a cake felt heartfelt and extreme.

'I'm really bad at receiving things,' he said at last. 'I'm much better at giving. I've always been that way. But I know it's something I need to work at. I need to learn how to receive.'

'Well, a cake isn't a bad place to start,' I suggested.

Bachi's reservations reminded me that, while we often talk about the art of giving, we rarely ever acknowledge the art of receiving – yet there is a real art to it. It requires relinquishing total control, being permeable to others and open to what they might bring to our lives, even if there is always vulnerability in that. It is an art that Nick and Pascal have perfected. Through their mastery of receiving, they offer people the possibility and pleasure of giving. Bachi, of all people, knows that pleasure.

'Coffee cake? Carrot cake?' I persisted.

'Well, if you must . . . chocolate,' Bachi offered. 'I do really love a very fudgy chocolate cake. Without nuts, obviously. That would be very nice. Thank you.' There was warmth in his voice even if it took us a while to get to the point of acceptance.

'I think I should be able to manage that,' I said.

But that was before I realised that Bachi's birthday was going to coincide with something else – a memorial for Lizzie, his much-beloved dog.

For some time now, I had been aware of Lizzie's declining health. Bachi had in fact been texting me with almost daily updates over the last four weeks. At first they were descriptive: Lizzie's eyesight was getting worse; she seemed to be struggling with her walking; she was lethargic, was losing her balance and was off her food. 'I'm rather worried about her to be honest,' one text read. Soon Lizzie's kidneys, lungs, intestines, hearing, eyesight and muscular functioning were being tested, then she was referred to the Royal Veterinary College at Hatfield, where orthopaedic, dermatological and neurological specialists were brought on board. Finally CT and MRI scans confirmed that she had a large tumour on her pituitary gland.

Lizzie's sickness made it difficult for her and Bachi to come to the park, but Nick and Pascal always asked after them both, so that now, along with food and hot water, I became a purvey-or of news of Lizzie's health and Bachi's frame of mind. I would read out his latest texts and together we would look up information on my mobile about pituitary glands and tumours.

'How is Bachi in himself?' Nick would ask, concerned. And I would answer as best I could. 'Anxious.' 'Hopeful.' 'Bearing up.'

'He won't let Lizzie suffer,' Nick stated. Of that we were all certain.

Various options were presented: radiotherapy, steroids, surgery. Eventually the decision was made to operate. There was even reason for optimism. If the operation was successful, Lizzie might regain some of her eyesight, we were told. She was sent home and put on drugs to shrink the tumour, and a date was fixed for the operation. 'Keep your fingers crossed,' Bachi would say at the end of each text message, and I would try to offer words of encouragement along with whatever emojis seemed most appropriate – crossed fingers, praying hands. From time to time when I was in the middle of preparing lectures little videos would appear through WhatsApp of Lizzie looking blissfully serene, sleeping with her head on Bachi's lap.

On the day of the operation, Bachi drove Lizzie to Regent's Park to see Nick and Pascal on her way to the hospital. No doubt he realised at some level that this might be their last encounter. During an operation that lasted five hours the tumour and pituitary gland were successfully removed but there was excessive bleeding, which signalled a possible stroke or brain damage.

'I know if there's any chance at all she's in the best place possible and she will fight as hard as she can, but if her quality of life isn't what she deserves, then I know what I have to do,' Bachi texted on the morning of 11 November, two days after the operation. A few hours later he texted to say he had had to let her go.

'She did her best, as did everyone else,' he wrote. 'I'll miss her but I had the pleasure of her company for four amazing years. She made my life better and had a positive effect on so many people (and dogs!) and that's how she should be remembered.'

I offered to go round to Bachi's apartment but he suggested we meet in the park in an hour's time to tell Nick and Pascal. He would see me there.

It was cold and drizzly out. The light was low and the canal awash with golden leaves that floated on the surface like teardrops that refused to dissolve. The trees leading to the secret passage bore a poster of a missing girl from Cricklewood. I wondered if she could be the girl I had sometimes seen bundled up asleep on a bench in the Broad Walk on early mornings in October, but had no way of knowing since I had never seen her face.

When Bachi arrived, skidding through the mud, he was bearing food and freshly washed clothes for Nick and Pascal, taking comfort in his role as giver. He looked depleted and exhausted.

'It is what it is,' he said with a long sigh, followed by a slight smile.

'She was a very special animal,' Nick said. 'She brought you so much pleasure and she brought me pleasure too. I loved the way she would come right up to you and stare deep into your face with her dark eyes. I used to look forward to her coming every day.'

'She was an incredible dog, quite unlike any other dog I've had – more intelligent, more reactive,' Bachi said. 'Even the surgeon and nurses at the Royal Veterinary College said they just wanted to spend time with her. She converted dog haters into dog lovers,' he added, looking spontaneously at me and then apologising for doing so.

'I'm not a dog hater,' I suggested, 'just more of a cat person than a dog person!' I think we were all relieved to have an excuse to laugh.

'I'm just glad that she had four good years after the first four bad years of her life,' Bachi said. 'When I brought her to the park on the way to the hospital she seemed to have a last burst of energy. She went straight up to Nick and licked him.'

I mentioned that my mother had also had a last burst of energy the day before she died, when she suddenly seemed a bit more perky and talkative. We stood around in the cold drizzle in silence for a while, allowing the sadness to be what it was. Bachi told us he had decided to leave Lizzie's body to science in the hope that some good might come of it. Then he said he was going home to upload videos of Lizzie. He wanted to make a YouTube channel dedicated to her as a memorial. We watched him lumber desolately through the drizzle, past the nubbly black crab apple trees now bereft of leaves.

Two days later, when I am sitting with Nick and Pascal at dusk, having delivered some curried parsnip with apple and ginger, Nick begins to tell me something very quietly, as if he is almost embarrassed.

'This might sound foolish,' he says, 'but on the night just after Lizzie died I stood outside Bachi's apartment in Camden Town. He once showed us where he lived. I was under a lamp post, looking up and just watching. I could see the lights on in his apartment and the television flickering, so I knew he was there. I stood around in the dark for some time, feeling like a shady character out of a film. I saw someone look at me with suspicion. I contemplated ringing the doorbell.'

'And did you?' I ask.

'No,' Nick replies.

'Why not?'

Nick hesitates, and then says, 'It's the tramp in me. I can't help it. I don't recognise it but it's there.'

'I'm sure he would have been really touched and comforted by your visit if he'd known,' I say.

'It was solidarity,' Nick replies. 'I wanted to show solidarity. I love that man.'

I am moved by this story, not least because I have never seen Nick leave the park before except to collect or deliver flasks down by the canal.

That night I ring Bachi to find out how he is doing. 'I'm OK,' he says, 'but it's very tough. I knew it would be, but it really is. I keep hearing sounds and thinking it's Lizzie.' He says he wishes he could have had a few more years with her. He keeps wondering if he could have picked up on the signs of the tumour earlier. Could he have given her a better life? She had given so much and brought so much joy.

I decide to tell Bachi about Nick's silent visit on the night of Lizzie's death.

'He should have come in. He would have been welcome,' Bachi says. 'Why didn't he ring the bell?' I repeat Nick's phrase about how the tramp in him had prevented him, and Bachi responds softly, 'I can understand that.' I tell Bachi that Nick said he loved him and I can sense that Bachi is moved to hear this. He goes on to tell me that he once showed pictures of Nick and Pascal to the porter of his building, saying that if they ever came round they should be let in. But they never have.

I ask how he is getting on with uploading Lizzie's images to YouTube.

'I can't do it,' he says. 'As soon as I try I just break down, so I'm painting the inside of all of my cupboards instead. The place is a mess. I've emptied everything out. I couldn't do that when she was here as she would have tripped over everything with her blindness, but now I can – but then that reminds me that she's not here.'

Bachi is in a state of grief. His life is upside down, so why not his cupboards? Why not his whole apartment? Over the next few days he goes into overdrive, turning everything upside down, pulling out wires, rigging new lights, fixing cables and reorganising his entire environment. Images of his upturned apartment appear on the screen of my mobile. I have never seen such a literal manifestation of the chaos of grief. He seems to have lost sight of the difference between day and night and by the sound of it has done very little sleeping. When he does sleep he dreams of Lizzie and thinks he can feel her kick in the night. When I phone him over this period he is generally either up a ladder or with his head inside a cupboard and I can't help feeling worried. I ask if he has been outside and he replies, 'I'm following the guidelines – staying in unless strictly necessary.'

'Perhaps it *is* necessary to get some exercise,' I suggest.

'I'm getting exercise up a ladder,' he retorts.

'How about going to the park?'

'I can't go to the park. The park *is* Lizzie,' he says, and that is that.

One thing he does tell me is that he has changed his mind about the disposal of Lizzie's body. He now wants to recuperate the ashes after the scientists have made their investigations and to scatter them in the park with Nick and Pascal, if they are OK with that.

'I'm sure they'll be OK with that,' I say. 'I think they'll be pleased.'

'Well, that's what I want. It's where Lizzie was happiest and with the people she was happiest to be around,' he states, asking if I would join them. 'Lizzie had terrible experiences in life but decided to make the most of things and be sociable with everyone,' he adds.

'That sounds rather like Nick,' I say. 'He had a difficult past but hasn't let that stop him from becoming sociable, outward-looking and kind.'

'Yes,' Bachi responds. 'I think Lizzie recognised that in Nick. She was drawn to him and Nick recognised that in Lizzie. They were close that way.'

I tell him I will sound out Nick and Pascal on the idea of scattering Lizzie's ashes in the park and will let him know their response.

It is already dark when I put down the phone at 6.30 p.m. but I feel an urgent need to communicate Bachi's wishes, so I heat up some couscous, dhal and red cabbage, fill the tiffin and some flasks and head to the park. Needless to say, the gates are already locked, so I have to leap over the railings to get to the other side. I then pad slowly through the leafy shadows to Nick and Pascal's spot. But to my surprise neither they nor their stuff are there.

The park looks expansive in the misty November darkness. I am struck by the beauty of the stillness. I am surprised to find that I do not feel afraid but instead experience an incredible sensation of freedom and connection to the earth and sky. I stand still for a while, just breathing in the cool night air, and then I begin to move very tentatively across the grass, taking care not to slip in the oozing mud. Eventually I spot the hazy shape of a figure in the darkness.

'Is that Pascal?' I call out. 'Have you moved?'

'Yes,' he says, coming towards me and pointing to the corner of the park. Tucked away discreetly behind some bushes is Nick, sitting in his sleeping bag and rolling a cigarette. He invites me to sit on a tree stump and offers me a sleeping bag to drape over my shoulders to keep out the cold. The longer I sit there the better my eyes adjust to the darkness.

The world looks and sounds different from this new location, which is more hooded by bushes and branches. An owl hoots from above our heads and in the distance the only thing visible is the BT Tower, which glows luminous pink, red and purple like something out of a fairy tale.

Nick offers me a piece of banana and walnut cake, which it turns out has been made by someone I know. I accept. And as he eats the dhal and red cabbage and I eat the cake I tell them of Bachi's desire to scatter Lizzie's ashes with them, since they were the most meaningful people to Lizzie and their corner of the park was the most meaningful place. They approve.

'That way, he'll be able to come and spend some quiet time with her on his own if he likes,' Nick comments. 'She represented so much to him. He's one of the kindest men I know – perhaps *the* kindest.'

I tell Nick that Bachi was touched by his visit to his apartment the other night, and that the porter has seen pictures of him and Pascal so that, if they ever go round, he will recognise them and let them in. Now it is Nick's turn to be moved.

'Why don't you text Bachi now and tell him that we like the plan for Lizzie's ashes?' Nick suggests, and so I do. Bachi immediately texts back. I ask Nick if he'd like to speak to him directly but he declines, saying he prefers contact to be face to face. So I make do with just sending Bachi our best wishes from the park, along with an image of the BT Tower glowing in the darkness from their new location.

That night we talk about ashes and where we would want to be buried. Nick asks Pascal if he would want a funeral. Pascal says no. I ask Nick if he would want one and he says he'd want his ashes scattered on the shoreline, but that if there were people who cared for him and wanted to give him a funeral, then he wouldn't object. 'If I can get to the end of my life without any regrets and can turn around to face the angel of death with a smile, then I will be satisfied.'

The talk of ashes reminds me of a conversation I once had

with the lady who used to run our local hardware shop. Her husband had recently died and she was telling one of her customers that she was off to Wales for the weekend to scatter his ashes in his favourite spot, when the customer piped up: 'Will you take my husband's too? They've been sitting around on the mantelpiece for years and I don't know what to do with them.' The shopkeeper was taken aback. She had never even met this woman's husband but somehow couldn't find a way of saying no. So off she went to Wales armed with two urns of ashes, those of her beloved husband of several decades and those of a husband whose wife was happy to outsource his disposal. A reminder of the potential intimacy and alienation of human remains.

The return of Lizzie's ashes from the crematorium seems to be happening more rapidly than anticipated. It now coincides exactly with Bachi's birthday. What does a birth-and-death-day cake look like, I wonder? The knowledge of these two events coinciding adds gravitas to the preparations. It is not that a cake can do anything to relieve the pain of Lizzie's death, but perhaps it can help towards the celebration of her life and its deep entanglement with Bachi's.

So here I am in the kitchen, piling a rich and creamy chocolate butter icing between layers of cake and pouring melted white chocolate over the top. I dip a matchstick in a small pot of melted dark chocolate and swirl it around in the white chocolate, creating a marbled effect. Light and dark. Life and death.

The cake feels up to the occasion, but am I? And, more to the point, is Bachi? I am anxious about how this combined memorialisation and celebration will go. If the thought of Bachi without Lizzie is hard for any of us to imagine, what must it be like for Bachi?

I root around in the kitchen cupboards to find a suitable tin, plate, knife and a birthday candle. But there are logistical issues to think of. How can I keep the cake upright when cycling, given that the tin is far too big to fit into my bicycle basket? A net bag on the handlebars seems like the best option. I have picked up some flowers in Camden for Lizzie's memorial: red and orange roses. I separate the petals from the stems and pile them under the copper dome, where they look and smell like a ritualistic offering in a Hindu ceremony. I then find some old leaf plates that I brought back from Gujarat some thirty years ago. In those days, and probably still today, they were sold in stacks of one hundred and commonly used for wedding feasts and other big events. I like the leaf connection with the park. In Gujarat I saw women stitching the leaves together with small sticks and brought a pack back to London to use as an ecological alternative to picnic plates. We often used them to have picnics in the Secret Garden on summer evenings. But there is another park connection. When my son was at nursery school I did a project with his class where we examined an Indian leaf plate, then collected our own leaves from the park, stitched them together with twigs and ate Indian sweets off them.

I decide I would like to offer Bachi a small present, but I'm not sure what. All the shops except food stores have been closed for weeks. I wander around the house, looking at the eclectic objects on the shelves, and alight upon a tiny, ingeniously made articulated metal dog that I bought from an old Italian crafts-man in a back street in Venice, where he had a workshop filled with drawers of tools and wires, from which he enjoyed cre-ating quirky objects. With its canine theme, I hope it might miraculously connect Bachi's birthday to Lizzie's death, as well as appealing to the bricoleur in him. I wrap it up tentatively in some coloured paper and decide I will give it only if the mood feels right.

As I climb onto my over-encumbered bicycle I notice that the clouds are beginning to lift and a hazy sun is starting to emerge. I ride carefully through the streams of water that have accumulated at the sides of the roads. The secret pas-sage is still soggy with puddles and as I enter it I see Bachi just ahead of me, walking with extreme caution through the mud. Nick and Pascal are standing up to receive us, and the sight of them both standing immediately creates a sense of formality by comparison to our usual encounters. Bachi delivers a bag of food for them and then pulls out a long, dark-green, cylindrical box that looks like it should contain a bottle of whisky.

'So, this is Lizzie!' he says, as if introducing us. And we all stare in wonderment at Lizzie's new form.

'Well, we've already had ashes down here today,' Nick muses. 'Human ashes this morning. Daisy – she's an artist – was down here with a friend scattering some of her mother's ashes under the hornbeams. It was one of her mother's favour-ite spots. Humans, animals – it's all the same.'

Bachi takes a deep breath, then hands Nick the green urn and says, 'I'd like you to start. Scatter them wherever you like.'

Nick peers into the urn, pushes the stopper tab and sniffs the ashes with curiosity. Then he walks off with slow solemn steps, wandering here and there, scattering the ashes around the trees and bushes where Lizzie used to enjoy sniffing and the places where they have slept.

'It's a rehearsal for our own death,' he declares as he hands the urn back to Bachi. 'There are a lot of ashes in this box. More than you'd expect.'

'That's Lizzie's generosity,' Bachi declares as he takes the urn. 'Generous to the end.' Then he begins his own scattering before handing the urn to me.

I take out a handful of coarse, dry, charcoal-like ashes, realising I have never touched either dog or human ashes before and remembering Nick's comment about their equivalence. With them I trace the socially distanced triangle where we sat on those long spring and summer evenings, Nick against a backdrop of mauve vetch, Bachi and Lizzie on their stripy rug and me equidistant between them, sitting either on Nick's jacket, a tarpaulin or my own wooden stool. When restrictions were lifted we reduced the space between us from two metres to one and a half, but kept the same formation. It was a triangle that Lizzie etched out many times, moving from person to person and keeping us connected. If the conversation got heavy she would keep it light. If anyone felt awkward she would distract them by creating an atmosphere of conviviality with her panting, licking and nuzzling. Now she was bringing us together once again through her death.

I hand the urn back to Bachi, who hands it to Pascal. And so we each make our own ritual scattering. I retrace the triangle in rose petals, which glow the colours of blood oranges and saffron against the backdrop of faded autumn leaves. When I hand the copper vessel to Bachi he tosses the remaining petals into the air and we watch them disperse in the wind. Finally he releases the remaining ashes in one gesture and they blow back over him. He tips his head back and inhales them with his eyes closed.

'That was deliberate, by the way!' he says.

'Interact with Lizzie and you're interacting with Bachi. Interact with Bachi and you're interacting with Lizzie,' Nick once commented.

There is a sense of relief at having released Lizzie back into the park.

The afternoon has been kind to us. No rain. No passers-by staring or asking awkward questions. The ground may be sodden but the golden leaves at the tops of the hornbeams are shimmering in the light.

'Sometimes I wonder if she was how she wanted to be or if she became what I wanted her to be, or perhaps they were the same thing – which would be good,' Bachi says hopefully.

As the sun starts setting behind the trees and the temperature drops, I suggest it is time we celebrate Bachi's birthday. We huddle under the hornbeams and I balance the cake on top of a log. Nick lights the candle with difficulty in the wind using his cigarette lighter. The leaf plates make their appearance. Nick and Pascal admire their structure and will continue to use them for some weeks after. We all enjoy the sensation of sinking our teeth into a rich and sludgy chocolate cake and we manage to switch to a more light-hearted mode of conversation. Finally I present Bachi with his gift, knowing full well that he is likely to be embarrassed to receive one. 'It's only small, a little token,' I reassure him to reduce the pressure. But when he opens it his eyes light up. 'A metal Lizzie!' he declares, testing out its articulation and admiring the workmanship. Each time he looks at it, standing or sitting in the palm of his hand, he smiles.

After a while Bachi says he is cold and that he is going to head home. He won't take the cake with him as he is conscious of having put on several kilos, what with the worry of Lizzie's illness and the lack of exercise, and he knows that if the cake is in the house he will just eat it. Before he leaves I ask if I can give him a hug, but he steps back. 'If anyone hugs me I'll break down in tears,' he says, 'and then I won't be able to drive home.' As he begins to make his way out of the park, Nick asks if he can accompany him, and Bachi agrees, so they walk along the soggy path together, leaving me and Pascal with the remaining cake in the sunset.

The next morning I come to the park with coffee, half hoping to be offered a slice of chocolate cake, but Nick and Pascal have eaten the whole thing in the night. They say the temperature dropped very suddenly to freezing and the cake was going hard, so they decided to eat it. 'Especially Pascal, with his penchant for chocolate,' Nick adds.

As the rainy November days and nights draw on, I am conscious that it was at this time last year that my mother's life was drawing to an end. Her death was so gradual and so surrounded by encouraging friends and family that, when the moment finally came, my last words to her were, 'Well done! You've done it.' This wasn't a sign of lack of love but of acceptance that at this particular moment in her life there was no other path she could possibly take, and yet taking it was still palpably difficult. It required her to stop doing the one thing she had done all her life – breathe.

As the anniversary of her death approaches, I sit down and write her a letter. In it I remember her last days and celebrate the fact that she is tucked away peacefully, embraced by a blanket of mud and memories in her local churchyard, entirely oblivious to the pandemic that has played havoc with all our lives in such strange ways. I congratulate her again, this time for getting out on time – just two months short of her ninetieth birthday – when Covid was little more than a distant rumour in China.

How we react to death seems very much linked to how well we are prepared for it and whether we feel the dying have led a full life. When my father died some fourteen years earlier I was much less prepared and the loss felt more raw and unbearable. Whereas my mother had been fading away gradually with Alzheimer's for several years, my father had a sudden diagnosis of a brain tumour and within three months he was dead. I can still remember how the shock of the realisation of his death would wash over me quite suddenly and unexpectedly at the strangest of moments, and I'd be overcome with grief. I remember how, like Bachi, I couldn't risk being hugged as I knew it would trigger a torrent of unstoppable tears.

I am conscious of Bachi inhabiting that state of rawness. It is as if a part of him has been amputated. When I speak to him on the phone he tells me how if he walks in the park he keeps looking round and expecting to see Lizzie. His sleep patterns have gone haywire. Sometimes he is up all night because he can't bear to go to bed, busying himself with disassembling and reassembling yet another element of his apartment. 'I make sure there is something else to fix before I finish the last job so that I'll have something to keep me occupied,' he explains. It was Lizzie who structured his day with regular morning and evening walks and with her physical presence and requirements. If he does get to sleep, he wakes up feeling her beside him and then has to relive the realisation that she is not there.

'I've been trying to throw away an old water bottle of hers,' he tells me one day. 'It was all old and chewed and was due to be chucked anyway. But each time I put it in the bin I find myself taking it back out. I actually salvaged it three times and then I forced myself to put it in a bin liner and carry it to the bins downstairs so that I won't recuperate it.' Six months later when I meet him in the park he tells me he has just had the outside of his car cleaned at a garage, but he wouldn't let them clean the inside because it still retains a hint of Lizzie's smell.

As he struggles with the painful mechanics of detachment, Bachi simultaneously maintains his attachment to Lizzie by developing her YouTube channel. Within a few months it contains over a hundred videos of Lizzie, documenting every aspect of her life, from eating, playing, yawning and sleeping to interacting with other dogs and humans at home and in the park. Some of the clips have over two thousand views. Amongst the other videos are two short films of Nick playing with Lizzie. One is accompanied by the words:

She may have been virtually blind, struggling with old injuries and, as I later found out, a brain tumour, but when she was in the park playing with Nick none of that mattered and it was like she was a puppy again, curious, playful, energetic. It takes an innocent animal to see through the stereotypes, to see the reality behind the mask. Lizzie instantly took a liking to Nick and was rewarded with a true friend not just for her but for me too.

Bachi intends the channel as both a tribute and a memorial to Lizzie, but also as a message of hope in relation to other dogs who have been abandoned, mistreated or considered beyond redemption. 'I know I didn't rescue her,' he writes. 'Lizzie saved me . . . The way she saw the world living in the moment, letting go of past trauma without rumination, taught me so much. How could I worry about the bad things that had happened in my life when she had endured and let go of so much pain and suffering?' He goes on to say that Lizzie taught him to be a better human being and inspired him to give something back to the canine friends who have given humans so much. He is now retraining as an animal behaviourist and will use his time rehabilitating other innocent souls like Lizzie who have been maltreated, so that they too can enrich people's lives. The post ends 'Rest in Peace my brave, beautiful, gentle friend, I will honour your life.'

So Lizzie not only defined Bachi's past but is now directing his future.

Reading all of this, I am reminded of something Nick once said as we were talking about people's relationships with their dogs.

'Look at Bachi. He's a saviour. Save the dog and you save yourself.'

10 Stuff

Today Nick offers to accompany me across the park as I am leaving. His reason is that he wants to dispose of a pillow that someone gave him yesterday. He tries to persuade me to take it but I resist.

'I already have two pillows from you!' I point out. 'And I'm trying to get rid of stuff from my house at the moment, not accumulate more.'

'Well, I can't do with another pillow,' he retorts. 'I don't need it and haven't got anywhere to store it. And I don't want to build up too much stuff. It will only get thrown away if you don't take it,' he adds persuasively, knowing full well that this argument often works with me, but this time I do not succumb.

'You're not interested in it, Pasc?' he asks rhetorically, knowing the answer all too well. Pascal shakes his head. He doesn't even use a pillow, preferring to lie completely flat.

'Well, I can't throw it away in the bins near here,' Nick explains. 'I wouldn't want to offend the woman who gave it. It was very good of her to take the trouble to bring it down.'

So we set off along the path together, Nick carrying the pillow and me transporting various empty vessels and flasks. When we reach a far-off bin, I watch him lean over the edge, taking care to bury the pillow deep inside, where it will not be seen. I am aware that anyone watching is likely to assume he is looking for things to take out of the bin rather than carefully concealing an unwanted gift so as not to offend the donor.

Stuff. I am reminded of how entangled it is in relationships and of how it sticks to us and becomes difficult to relinquish, whatever our circumstances. I remember Bachi telling me how he had repeatedly retrieved Lizzie's chewed-up water bottle from the bin, unable to part with it because it meant parting with her last traces.

That weekend I drive to my mother's house near Worcester, where every object still reverberates with both her presence and her absence. The house has been put on the market and needs to be emptied of its remaining contents. My sisters and I have already put stickers on the few items we think we might be able to absorb into our lives, even if we have no idea where we will put them in homes that are already brimming over with stuff. My elder sister has selected my father's desk, my younger sister the bookcases and piano, and I have selected an old cupboard which contains my mother's diaries.

Two men are due to come to the house on consecutive days to review the rest of the furniture and objects with the idea of purchasing some of them – one describes himself as a second-hand furniture dealer, while the other calls himself an antique dealer. First to arrive is the second-hand furniture dealer, who makes it clear as soon as he sets foot in the house that everything in it is pretty much worthless in his eyes.

'I don't take any white stuff,' he clarifies as he comes through the front door, dismissing such items as the fridge and the washing machine, which the estate agent has told us we are expected to remove. 'So we're talking what we call "brown stuff" in the trade,' he says as he casts a dismissive eye over a combination of mahogany dressing tables, stools, elegant chairs, framed mirrors and chests of drawers that my mother inherited from her mother, and a large polished dining table with chairs that my parents, unusually for them, splashed out on two decades back, thinking that one of their daughters would one day be grateful to inherit them. But none of us has the space or the lifestyle that accompanies a large polished dining table with eight matching upholstered chairs.

'I might be able to shift the chairs, but not the table,' he declares. 'Nobody wants this stuff nowadays. Impossible to shift and difficult to store, especially now in the pandemic, when the shop isn't even open. Pity, really,' he continues.

I am not sure if what he is saying is entirely true or if it is partly a bargaining technique designed for obtaining the maximum amount of stuff for the lowest possible price, but either way it is discouraging. I see him bunching things together in his mind, viewing objects with a combination of disdain and self-interest that I find painful to observe.

'Oh, a click-clack,' he says, amused, as he eliminates the sofa-bed upstairs. The beds themselves have already been rejected.

I lead him into the sitting room, where my parents had their formal sofa and armchairs, on which they entertained their friends over the years.

'Doesn't fit today's fire regulations, this lot, so I can't take any of it and the charity shops won't take it either,' he says.

'You'll have to pay house clearance to shift those, I'm afraid.'

There is something deeply disturbing about the ease with which he is deflating the entire material world that my parents built up over their lifetime. It is as if he has walked into the house with a needle and gently pricked the bubble of their existence, exposing the fragility and apparent futility of everything they possessed. Somewhere in that edifice was my childhood, which seems to shrivel with the rest. As I watch everything dissolve into the categories of white stuff, brown stuff and useless stuff, I have to remind myself that I don't have the space for it or the need, and I don't even want it, even if it is saturated with memories which make it difficult to relinquish.

'I'll give you two hundred and fifty quid for the lot,' he says, as if he's doing me a massive favour. I try to bring him up in price a little, in honour of my late parents' pride in the objects, but he isn't willing to budge. So I watch my mother's carefully polished, unscratched mahogany furniture disappear into the vortex of his van. I know from her diaries how much the things from her own mother's home meant to her. I have read the description of the furniture arriving in the house in 1971. Religious divisions in the family meant that contact with her parents had become impossible in later years, so to receive the furniture was a surprise and offered a glimmer of solace, showing her that her parents had not forgotten her, even if they refused to ever see her in her marital home.

The next day it is the turn of the antique dealer. He is very different in his attitude. He views the various pictures and objets d'art lined up against the walls with interest and respect, even if they do not correspond to 'his type of thing', which turns out to be eighteenth-century antiques and French brasses. He selects an etching of Worcester Cathedral, some medieval-looking stone religious sculptures and a couple of large brass herons that used to sit in the garden and which, he says, he wants to keep for his own garden.

'There are two types of people in this business,' he tells me. 'The ones who are in it purely to make money and the ones who are in it because they love the objects. I'm the latter type. When I buy something I really like I don't want to sell it. I want to keep it, and quite often I do!'

I can't help liking this man who, instead of merging everything into the amorphous category of stuff, understands the permeable relationship between people and objects. I tell him that I am happy for the herons to go to a good home since they meant a lot to my parents. They were a twenty-fifth wedding anniversary present, but after sitting in the garden for ten years one of them was stolen. My mother was very upset and even went to the length of writing a piece in the local paper explaining the sentimental value of the missing heron. To her surprise she awoke one week later to find it lying in the grass. It had been returned.

The antique dealer pays £150 for the things he selects, and I throw in the hat stand I purchased from a jumble sale as a teenager and was extremely proud of at the time. He says it will be really useful for hanging things in his workshop. I am relieved to be talking about use values rather than exchange values. It seems to bring the objects back to life.

After he leaves I linger in the garage, where my sister and I have boxed up kitchen stuff, ornaments and clothes, hoping to give them to local charity shops, only to find that they are already chock-a-block with stuff people have cleared from their houses during the pandemic and that they don't want any more donations. Their storage facilities are already full – a reminder, if one were needed, that we are living in a culture of over-consumption, where the challenge for many of us is how to divest ourselves of excess stuff.

Amongst the boxes I unearth are two old trunks that I haven't opened since the 1990s. To my surprise one of them contains two sleeping bags, which date back to my childhood and teenage years but are in good condition. I remember the excitement of receiving my first sleeping bag, which I took to France on a camping trip with my best friend's family, and my second, which was lent to me by a boyfriend and which I took to India the first time I went there. I decide to take the bags back to London to see if Nick and Pascal might find them useful, knowing full well that, despite their lack of involvement in consumer culture, they too have problems with how to regulate the flow of stuff.

Once, when we were in the park in late summer, Bachi took a photo of Lizzie nuzzling up against Nick. What Bachi saw in the photo was the close affection visible in this human–canine relationship. But when he showed it to Nick, Nick saw something different.

'What on earth is that block of flats behind me?' he said with a frown. He was referring to his skipper, consisting mainly of objects given to him by people who use the park, piled up and tucked under a tarpaulin. The photograph made him conscious of its volume and he determined to set about sorting through it and reducing his affairs.

This desire was further precipitated by the arrival of a new deputy park manager, who was surprised to come across Nick and Pascal in the park and issued them a warning, telling them they didn't have a right to sleep there and that they could not store their stuff there. 'You're welcome to sit in the park like anyone else,' he told them, 'but you don't have the right to sit in your sleeping bags.'

'Are you trying to kill us?' Nick asked with a smile, pointing out that without their sleeping bags they would not be able to survive outside, and that if you live in the street you don't have anywhere to store your stuff so you have to keep it with you at all times.

'He's only doing his job,' Nick said afterwards. 'He's born into rules and regulations, and it seems to be all he knows. That's what the system does. The algorithm reaches an end and then it reverses. So I don't blame him. He's just part of the algorithm.'

The park official appeared three or four times to check up on them over the next two weeks before fading into obscurity and leaving them be under the hornbeams. But the episode caused a lot of anxiety at the time and led Bachi and me to write to Michael Wood, the park manager, and to offer Nick and Pascal the possibility of storing some of their stuff in our homes if they wanted in order to reduce its bulk. Over the next few days Nick and Pascal could be seen sorting through their possessions, dividing them into things for chucking and things which might be worth keeping for the future. Bachi took the clothing and other stuff, which he washed and stored in his apartment – making it clear they could access it any time they wished – and I took in the books and papers that Nick wanted to keep. I also offered to take back my stool, but Nick suggested I leave it there for the time being, as if my taking it would mean my withdrawal from the park. It was then that he gave me two brand-new pillows, still wrapped in their Marks & Spencer packaging, along with pillowcases and undercases – gifts from well-wishers that had been buried in his skipper for over a year. He told me to use them as he didn't require them. In my letter to the park manager I couldn't resist hinting at the irony of forcing people without shelter to downsize, and of them offering me gifts of pillows. I also pointed out that whatever Nick and Pascal had accumulated was proof of their sociability and the high esteem in which they were regarded by many frequenters of the park, who, like me, valued their presence.

'I should throw most of this stuff out but I can't,' Nick told me as he struggled to get rid of things. 'It would be like throwing away the people who gave it.' I knew exactly what he meant, having lugged some of my mother's clothes back to London in the summer even though they were neither my size nor my style.

'These are Jim,' he says, pointing to the trousers he is wearing. 'And these shoes are Roger. The jacket is Mark. This puffer jacket is Philip, the same man who gives me cigarettes. The black top I'm wearing underneath is something a cyclist had flung off and left. Each thing is a memory and a person. A relationship. It's Walter Benjamin. God isn't out there but in the material things we connect with.'

Bachi delivered the books and pillows to my house by car late one evening since they were difficult for me to carry on my bicycle. So just as I was getting ready to empty my mother's home of yet more stuff, as well as clearing piles of books and papers from my study at home, I found myself taking in some of Nick and Pascal's stuff – because I knew that stuff is never simply stuff, in spite of the opinion of the second-hand furniture dealer.

When Nick's books and papers arrived in my house, I unpacked them from a large orange Sainsbury's bag inscribed with the words 'I'm strong and sturdy' and spread them out on the kitchen table to air them. The mossy odour of the park filled the room. These were favourite books, many of which he had read several times and inscribed with comments and underlinings. They reflected a meeting point between his interests and those of the people who conversed with him in the park. Amongst them were Yuval Noah Harari's *Homo Deus* and *Sapiens*, Walter Benjamin's *Arcades Project*, Harold Pinter's *The Birthday Party*, Bertolt Brecht's *Mother Courage*, Norman Lebrecht's *Genius & Anxiety* and Neil MacGregor's *Germany: Memories of a Nation*, as well as books by Herman Melville, Amos Oz and Aldous Huxley. There were also some books given and dedicated by hand by authors local to Regent's

Park: Nick Crane's *You Are Here: A Brief Guide to the World*, Martin Sheppard's *Regent's Park and Primrose Hill*, and one of my own books, *Entanglement: The Secret Lives of Hair*. I was touched to see that Nick had written me a message inside it, saying how much he had enjoyed reading it both to himself and aloud to Pascal, and thanking Bachi and me for what we had done for them, which he said would never be forgotten. Also in the bag were Nick's diagrams, drawings, notes, newspaper clippings, cards and obituaries, which he had been keeping carefully, stored under tarpaulins, and which had survived the sun, wind and rain. Nick had told me I was welcome to look through them. 'I would have binned the lot if you hadn't taken them in. I've lost books and paperwork before but I like to keep the ones that are relevant.'

'We collect books in the belief that we are preserving them,' Walter Benjamin, Nick's favourite author, once said, 'when in fact it is the books that preserve their collector.' Taking in Nick's books was my way of respecting and preserving his voraciously curious mind.

My mother's books pose an altogether different problem. They are mainly about prayer, suffering, silence, the lives of saints and various other aspects of Christian faith. They represent those aspects of my mother I am least intimate with and least anxious to preserve. They symbolise what she strived to be, unlike the diaries, which represent something much closer to what or who she was – the mother I knew and want to preserve. I select just a few of her books, for the insights they might offer into her religious life, and leave the rest to be recuperated by the local church or second-hand bookshop. But they too seem to be suffering from a surfeit of unwanted stuff.

My bookshelves at home and in my office at the university are filled with a mixture of books read for research, teaching and pleasure. In the next few weeks I am going to have to cull them down to more reasonable proportions. At work I find myself photographing collections of books on particular themes and offering them to my colleagues via WhatsApp. I know I don't have room for them in my study at home and would prefer them to be used by colleagues than to stagnate in piles on the floor.

There was only one thing of Pascal's in the bag Bachi delivered from the park. It was a small Collins pocket French–English dictionary and it was soaking wet, discoloured from mould and swollen up like a puffball. A tiny spider scurried across it when I took it out of the bag, no doubt disconcerted by the change of atmosphere. The saturated pages covered in minute type had become transparent but were still intact. It took nearly three weeks for the dictionary to dry out. Each time I entered the kitchen I eyed it with fascination. It seemed to swell daily as the pages slowly dehydrated and separated out. By the end it looked like a piece of desiccated driftwood, as if the paper had returned to its material of origin.

'Ah, that goes right back to the Lincoln's Inn days,' Nick recalled when I mentioned the dictionary. Pascal laughed as I recounted the amount of time it was taking to dry.

Two months have now passed since the deputy park manager's visit and life has returned to normal in the park. As the

November days get colder and shorter I ask Nick and Pascal if they might be interested in the sleeping bags I have salvaged from my mother's garage. To my surprise they both say yes, so I cycle them to the park. Nick takes the sage green one that belonged to my boyfriend and spreads it on top of his more contemporary hi-tech bag, and Pascal takes the blue one, which he puts under his decrepit sleeping bag to create a layer of insulation between himself and the ground. And so, after lying dormant in my mother's garage for three or four decades, my childhood sleeping bags are given a second life in Regent's Park, while the pillows that have been buried in Nick's skipper for over a year take up residence on my bed at home. Meanwhile their spare clothes have found a new resting place in Bachi's storage cupboard. And so my stuff becomes their stuff and their stuff becomes our stuff as our lives become further entangled.

One night as I sit on a log in the park, wrapped in the jacket from Pete, Nick's friend of Dartmoor fame, with my ex-boyfriend's old sleeping bag lent to me by Nick to drape over my knees, I tell Nick about the difficulties of trying to sort through my mother's stuff, given that she never threw anything away and had kept every paper and letter.

'I only wanted one thing of my mother's,' Nick tells me. 'It was a photograph of her with a man she knew before she met my father. She looked happy and beautiful and carefree in that picture. But my brother kept it for himself. He made a photocopy and said I could have that. I didn't want the photocopy. I wanted the original. It's the original that has the aura.'

Nick did not keep the photocopy; it had felt like an insult. But he does unpack a small packet of documents relating to his own life: passports from 1993 and 2003, an old bank card, a driving licence and a work permit for New Zealand – the accoutrements of an official identity. I see that he was born in 1956.

'Do you recognise me?' he asks, handing me the old passport from 1993.

I stare at the picture of a clean-shaven young man with laughing eyes who looks neat and preppy. 'I can't say that I do,' I say, peering deep into the image and thinking that he looks more interesting now. Later, when Bachi sees it, he says Nick looks like the man from the Milk Tray ads of the 1980s, which he gets up on his mobile so we can all enjoy the comparison.

I am struck by how the problems posed by stuff, far from diminishing when you have nothing, seem to increase, since you are forced to keep whatever you have with you at all times for fear of it getting lost, stolen or damaged. Knowing this, I become more alert to the amount of stuff that is discreetly concealed in the urban fabric around me. Stuff I have never noticed before. One day as I am entering the park via a different route, I spot a pile of cardboard boxes wedged into some blackberry bushes. The boxes sit there full of stuff for several days, and then suddenly one morning they have been emptied. Someone's treasured possessions, perhaps? And walking under one of the bridges over the canal I notice a sleeping bag stuffed into a hole that forms one of its architectural features. I see pop-up tents emerge and disappear under bridges and in public squares. And outside Marylebone Church I find myself drawn towards a pile of words and things that have been care-fully arranged, in this case not discreetly but for maximum visibility.

Scrawled on flattened cardboard boxes in capital letters written in alternate red, green, blue and black felt-tip pen is someone's life story, replete with doctors' letters stuck onto the display. As soon as I start to read it, its author appears and recounts his life story – how he used to earn a living through manual labour, which he can no longer do owing to a combin-ation of osteoporosis and arthritis; how he lost his disability allowance and was forced out of his accommodation; how he lived in a tent under Tower Bridge for eight months and is now camping outside Marylebone Church. His sleeping bag is rolled up beside him, and all his possessions are stored in one large suitcase without a handle that a woman gave him and which he says he uses as a cupboard. He is weary and des-perate and is awaiting further medical attention. As he talks, he gets out X-rays of his legs and shows them to me, even though I admit to having no medical knowledge. It is as if he has reached a point where all he can do is make his loss and pain transparent to the world, and all I can do is bear witness to his woes, which feels hopelessly inadequate.

'Ah. That's his pitch,' Nick tells me. 'Did you give him a drop?' – 'drop' being the street term for a gift of money.

'Yes,' I say, mentioning that I was with him for an hour and a half, as he seemed to need to have his story heard and it didn't feel right to move away.

'Yes, well, the thing is, people won't usually listen, and he will have picked up that you are someone who will. And it's important. I remember once, when we'd gone for a handout in a shelter, there was a man who was clutching at his arm and calling out for help. He said he was in terrible pain. So I listened to him, but when I looked closely I saw that he had plastered bacon and tomato ketchup to his arm to make it look as if it was wounded!'

I am not reassured by this tale, but I am reminded of how different Nick and Pascal's way of living without shelter is from that of the man outside Marylebone Church, who embodied the raw desperation of enforced homelessness. For Nick and Pascal, living outside is not just about hardship. I have often heard Nick quote the Bedouin saying: 'When you sleep in a house, your ideas are as high as the ceiling. When you sleep in nature, your ideas are as high as the stars.'

While the downsizing project in the park was initially successful at reducing Nick and Pascal's stuff, it soon becomes clear that keeping things to a bare minimum is a constant challenge owing to the number of things given by members of the public. It is as if people cannot bear to see them exposed and feel a human compulsion to give food, clothing and equipment, regardless of whether or not such things are desired. Being polite and appreciative of people's good intentions, they find it difficult to refuse things.

'Can I bring you anything?' I hear a man ask as he stops on his jog.

'No, we're fine, thanks,' says Nick. 'I don't think we need anything but thank you for asking.'

'There must be something you need!' the man insists.

'I don't know. Can you think of anything we need, Pasc?'

Pascal hesitates. 'Sugar,' he says.

The man returns later that day with a one-kilo bag of sugar.

'It didn't use to be like this, with people giving so much stuff all the time,' Nick comments. 'You used to get people walking past and looking the other way, pretending not to see us. I don't know if it's the pandemic that means people are noticing each other and looking out for each other more. But it seems there's more of a community, which must be good.'

Not everything people bring down is as easily disposable as sugar, though. One day, while I am sitting on a log in conversation with Nick, a woman wades over with two huge carrier bags full of novels.

'I've been meaning to bring these down to you for two years!' she confesses. 'I've always seen you reading books so I thought you might want these. I usually walk to the park and couldn't carry them all the way from my home. But today I came in the car so I thought I'd bring them down. I'm sorry it's taken me so long!'

'Well, that's very kind of you to think of us,' Nick says with genuine appreciation of the effort this woman has made to bring the books.

When she has gone, he starts looking through them. Most of them are light contemporary novels, which don't interest him, but he does keep a more serious book by Amitav Ghosh. He asks me if I want any of the others. 'They're not really my thing either,' I say, reminding him that I am trying to clear space on my bookshelves at home rather than add to them.

'If my books are in the way, just let me know,' he says considerately.

'No, I'm happy to store your books,' I say, 'but I don't want to add this woman's books, which I'm unlikely to read. I'm still trying to deal with all my university books.'

In effect, this woman has inadvertently dumped her unwanted stuff on Nick, thinking she is doing him a favour, when in reality she is simply shifting the problem of excess stuff from herself to him. She is also treating books as if they were all of equal interest rather than noticing what sort of books he actually reads.

'Well, I'll leave them on a bench near the bins,' Nick says. 'That way, if anyone wants them, they can help themselves.'

Another day when I arrive in the park, Nick tells me, 'I've put some stuff together for you if you'd like it. We can't keep it here. Pascal doesn't want it and I don't need it. There are some brand-new clothes here. Some kids brought them down.'

'No, thanks,' I say. 'I'm trying to get rid of stuff!'

'I know that,' Nick replies, 'but it's good to share things so the giving isn't all one way.' I recognise this and as time goes on get used to the fact that it makes sense for me to accept gifts of stuff from Nick and Pascal from time to time, just as they accept stuff from me.

Nick gets out a black T-shirt, a grey sweatshirt and a thermal vest. I say that if they really don't want them I'll ask Julius or Denis if they might. Then he produces some fine high-quality woollen jumpers brought down by a Danish man.

'I've kept two of them,' Nick says, 'for wearing under things, but I don't need more.'

'They'll be too small for my men,' I say.

Next, he produces some tins of baked beans. 'Want any of these? We've got loads. It's the sort of thing people like to give to hobos.'

'I'm not really keen on baked beans,' I confess.

'Biscuits?' He produces a box containing fourteen packets of digestive biscuits, given to them as a job lot.

'Well, I could take one packet,' I say, 'in case I make a cheesecake.'

'Dates? Tangerines? We've got too many of both.'

I go home that day with a strange combination of clothes, digestive biscuits, dates and tangerines.

On another occasion, Nick produces a black jacket given by an Italian woman. 'Try it on,' he insists. 'We won't wear it and if you don't like it you can always take it to one of the charity shops. It seems to be new.'

I try it on. It is a lightweight waterproof jacket that fits me remarkably well and corresponds to something I actually need. So after considerable persuasion I take it, feeling guilty nonetheless that the woman who brought it down certainly wouldn't have wanted me to have it. On the other hand, by taking it I am accepting a gift from Nick and preventing it from going into the waste stream.

One day I am about to cycle to the park with food when I remember that I've left my revamped orange bicycle locked to the railings of a house around the corner, just opposite a shop where I went to buy some milk. When I go to collect it, I am unable to find it. Looking on the ground, I find that my high-security lock has been sawn open and is lying in pieces in the gutter. Unbelievably – given the age and condition of the bicycle – my new old bike appears to have been stolen. But this turns out not to be the case. I discover, two months later, that the owners of the house asked a builder to cut the bicycle off their railings as it was lowering the tone of the property, which they were trying to sell. Whilst I had accepted the idea of the bike re-entering the circulation of stolen property in London, somehow the idea that it was deliberately cut from the railings and disposed of enrages me, especially since it had been left there for only one night. By the time I learn this, the owners have sold their house and moved to Venice. To them the bicycle was nothing more than junk – a stain on the value of their property. To me it was my lifeline to the park and a means of distributing food.

So I find myself going straight down to the second-hand bike shop in Camden and purchasing the cheapest bicycle they have – my third of the year. Since meeting Nick and Pascal the bicycle has been elevated to the category of stuff I simply can't do without. Essential stuff.

11 Work

Today I open my eyes to stillness. It is late November and the world seems to have forgotten to waken. When I draw the curtains I am greeted by a blanket of white felt-like fog. It is thick and boundary-less. The street where I live no longer seems to exist. The gibbons are either asleep, dormant or simply muted by the mist. The birds are silent. Everything has been absorbed in blankness and I too feel the allure of the possibility of submergence. I dress quickly, make a flask of coffee and head for the park, entering cautiously on foot and setting off along the Broad Walk, enjoying the sense of plunging into nothingness. It is the disorientation of blankness that Antony Gormley produced some years back at the Hayward Gallery by creating a cube of mist. In the gallery there were walls to bounce off; in the park there are no edges. Even the giant plane trees and horse chestnuts that line the Broad Walk have temporarily disappeared.

Something is looming towards me through the gloom – two small, hazy, red points of light bobbing up and down and glowing like the eyes of a mythical dragon. It takes me a while to realise that what I am seeing are headlights strapped to the foreheads of two joggers, whose breathy conversation I catch wind of as they jog past then disappear. Later I hear the panting of a dog and see a ring of low-lying lights flicker past then dissolve into the whiteness. I spend an hour or so just wandering about, enjoying being suspended in this timeless landscape populated by strange ghostly beings. I take photos of the smudged silhouettes of distant trees as they begin to emerge on the horizon. Then finally I set off in the direction of Nick and Pascal. By the time I get there I must have been in the park for two hours. The mist has almost lifted and shafts of low sunbeams are penetrating through it, casting stripes of intense light across the grass. I spot my old green sleeping bag, now saturated with morning dew, stretched out like a swollen skin to dry.

Nick is in an ebullient mood.

'I thought of you this morning,' he says. 'When I woke up I looked out and could see waves of white rolling towards me – different shades of the same colour. It was as if the paddock had become an ocean. It was one of the most amazing mornings I have ever seen.'

We exchange images, me showing pictures of trees transformed into phantoms on my mobile, he conveying the sights and sensations he has retained in his mind specially for sharing.

'I was up late last night preparing a lecture on witchcraft,' I tell him. 'This morning's fog made it easy to imagine a world plagued by fear of witches, which is really the fear of the unknown or of anyone who doesn't conform.'

'Imagine what they'd make of us,' Nick interjects. 'Especially Pascal with his quietism!'

'Well, you said the other day that you wanted your ashes scattered by the shoreline. In Scotland they recently rediscovered the watery burial site of a woman accused of witchcraft in 1704. They'd left her body on the shoreline, between the low and high tides, weighted down by a sandstone slab to stop it from resurfacing. They wouldn't bury suspected witches in graveyards for fear that they might come back to life through the devil. Most were burned. There's a campaign today to get an official pardon for her and the thousands of other Scottish women persecuted as witches.'

'Well, I suppose recognition counts for something, even if it's a few hundred years too late,' Nick says.

Now that the veil of mist has lifted, the grass is glowing acid green. The dew is starting to evaporate but still gleams in the morning sun.

'Everything was soaking wet this morning,' Nick remarks. 'The sleeping bags, even my beard. Keeping books dry in this is getting impossible. But just look around. The earth, the universe, creation, life, death – it is all here and we are just tiny particles within it. It's incredible, really.'

Nick looks ahead at the copper beech and then back at Pascal and me and adds, 'The chances of the three of us being here at the same time are infinitesimal and yet here we are, so we might as well enjoy each other's company!'

The fog, the dew, the sun, a sense of shared enthusiasm for this exceptional morning all combine to make a perfect start to the day. And for a while we just sit there in silence absorbing the beauty and stillness. Then eventually I get out my flask and start pouring the coffee, and Nick begins carefully arranging tobacco on a paper and rolling himself a cigarette.

'I like to roll my own,' he murmurs. 'I tend to get out the tobacco whenever someone comes to talk. The act of rolling stops my mind flying about and gets me to focus.'

Once he is settled with a cigarette and a mug of coffee he starts talking about life working on a kibbutz in the 1980s. It is a memory triggered by the morning light.

'I remember sitting in a Massey Ferguson tractor in the Golan Heights in the early mornings when everything was quiet. You'd have the pink dawn sky lighting the fields with their great white heads of cotton bursting from the kernels. Completely luminous, they were. You'd have loved that sight. And I'd be looking down over the fields and listening to the BBC World Service. Have you ever seen fields of cotton?'

'Yes, I have,' I say, 'in Gujarat. It's an amazing sight but for me it's forever associated with a slightly perilous episode when I was doing fieldwork in my early twenties. I was trying to travel to a nearby village where I'd been invited to a ceremony, but the bus never arrived. Eventually a young man who was also waiting with several others offered to go home, fetch his scooter and drive me there. He said he was the nephew of the person I was going to meet in the village.'

'I don't like the sound of where this is heading,' Nick says knowingly, and Pascal nods and smiles.

'When he was gone, a truck arrived and everyone piled onto it – humans, goats, hens, all jammed together standing up. It was stiflingly hot and difficult to breathe. Then the young man appeared on his scooter alongside the truck and everyone pushed me out, encouraging me to accept the lift. As soon as

I got on the back of the scooter I realised it was a foolish idea. But it was too late. We were off, whizzing through empty fields of ripe cotton. Part of me was loving the sense of freedom and the sight of the cotton fields, which I'd never seen before, but the other part of me was scared by the emptiness and the fact that if this man had ill intentions he could rape me and leave me in a ditch and there would be no one around to stop him. Then he started turning his head round and grinning madly, as if he were starring in a Hindi film.'

'And did he abuse the situation?' Nick asks, frowning.

'He just started saying, "Madam, please give me one kiss! Just one kiss!"'

'And did you?' Nick asks.

'No way! I'd read somewhere that references to family honour were an effective defence in such situations, so I said in the best and most outraged Gujarati I could muster, "Have you no shame? How would you feel if someone asked that of your sister? What would your mother think if she could hear you now?" Anyway, it seemed to work as he immediately changed tack and started saying, "Sorry, madam. Sorry, madam" – and from then on he kept his eyes on the road ahead, and when we arrived in the village he scarpered.'

'Why do men feel they can try to abuse women any time they get the opportunity? That's why I always say men are the inferior sex, Pasc,' Nick says, turning to Pascal to confirm what he has apparently always said.

'How long were you in the Golan Heights?' I ask, returning to the cotton fields. 'And what were you doing there?'

'I was working on a kibbutz. I always knew there was another world out there and taking off to Israel was enlightening.
I went as a volunteer for six months but ended up staying
two years. And I loved it. Kibbutz Amir, it was called, high up
in the north of the country. You couldn't choose which place
you would go but they did speak to you and try to put you in
the kibbutz that matched your politics. Amir had a left-wing
reputation. There was a right-wing one with lots of South
Africans nearby.'

'So you were picking cotton?' I ask.

'Not exactly. The combine harvesters gathered the heads
and separated out the cotton from the pods. I was in charge
of the tractor, which I'd have to align with the harvester so it
could be filled with cotton for delivery to the diaper factory,
which was on the kibbutz. It was making stuff for export to the
US. Everyone, myself included, always tried to avoid working
in the factory. But being outside in the fields was good. I was
happy there. I loved the kibbutz life. And whenever I got time
off I would go travelling to Egypt to look around.'

'Did you ever contemplate staying on the kibbutz for good?'

'Not really. Most volunteers only stayed six months, but
they kept encouraging me to stay on. But to live there permanently you had to learn Hebrew and do two years of military
service. And I'm not a killer. I think all sentient beings have a
right to life. Also, there was pressure to get married and start
a family, that sort of thing, and I knew I never wanted that, so
it was time to move on.'

'What sort of age were you?' I ask.

'Twenty-three, twenty-four, something like that. I don't really keep track of dates and times.'

I find myself trying to piece together Nick's working biography, fragments of which have come out in passing conversations like finely textured patches in a multicoloured quilt, triggered usually by something in the present – the light, the ripening fruit, the ingredients of a soup, a reference to a book or film or something in the news. This is the first time I have heard details about his working life on the kibbutz. But there are certain recurrent themes that seem to be emerging – a desire to see the world, to explore alternatives, to be master of his own destiny, to avoid being tied down and to spend as much time as possible outside. These preoccupations and patterns seem to have developed early on, stimulated in part by a desire to get away from the more oppressive aspects of life back home.

'I could always sense that something better was possible,' he told me once when talking about his father and brother. 'And I went in search of that. I think I always knew I wasn't going to toe the line. Obviously as a child I had to, to some extent. I had my mum saying, "Now come on. You're going to have to engage with the world on its own terms at some point." But I never did. I found my own way. My brother chose convention; I chose freedom.'

On another occasion, as we were walking over the canal bridge, he told me, 'I left my family at the age of fifteen, really. I'd read Jack Kerouac's *On the Road* and it made an impression. I thought, let's try and work for a bit and then move on, but in fact I found that I liked work. I liked the social side of it and the experience of different places and work environments, even if you sometimes saw some ugly things. And I don't regret the path I've taken.'

The furlough scheme is back in the news again and I mention one morning that I had never heard the word 'furlough' before the pandemic.

'Oh, I was familiar with it from my days in the merchant navy,' Nick replies. 'I joined the merchant navy after I'd left school. I was working on what you'd call the bourgeois side of things – checking and deciding on the weights and balances of cargo on ships. It was just at the time when containers were coming in, and they changed everything. Before that in Liverpool you would see people siphoning goods off the ships and selling them on street corners at the end of the day – alcohol and other stuff. But the containers stopped all that. Everything was regulated and accounted for.'

Nick seems to have good memories of this time, saying that if he ever might have stuck at a single job it would have been this one. He remembers the naval officers at the training school wanting the best for him and has fond memories of the vibe in the Liverpool streets and down by the docks. But within eighteen months or so he was looking for alternative work.

'There weren't many jobs in the north of England at that time. Margaret Thatcher soon saw to that. They destroyed all the industry and were pushing people into the sink estates. Thatcher was from a bourgeois working-class background and she hated the working classes for what they were or what she thought they were, which is a tribe with solidarity. "If you have any brains, go south, young man," I was told. "Get yourself a job in London." And I did. I didn't want to go on the dole. In London there were more opportunities and better pay, not that pay is all that counts in life. I think of money as an illusion, really. I got a job with Trans Containers. It was a shipping container company, based in Sloane Square, run by an American called Jerry Ratz, who was married to a bunny girl. And that was when I first came to Regent's Park and walked around. Must be nearly forty years ago. I took a liking to this area from the start.'

The docks of Liverpool, Felixstowe, Sydney and Mumbai all feature in our conversations. Evocative descriptions emerge of bars open late into the night where people would hang out – dockworkers, printers, reporters and others who were either looking for work or whose work was not confined by daylight hours. If a ship was delayed Nick would wait up amongst them, imbibing the atmosphere and observing the people around him.

'The observer and the observed: they're separate, and yet they're the same thing. They merge,' he announces out of the blue one afternoon as I arrive with a spicy parsnip hotpot.

'You sound exactly like an anthropologist!' I say. 'We do research through what we call participant observation. What we write emerges from the convergence of our lives with those about whom or with whom we write.'

'I always sensed you were a fellow traveller,' Nick retorts. 'I purposely set out to see if I could fit in and experience different environments and I saw a lot of things on my travels and mixed with a lot of different types of people – like you do, in a way. I'd like to go walking again sometime,' he adds. 'Of course I'm walking when I'm sitting here – walking in the mind. But that's a different kind of walking.'

Nick knows quite a lot about my research, partly from our conversations but also because he attentively read my four-hundred-page book about the global trade in human hair. In it I move between hair workshops, temples and markets in India and Myanmar to wig factories in China and salons in Britain, Senegal and the United States, tracing the movements of hair and the lives and preoccupations of people engaged with it. Through having read my book, Nick has accompanied me on these travels, and before I took his library into storage he even shared the experiences with Pascal through reading it out loud to him. I was touched to see the book, strewn with leaves, beside Nick's sleeping bag, alongside his smoking equipment, flasks, garlic and other paraphernalia of everyday life.

Nick passes one section of the tiffin to Pascal and takes another segment for himself, inhaling the aromatic steam of the hotpot, which I've made from parsnips, leeks, onions, sweet potatoes, apples, raisins, mustard seeds, chilli, coriander, cinnamon and fresh ginger.

'I hope you both like parsnips,' I say, 'because I seem to have made industrial quantities of this dish. We just had some for lunch and it's a bit sweeter than I intended. It might be more to your taste, Pascal, than Nick's.'

'I love parsnips,' Nick interjects. 'I lived on parsnips for a whole month once. I didn't have any money 'cos you got paid at the end of the month and I'd got a job sorting carrots and parsnips in a factory. They didn't mind if you went home with a few parsnips at the end of the day. There's a lot you can do with them – roast, boiled, mashed, fried. I've tried them all!'

'This dish tastes a bit like a solid savoury version of mulled wine,' I suggest. 'I think I may have added too much cinnamon and fruit.'

'Yes, but it tastes much better,' Nick says, tucking into it. 'I don't really like mulled wine. And, by the way, would you like some? Someone gave us a bottle.'

And when he has finished eating, he rummages around in a bag behind him, pulling out socks, trousers and then a bottle of mulled wine, its base caked in a thin layer of mud.

'What don't you have in that bag!' I ask, amused.

'Take it, take it,' he says. 'Pascal doesn't drink, as you know, and I don't want it. And it's always nice to share.'

Once, when I am walking in the long grass with Nick, I ask him, 'I imagine in your life you must have had times when you've experienced extreme hunger or real anxiety about food.'

Nick hesitates, then replies indirectly: 'I read somewhere that if you learn to fast, then you won't ever have to do a job you don't want. It's a good principle, I find.'

Armed with this intrepid attitude and a willingness to try his hand at a variety of jobs – from fruit and vegetable picking in Britain, Australia and New Zealand to tree planting in Vancouver, driving in the UK, hotel work in Austria, fish sorting in

Scotland and factory work in the Netherlands and elsewhere – Nick spent most of the 1980s and 1990s navigating his way through different working environments, earning enough to get by, then travelling and often living off the foodstuffs he was processing, whether blue-lipped mussels in New Zealand or scallops on the Isle of Skye. And in doing these various jobs he met and interacted with people from a variety of backgrounds, many of them struggling at the precarious bottom end of the economy. As he'd told me earlier, some of the scenes he encountered were ugly – particularly in Britain, it seems.

'I worked as a driver once where they were picking broad beans, somewhere near Stratford. Most of the workers were Bangladeshi women. One day I saw the aftermath of a terrible collision between a van and a train. Sixteen people died. I will never forget coming across the sight of fragments of colourful sari and body parts strewn on the ground. It was horrific. I've worked in factories in Scunthorpe, Preston and Blackpool, which could be depressing places, and on a fish farm up in Scotland. That was a miserable place where the fish had some form of venereal disease and had been condemned. They had to be consumed within three months. There were all these African lads working there, killing fish, then beheading, filleting, packing it for freezing before it was sent off to the supermarkets. I got into trouble for defending a South African trans guy who they kept forcing into the freezer.'

'What, pushing him into a deep freeze?' I ask, horrified.

'Working in the freezer room was the worst job. The temperature was very low in there so you were only meant to do short stints, but they kept putting that guy in there day after day. It was prejudice and high-level abuse. The eighties and nineties were a time of gangmasters in this country,' he recalls. 'It was a light-touch economy and they could get away with anything. The pay was poor, the lodgings bad and most of the workers had no rights 'cos many of them were working illegally. I remember seeing Somalis bundled into a van. They'd done all this work picking fruit, but they just took the money off them and sent them back home. And one time I travelled to Penzance in Cornwall to check out a flower farm where I'd seen work advertised. But when I arrived I saw they were crooks running the enterprise. They took me to a caravan, where I met Russian women who were working on the farm. They showed me their hands, which were swollen up 'cos they hadn't been given gloves and the fertilisers were damaging their skin. The workers were all Russian, Ukrainian and Estonian. I told them they should go to the police, but they said they didn't dare because their passports had been taken away by their employer and they were worried they wouldn't get them back. I didn't stick around that place. I left straight away and hitched a lift back north.'

One day, when I arrive with a flask of leek and potato soup, it triggers memories of picking various vegetables on farms up and down the country.

'I got one job picking potatoes and broccoli on the Herefordshire–Wales border where the workforce was all Portuguese, and another picking leeks and asparagus with Moroccans who were all here illegally, not that I was bothered by that. If you can help a person out, it doesn't matter who they are or where they're from. When I went to Kent to pick hops I found a workforce of five hundred Poles all crammed together. That was in the early eighties and they'd stacked them up in bunk beds built ten bunks high in these massive barns. If you fell from one of those you'd break your neck, but there was no regulation so the gangmasters could run riot.'

It seems that the poor pay, migrant exploitation and grim working conditions in Thatcher's Britain, combined with a curiosity to see and experience the world, motivated Nick to seek employment abroad, where you could earn more money and then travel more freely. Another day, when I come to the park with warm loaves of bread, the smell unleashes memories of working in a bread factory in the Netherlands.

'In those days you could nip over on a ferry direct from Newcastle to Ijmuiden. Maybe you still can? One job I got was in this bread factory. The whole place had the most amazing smell of bread that infused everything and I remember all these beautiful young women from Surinam lined up, dressed in white, working at the conveyor belt. You'd think they might be depressed doing that job but there was a good atmosphere and they were all chatting and laughing and checking out the men.'

On another occasion I arrive in the park jubilant after finding one of our cats, Fudge, who had been missing for four days. She had climbed into a deserted office block through a window that had been left open, and we struggled to detect where she was for days and then had trouble enticing her out. I show Nick an image of Fudge in my arms. She is moulded over my left shoulder and I am clinging on to her as if she is a newborn baby.

'She's gorgeous,' Nick says. 'I can see the relief in that picture. But how did you get her out in the end?'

'With cat food,' I say. 'She couldn't resist the smell, which isn't surprising given that she hadn't had food or water for four days.' The mention of cat food reminds Nick of when he worked in a cat food factory in Ijmuiden. He gives a vivid description of the atrocious smell and how everyone who worked there got diarrhoea at first, until their senses were dulled. He also describes a huge clock on the wall of another Dutch factory.

'That clock towered over you and dominated your life. They had colour-coded the time and they clocked you in and out even if you just went to the loo.'

'Sounds like *Modern Times*!' Pascal interjects with perspicacity. This is the first time he has spoken but, as usual, he has been listening all along. He is referring to the 1930s film in which Charlie Chaplin plays a disaffected worker who goes mad trying to conform to the insane rhythm of the modern factory.

'Well, it was a bit like that,' Nick concurs, and our conversation digresses into discussing Charlie Chaplin films, most of which they recall far better than I do. Pascal supplies the missing titles and dates.

Of all the jobs Nick describes, fruit picking is the one he speaks of with the most affection, adding that he may pick fruit again in the future one day.

'I've always loved picking fruit,' he tells me. 'That may sound strange to you but it's a job with lots of advantages, as far as I'm concerned. It gives you a bit of money in your pocket – and that can be useful if you want to travel – and you can be outside most of the time, work to your own rhythm, and you're not tied to anyone so you can leave. I spent a couple of years picking fruit in New Zealand, and after that I used to go back there every year for the apple season. They paid much better wages than over here and I liked the way of life. Most of the workers were Māoris and they were all good men, as far as I could see. We used to hang out together after work. I loved New Zealand. The houses were dispersed. There was space and there weren't any police around. I even thought of settling there and I still have my old New Zealand work permit, even if it's out of date. I learned to turn apple picking into a kind of dance in the orchards there.' Nick illustrates the point by stretching his arms and legs out as if suspended weightless in a tree and making references to Nureyev and the figure skater John Curry. 'And I was good at it,' he adds. 'You might wonder what that means, but there really is an art to picking fruit and I really came to love that work.'

'I believe you,' I say, remembering the pleasure of getting lost in the act of picking strawberries in the summer on farms in Worcestershire as a child, and the joy I still get from picking blackberries and sloes in hedgerows and in selecting which ones are at the perfect stage of ripeness.

'When I first started picking apples in New Zealand, I thought it was all about speed and I'd be picking hell to the grave as fast as I could, as I was getting forty dollars a bin. You'd only get six pounds a bin over here. But then this Buddhist ex-farmer guy came up and said he'd been watching me pick and that I wasn't doing it right. He taught me to go lightly on the fruit, and that has stuck with me all this time. Stewart, the employer, liked me and liked my work, so I'd go back to the same place every year. But later he started getting more into the money side of things. I saw a shift in how things were run. There were lots of small-scale farmers in New Zealand. They hadn't been in it for the money. For them it was a way of life. But suddenly they changed the rules and only farms with a big acreage were allowed to supply the supermarkets. It's pure Adam Smith – when you get to a certain scale, you lose the human element. People lost their livelihoods and their sense of purpose. There were suicides on some of the small farms. When Thatcherite ideas started setting in, the whole atmosphere changed and I stopped going back.'

I can easily identify with Nick's aversion to the corrosive and emotional consequences of untethered expansion and marketisation. I feel it in my own working environment. I have watched universities transform from institutions of learning, where lecturers and students shared a sense of inspiration and common purpose, to businesses, evaluated by new criteria of productivity. And I have seen how staff morale is eroded and student expectations shift as they are encouraged to perceive themselves as discontented consumers comparing prices and wanting a better deal. I am still serving out my three months' notice and the more time I spend trapped on my laptop in meetings for which I can often see little purpose other than to create the need for further meetings, the more I feel the yearning to be in the park, whether in sun, wind, rain, frost or hail. The outside has become a magnetic force in my life. I feel its pull from my bedroom, kitchen or study. It is a place of refuge, peace, imagination and renewal, where other ways of living and being seem possible. I no longer find it hard to understand how Nick and Pascal greet each day with such enthusiasm, whatever the apparent bleakness of the conditions in which they live.

One morning when I am out walking on the hardened frosted earth I get into conversation with one of the rubbish collectors. I have seen him before, a young man walking about the park in the early mornings with a bin liner and a metal stick with a pincered end with which he picks up waste. We chat and I ask him what time he starts his working day.

'Around seven o'clock,' he says. 'Sometimes it's pitch dark. But I like the work – you get to walk around and you're outside all the time. I wouldn't work inside again after doing this job.'

'What sort of work did you do before?' I ask.

'Bricklaying,' he says. 'That was outside too, but with this job you get to walk around. It's a four-hour shift and after that you're free for the day.'

'The art of living!' I say, and we walk alongside each other for a while before splitting off in different directions through the frosted grass.

On another morning I get into conversation with a gardener in the Secret Garden. She tells me that she and her colleagues are employed by the French company Idverde, who have a contract with the Royal Parks. The pay is low and the perks minimal, regardless of the gardeners' levels of skill and experience. But she loves the Secret Garden.

'I've been working in this garden for five years. I've planted the beds and watched them grow. You get more variety of birds in here than anywhere else in the park. Did you see the heron on the pond this morning?'

'No,' I say, 'I must have come too late.' As I speak, the sound of the gibbons warming up their vocal cords wafts over and we both stop to listen with a smile of recognition.

'Sometimes you can hear the lions roar from here,' she says, and then starts talking about how the toads attack the plants.

'I work from seven a.m. to three p.m., even in winter when it's totally dark in the mornings. It's physically tough at my age but I love this place. It's my patch. If they put me anywhere else, I'd leave.'

On another morning I pass a young man weeding near the pond in the Secret Garden.

'Beautiful day,' I say, having drunk my coffee sitting on a bench in the winter sun, with a robin perching impudently and irresistibly on the edge of my mug.

'Oh, it's so peaceful in here you never want to leave!' the gardener replies as he keeps on digging, and I know exactly what he means.

'I've been living outside most of my life,' Nick says one winter evening as we are gazing at the sky. It is only 4.30 p.m. but the sun is already setting, and I have come to deliver chicken soup and chocolate brownies. The cloud formations have been spectacular all day. I photographed them fringed in pink at dawn, with their reflections shimmering back from generous puddles. Now as darkness descends they are glowing dusky purples, greys and mauves. Watching the colours change is like watching a film in slow motion or an oil painting being executed before your eyes. It is impossible not to feel exhilarated.

'I've got a never-ending battery, it seems,' Nick continues at last.

'That's because you recharge it here in this landscape,' I suggest.

'Yes, I recharge myself. This is where I find peace.'

'That's something we share,' I confess.

'Even when I was picking fruit I was outside, really,' Nick continues. 'The only time I've been inside was when Pasc and I looked after someone's flat for a month when we were dog-sitting in Somers Town over a couple of winters. And I started feeling ill, being inside. Other than that, the last time I lived indoors was when I rented a bedsit in West Hampstead in the early nineties.'

As the temperature drops and we head into December, Nick is attentive to how cold I must be sitting on a log without a sleeping bag. He always hands me a jacket to sit on or put over my legs and the conversation turns to jobs he did in cold climes. He describes the icy beauty of the Isle of Skye in winter, where he worked on a scallop farm in Broadford. His job was to set out early in the dark by boat to the area where the scallops were growing on ropes, then pull up the ropes and knock off the scallops.

'Your hands froze but you adapted after a while. I lived on scallops for breakfast, lunch and tea,' he reminisces. 'The landscape was empty and beautiful. You would have loved those skies.'

Another winter memory is of the time he spent in Oberlech, a high-end ski resort in Austria, where he'd gone hoping to learn to ski. He got work doing odd jobs for a hotel. He remembers how the town was as pretty as a Christmas card but his boss was a nasty piece of work.

'I had a Jewish girlfriend at the time,' he recalls. 'My boss cottoned on somehow and asked, "Are you a Yid?" He had right-wing posters on the walls. The head cook hated him – he told me he wouldn't come back the following year. Then one day he looked me in the eye and cut his hand deliberately in order to claim the insurance. But I have good memories of the skiing, which was what I wanted out of it.'

Nick does not seem to have experienced difficulties in getting jobs, but retaining them was sometimes challenging.

'The last job I did was training to drive buses for Metroline. I did well in the tests and did the training, but then they found out that I didn't have an address. When they cottoned on that I was sleeping on Parliament Hill, I was dismissed. That was in the late nineties. You need an official address to be employed, it seems.'

I am aware that what I recount of Nick's working life are mere fragments of a much richer tapestry of experience to which I will never have access, and some of which he may himself have partially forgotten. Central to his working biography is a sense of controlling his own destiny, retaining his freedom and not putting up with petty rules, regulations or discriminatory practices. Being outside, both literally and metaphorically, is another recurrent theme. From early on in life – perhaps from the time when as a child he used to hide under the dining room table – he seems to have developed the critical distance of an observer, even if he later became materially engaged in a whole variety of jobs and working environments.

'I am pleased to have had the foresight and the fortune to indirectly and unconsciously challenge the mores of the system to some degree,' he tells me. 'And I do consider it fortune, not luck, 'cos I don't believe in luck. There isn't anything I've done that I'd do differently. I've had a wonderful life.'

I am left wondering how many people can say that with such conviction at the end of their working lives.

12 Care

Amongst the books Nick handed me to store in my house a few weeks ago is a bunch of neatly folded papers – clippings of newspaper articles, handwritten notes and quotes from radio programmes and books, a stack of diagrams and the memorial service booklet of a man I don't know named Henry. It is accompanied by a scribbled note from Henry's sister, which reads:

Please tell Nicholas and Pascal about the celebration. Tell them this is a special invitation from me and that I shall look out for them and accompany them to the refreshment around the corner. The ceremony is at 2.30 at St Paul's Church in Covent Garden.

With these documents is a small white paper bag of the sort given in shops. It is covered front and back with Nick's reflections about life, death and the meaning of existence, with references to Plato and C. S. Lewis. There is also a short eulogy he penned though – I later discover – never formally delivered about Henry, who was a writer and composer. It is written neatly in now faded biro on a scrap of cardboard. It reads:

Death of another recommends to the living an opportunity – not only to recall memory of that 'other' person but also to contemplate our own attitudes towards memory and life. For example: to remember to express our feelings for one-another in this life as opposed to waiting until it is too late and the opportunity passes us by. To paraphrase a poet: 'If I know anything, we are not born to avoid dying by lying low and playing safe. We are born to leave the Garden more beautiful than we find it.' I believe Henry did this.

I never met Henry, who died in 2017, but what I see in these paper fragments are traces of networks of care and respect that extend in and out of the park – the funeral invitation signalling Henry's family's recognition of Nick and Pascal's importance in Henry's life, Nick's care of Henry evident in his carefully penned eulogy, Henry's sister's care and respect for Nick and Pascal evident in her efforts to make sure they are not just invited but also made to feel welcome and included in the memorial ceremony and reception, which I see was held at Carluccio's in Covent Garden. Her offer to look out for them and accompany them in person to the restaurant suggests she is aware that they might feel out of place, unused as they are to being inside, let alone attending formal events, coming as they do from the outside, and with an aura of outsideness written in Nick's uncut beard and Pascal's matted locks. The fact that Nick has preserved these papers for several years, keeping them safe from rain, mice and squirrels in the park, and now continues to preserve them in my house, indicates how relationships such as this one matter and how they point to the force of human connection, which extends beyond petty distinctions of class, wealth or power.

'He came down here immediately after he had the diagnosis,' Nick tells me. 'He was disoriented. Incoherent. Completely in his own world. Then he mumbled something about having just been told. He said the only thing he could think of was coming straight to the park. I didn't even know what he was talking about at first. But he was talking about cancer.'

On the front of the memorial service booklet is a photograph of Henry walking in the countryside in winter, camera in hand, an Ordnance Survey map dangling around his neck and a cloth cap on his head. His expression is congenial. On the back of the booklet is an image of him looking out over a Welsh landscape of tufted hills and bare-leaved trees leading down to an estuary.

'He used to come to the park for peace of mind,' Nick continues. 'He loved the trees and the birdsong. He was tuned in to that sort of thing like you are. When he got ill he'd come here to relax and sometimes he'd lie down between us just looking up at the trees and sky.'

If Henry found solace under the trees with Nick and Pascal, he is not alone – even if he was perhaps unique in lying down with them rather than sitting on a log or remaining standing as many people do. As the year goes by I witness and meet many people who wander Nick and Pascal's way, not just for experiencing the beauty of this small fragment of wildness in the city (although, as Nick points out, it is the city that is built on the wildness rather than the other way round) but also for the pleasure of the interaction. Some stumble upon them in the course of jogging or birdwatching, and find themselves drawn into surprising one-off conversations on topics which stretch from the weather to politics, history and philosophy. For others, stopping off to chat to Nick and Pascal has become part of their daily routine as they walk their dogs each morning and evening. Others come by to deliver food and discuss the latest news or whatever is going on in their lives. Concerns about children, siblings, ageing relatives or dogs, experiences of bereavement or the break-up of relationships, fears and anxieties about the pandemic, worries about work, financial responsibilities, declining health or imminent death are all spilled out.

Nick and Pascal absorb these in their own distinctive ways – Pascal with silence and a gentle smile that makes all problems feel irrelevant, Nick with concentrated empathy and concern as well as wise comments and advice. There is something about their detachment from the everyday structures in which most of us are embroiled, along with their congenial and welcoming attitude, that makes conversation about difficult topics possible with them in ways that might not exist with family, neighbours or colleagues with whom our daily lives are more obviously connected.

'Great! Well, that's my therapy for the day!' I hear a woman say playfully as she gets up from a log where she has been installed in front of Nick and Pascal for some time recounting her struggles with her father. I have met her once or twice before and know Nick enjoys her visits. She sometimes brings them home-cooked food in Tupperware containers, carefully hand-labelled with contents and dates for consumption. Apparently they are from a restaurant where her brother works. Her father, who is undergoing treatment for cancer, is angry and aggressive towards her even though she is his primary carer. Spending time with Nick and Pascal offers her a much-needed escape where she can vent her frustrations and express feelings that she can't easily voice elsewhere. She is explicit about the therapeutic effects of talking to Nick and Pascal. Others, like me, may not perceive the interaction as therapy but nonetheless experience beneficial effects.

One of the unique things about encounters with Nick and Pascal is that they happen without having to be prearranged by email, phone or text. At least one of them is always there, guarding their stuff. And the fact that they don't have either mobile phones or computers means that the only way to see them is to simply drop by. This gives these encounters a refreshing element of spontaneity sadly lacking in most domains of life, where increasingly even making a phone call seems to require booking in advance by text or WhatsApp to check the timing is convenient. With Nick and Pascal you just arrive open to whatever or whomever you might find there and willing to back away if they seem preoccupied, are resting or are asleep. With them life retains a welcome improvisational quality and an openness to the unexpected.

'Don't tell me what I'm doing. I don't want to know,' Federico Fellini apparently told the press when they tried to explain his film plots. Nick has recorded this comment on some paper under the heading 'General notes and aphorisms'. Beneath it he has written:

> *NB, Life as a surprise . . . the Divine purpose of the mundane vernacular is to discover there is no 'purpose' at all. There is only living beyond mundane, earthly purpose while living in it! The Paradox of being – like quantum – in two places at the same time, but acting as one simultaneously.*

He is drawing on the works of Krishnamurti. When Krishnamurti was asked who should be followed, Jesus or Buddha, he apparently replied, 'Follow no one! Follow yourself!' Nick has underlined this response in red biro in his handwritten notes and it seems to summarise both his philosophy and his way of living his own life. For all the hardships that living outside might present – and there are many – Nick lives the experience as a freedom, and it is perhaps a taste of freedom that he offers people when they unburden themselves of their responsibilities in the park. His role has much in common with hermits of old or with ascetics in Hindu and Buddhist traditions who renounce the world but nonetheless play an important role in it, offering a space for reflection and an example of alternative values in action.

Perhaps part of what people appreciate in spending time with Nick and Pascal lies not only in their remarkable personalities but also in the taste of outsideness they offer. It is as if, by being outside the structures of society, they offer people the possibility of stepping back from their own everyday lives and viewing them from new angles and perspectives.

'Pascal calls me the agony aunt of the park,' Nick recounts one day, somewhat disapprovingly. He clearly does not like the term – just as he doesn't like being called 'the philosopher under the tree'. Pascal smiles cheekily in my direction and I smile back. 'I'm not an agony aunt,' Nick reiterates, 'but I will listen and I do love humans.'

Nick may be irritated by Pascal's analogy, but Pascal is merely alluding to the fact that so many people come to discuss their problems with Nick and that he not only listens but offers commentary which people appear to value, judging by their readiness to return. He seems to have a heightened capacity for empathy, born perhaps out of the difficulties he experienced as a child, and a skill for enabling people to see things differently.

One day near my home I bump into a friend who sometimes talks to Nick as she walks her dog in the park. To all intents and purposes she leads a comfortable and privileged existence replete with a house, a profession, a husband, four children and a dog. What strikes her when she talks to Nick, she tells me, is how he reverses the situation.

'I ask him how he is and he is always full of enthusiasm for the day. Then he says, "It's alright for me. I don't have the responsibilities you have of running a house and bringing up a family. It must be really hard for you raising four children and not having so much time for yourself." And I go away thinking, do you know, he's right! It is a challenge keeping everything going, and that isn't something people usually acknowledge.'

Spending so much time in the park, I have come to recognise the regulars – the ones who jog past with just a wave and friendly nod or who stop off for a quick chat versus the ones who come for more engaged conversation, some of whom, like Bachi, have been visiting Nick and Pascal for years. One day as we are seated on logs, deep in conversation, taking advantage of an interlude between two rainstorms, I sense that a woman is hovering nearby. Her enthusiastic dog has come to drink the water in the natural bowl made by the hornbeam roots, and Nick is clearly familiar with the animal, greeting it by name. Eventually the woman steps forward, hesitant perhaps because of my presence. Nick introduces me to Sandra and her dog, Rusty. I notice that Sandra has difficulty forming words. Nick asks after her health and whether a diagnosis has been reached yet, explaining to me quite openly that Sandra has been experiencing problems with speaking. 'It's either a stroke or cancer,' she says very slowly, forcing her mouth to articulate the words. 'I've had an MRI scan but have to wait two weeks.'

'Can't they tell you any quicker?' Nick asks. 'You've been waiting a while and the symptoms have got worse quite quickly.'

'I've got private health insurance,' she explains, 'but with Covid everywhere it's very difficult to get seen or to get a hospital bed.'

I am not sure if my presence is appropriate but Sandra is surprisingly forthcoming about her increased difficulty in speaking and swallowing, and it doesn't feel right to get up and walk away in the middle of her explanations.

'My voice has gone very quickly,' she concedes. Then, turning to me, she explains, 'I've got a dog, two cats and a demented stepmother who's Spanish. I can't speak Spanish and she's getting very frustrated by my voice. She can't understand what I'm saying or why I am speaking this way.'

The situation sounds extremely stressful – the pending diagnosis, the fear of what it might reveal, the demented stepmother who doesn't understand either literally or conceptually. But perhaps there is relief in being able to talk openly about it – to articulate the inarticulable under the trees, far away from hospitals and relatives.

'I'm on sick leave now – I'm a nurse with the NHS,' she explains to me, and then tells both of us, 'I've decided, if I recover, I'm not going back to work. I've had enough.'

'I can relate to that,' I say. 'I've had enough of my job too and I'm going for voluntary severance. I'm currently in the process of trying to sort out my pension, which seems very complicated.'

Our conversation ends with Sandra recommending me employment lawyers. She tells Nick she'll pop by to let him know the results of the scan. As she leaves, she breaks off a branch of the hornbeam tree to throw as a stick for Rusty and the two of them disappear off in the direction of the crab apple trees. Nick doesn't say anything to Sandra about this gesture, and nor do I, but I experience it as an act of amputation. 'I don't like the way she snapped that branch off,' Nick admits to me. 'That tree is my privacy.' But we recognise that Sandra has a lot on her mind.

What is palpable is that Nick and Pascal are Sandra's confidants – people with whom she has long been sharing the vicissitudes of life – and that my presence on the scene was acceptable to Sandra simply because of my association with them. When next I ask after her, Nick tells me that she's been told she has six months to three years to live.

'She's scared but she says she's done the crying now and is just getting on. She's got her seat here if she needs it. She likes to come from time to time for the peace.'

The next time I see Sandra, two months later, most of the sound has drained out of her voice but she remains impressively resilient. She is offering Nick and Pascal storage space in a garage if they need it. She says she is spending as much time in the park as possible. Rusty seems to be playing a big role in keeping her active and strong.

One day when I have just been playing tennis at the other side of the park, I see a man watching me attentively. He is seated at one of the tables outside the cafe, chatting animatedly to a group of tennis players, some of whom I know. I recognise him as Keert, whom I met on summer evenings when seated in the long grass with Nick and Bachi. I wonder if he will want to make the connection, given that we are in a different context, but I soon see him withdrawing from the conversation he is in and walking towards me.

'You know Nick and Pascal, don't you?' he says, his eyes lighting up behind his glasses. 'How are they? I haven't walked over to that side of the park in a while. I've got this weakness in my legs.'

'They're well,' I say.

'I've often gone to Nick for advice over the years and I still do,' Keert continues. 'I find him a very wise person to talk to about all sorts of things.'

I nod and ask how things are going in Ilford.

'It's too noisy,' he says. 'My flat looks out onto the main road and I can't stand the noise. That's why I come to Regent's Park, for the peace, but these days you get people having raves even in the Secret Garden and that makes me so angry. Did you know I spent a couple of nights sleeping with Nick and Pascal in the park during the heatwave in August? It was really nice and peaceful sleeping under the trees.'

I didn't know that Keert had stayed with Nick and Pascal. I was away the week of the heatwave. I picture him, heavyset with a lumbering gait, arriving in the park, sleeping bag in hand, finding temporary peace under the hornbeams, waking to the sound of birdsong and the light filtering through the trees, swapping the security of a roof over his head for a few nights under the open sky.

Throughout October I see a lot of Keert. Often when I arrive with food he is already installed on a log beside Nick and Pascal and I sometimes feel embarrassed that I haven't brought food for him too, even if he does have a roof over his head and arrives with gifts of cheese. He seems to be perpetually traversing the threshold between home and park – something I can relate to – but his presence is heavy and anxiety-laden.

'I like Keert. I can empathise with him. He just needs to talk,' Nick says. 'He's disappointed in himself. Angry. He wanted to be able to keep his parents' house but the bailiffs came and he got thrown out. He'd lost his job. I think he was an electrician or something. That was years ago but I don't think he's ever forgiven himself. He suffers from nostalgia for how things were. His parents were from Estonia. He was the first generation born here and there were expectations he hasn't been able to fulfil. It's melancholy, I would say, rather than depression. Melancholy at how things have turned out.'

One evening when I arrive at sunset the clouds are an explosive red and pink, which is reflected back in the water of the canal. The world looks positively atomic. The paths are still sodden with recent rain, glowing in the last light. Sitting on a damp log amongst wet leaves is Keert, dressed in his familiar long black coat.

'Ah, Emma! Can I ask you something?' he says as I approach.

'Yes.'

'Do you know any psychiatrists?'

'The only ones I know are child or adolescent psychiatrists,' I confess. 'Why?'

Then Keert starts recounting his problems: he can't stop listening to the news about Covid and it's getting him down and making him fearful; he feels dizzy and is worried he is going to fall at any moment. He is suffering from anxiety and wants to talk to a psychiatrist but can't bear the idea of doing it on Zoom even though he spends a lot of time on his computer at home.

I try to reassure him that speaking on Zoom is not as bad as you think for one-to-one conversations. I also mention that I too have had bouts of dizziness in the past which turned out to be labyrinthitis. He confirms that this is what he has but that it has taken the doctors a long time to identify it. Nick, meanwhile, offers kindly reassurance and an ever-willing ear to stories he has heard several times before. His calm and centredness seem to be precisely the therapy that Keert requires, and it is probably more efficacious than a half-hour session with a professional psychiatrist on Zoom, although I do also encourage him to seek psychiatric help.

Some evenings Keert's talk is of taking his own life, which fills me with dread. He introduces the topic almost with relish, accompanied by a dramatic gesture of pointing a gun to his head.

'Keert almost seems to be making fun of suicide,' Nick says afterwards. 'He can express these things down here because he thinks we're not associated with his life, but of course we are. He just wants to be able to say things. And we all need to do that. I'm doing it now with you, in a way, but I think we share a similar interest in human behaviour. If you have something to say, that can be helpful to him, but silence may be better on occasion.'

'He doesn't come to you for silence,' I suggest. 'He goes to the Secret Garden for that.'

'Yes. He goes there for solitude. That's the word. I love that word. Solitude isn't given. It has to be taken. That's why you need to know and understand yourself as best you can to be able to take it. I'm not really worried about Keert,' he continues. 'He's in that frame of mind where it's the eternal reoccurrence of the same thought – and that can be dangerous – but he doesn't strike me as someone who will act on it. If he didn't have people to talk to, that might be problematic.'

One evening Nick tells me that he recently interrupted Keert's excited fantasies of guns with the words: 'Frankly, the fabric of the earth wouldn't change if you did blow your brains out. We all come and go. If it's adventure you're after, go off travelling.'

'You mean you told him that his dying would be irrelevant?' I ask, somewhat disconcerted.

'Yeah, in a way. A bit of broken crockery, the odd tear. Why waste your life on small things? He feels stuck in a rut. We've all been there. It's like he's riding a wave and sometimes it's a straight line, which is fine, and other times he's sliding downwards and can't stop.' Nick uses his hand to indicate the difference between these two states.

The next time I see Keert, it's the beginning of November. He's depressed by how the days are so short and is panicking about the impending second lockdown, which is due to come into force in three days' time.

'Will I still be able to come to the park? That's what's really worrying me,' he says.

'Yes, you will,' I state with total assurance, even though I'm not sure what the next set of rules will be. 'It's essential for your mental health, and that's that.' But I also suggest that it might be good if he found some green spaces nearer to home and spoke to a psychiatrist.

In early December I ask Nick and Pascal how Keert is, and they say they haven't seen him for a few weeks.

'I heard on the radio that someone got run over by a bus in Ilford the other day and worried that it might be Keert,' Nick says. 'I never really took seriously the idea that he would kill himself. What if I was wrong? That thought crosses my mind every day. I always felt there was something a bit attention-seeking in how he spoke, rather than a genuine cry for help. I hope he's OK.'

At home I find myself scouring the Internet for information about an accident in Ilford but can't find any details of who was involved. But, thankfully, a few months later I spot Keert in conversation with someone back at the tennis club. He seems fine. I give him news of Nick and Pascal and tell him they have been worried about him. 'I must go and visit them,' he says – but he doesn't. It seems that he reserves his visits to them for when he is feeling especially anxious, going to the Secret Garden when in search of quiet and to the tennis club for more upbeat forms of sociality. It is as if he has plotted his emotional life onto the geography of Regent's Park.

As someone who walks and cycles between all of these spaces, I find myself becoming a conduit of information, transferring news of Keert back to Nick and Pascal under the hornbeams. 'I'll give him a hard time next time I see him!' Nick says. But he also says, 'That's good. I'm glad he's doing better. He'll come here when he needs to.'

Not everyone who hangs out with Nick and Pascal is in a state of mental or physical crisis. Some just enjoy a good discussion and a chance to relax and pass the time of day. In my own case, my visits are both a form of depressurising from the stresses and frustrations of my working life and an opportunity to enjoy good conversation and spend time with people I like under the trees, where we can have interesting discussions, laugh, relax, exchange stories and appreciate the changing cloud formations or the antics of a resident mouse or squirrel. Here I find myself able to convert painful experiences at work into amusing anecdotes that can at least entertain as well as offer food for uncensored reflection. It is freedom of thought that I seek to recover under the trees, and who better to recover it with than two men whose way of life is founded on valuing freedom above security?

'You're going to be free soon!' Nick reminds me. 'What is it, ten more days?'

'Three weeks!' I say, hardly able to believe that in three weeks' time I will bring to a close almost four decades' worth of engagement with universities, whether as a student, researcher, lecturer or professor. At this stage the prospect feels more unreal than daunting.

If Nick and Pascal are inadvertently helping me to grapple a path towards freedom, I like to think that I too am in an indirect way sustaining their capacity to live in freedom through the gifts of food and flasks of hot water I bring almost daily. Our relationship has never been one-way. It is based on an unspoken reciprocity – another 'arrangement without an arrangement'.

That Nick and Pascal leave a powerful impression on those

who engage with them is evident in all sorts of unexpected ways. There is Andrew, a farmer from Lincolnshire, who planted two hornbeams to represent Nick and Pascal on his farm back home. And there is Jerome, who, when his wife was pregnant with twins, said that if they were boys he would name them Nick and Pascal. And there is Darren, who has known Nick and Pascal from the days when they all walked and slept in the streets of London. Darren is something of a street poet and has told Nick and Pascal that he has written a poem about them.

I meet Darren only once. It is a bleak winter day and I have thrown a couple of extra potatoes in the oven so that after lunch I can quickly nip to the park and deliver them to Nick and Pascal before returning for a Zoom meeting. The potatoes are too large to fit in the tiffin so I have wrapped them individually in silver foil and put some butter and cheese in a separate container. I don't bother with salt since I know they have this in the park. Wrapped this way I reckon the potatoes will keep their heat for some time, offering the possibility of eating them hot later if preferred.

Darren is seated on the log Keert often used to inhabit. Nick introduces us and I am pleased to meet him, having heard a lot about him and knowing that Nick has wanted us to meet for some time, partly owing to the writing connection.

'I live in the street,' Darren says brightly, 'but the urban version, not the park. I find that more convenient. I did go into a hostel for part of the lockdown, but not for long. I've got my regular spot in the street.'

I don't ask where that is.

'These are my friends,' Darren continues. 'I've known them for years and I come and check up on them from time to time.'

There is a feeling of intimacy in this meeting. I really want to stay but am aware that a work meeting beckons, so I hand over the gleaming hot silvered baked potatoes, which look like shiny presents, along with the butter, cheese and flasks of boiling water.

'It's good that you sometimes think of them,' Darren tells me, assuming no doubt that my visits are occasional.

'Oh yes, I do think of them from time to time!' I reply ironically, looking at Pascal, who is laughing in the background. The fact is that, now that the winter has set in, I am coming with hot food and flasks of hot water once or twice a day if I can.

I explain that I have to leave, and Nick compliments me on the Cossack hat I am wearing, which comes out only when the temperature drops to near freezing. I rush off for my meeting, taking care not to skid in the ever more abundant mud.

'Darren was here once, greeting me and Pasc with a kiss and hug and telling us how he has written poetry about us,' Nick tells me on my next visit, 'but then Bachi turns up and he starts acting the rough geezer, saying, "Fucking this, fucking that . . ." because that's a nervous reaction from the street.'

'He wasn't like that when I turned up,' I say in Darren's defence.

'Well, that's because you're a woman and he pays respect to women. He's got an eleven-year-old daughter he had with his partner. They were going to get married but he didn't turn up on the day. Now he feels guilty towards his daughter, feels he hasn't done enough for her. But I tell him, "Look, you've put money there. You haven't walked away and she'll remember that when she grows up." Darren may be living in the street, but he can dodge and dive and he makes sure that he puts money in the kitty – six hundred pounds here, a thousand pounds there. He's juggling a lot of stuff but he does his best for the kid, and that matters.'

One time when Darren turns up he tells Nick how he took his daughter to a cafe but someone made a comment that set him off and he lost his temper and swung his bag. He now feels embarrassed. 'Sometimes small things take on enormous importance to Darren,' Nick comments. 'He's got a hot temper. Darren doesn't look as if he lives in the street but he does, and he knows that and it gets to him. But you have to understand, these guys have backgrounds. He's told me his. His parents were dysfunctional. Sometimes Darren will arrive and he'll say, "I don't know what to do, Nick," and I think that's why he comes from time to time.'

Another person from the street who turns up occasionally but whom I have never met is Ainsley, a young man of Caribbean descent. Years ago, when Nick and Pascal used to come into Regent's Park just in the daytime, Ainsley would often come along and they would all hang out together in the Rose Garden. Sometimes he would spend nights with them down by the canal if he wanted to lie low from his partner or the police. Nick and Pascal's connections with Darren and Ainsley go far back to long before they installed themselves in the park, as does their connection with Matt, whom I met several times over the summer, until Nick turned him away for swearing non-stop in front of Bachi and me, whose presence he resented.

What is striking is that, while Nick and Pascal have in many ways stepped back from society – 'cutting the tether', as Nick puts it – their social life is far more extensive than mine. Through them I have met a huge range of people, from sweepers and people living in the street to artists, academics, doctors, nurses, architects, journalists, entrepreneurs, gardeners, engineers and film producers. Throughout November, Nick can be seen reading and annotating the unpublished manuscript of a business entrepreneur and motivator. The author has asked him to take a look pre-publication and make suggestions. The constant wind and rain make such a task quite a challenge and I often see Nick trying to hold down the loose, damp pages of A4 paper in the wind while writing suggestions in the margins. On another occasion I find him writing a reference on the back of a piece of cereal packet for a woman who has recently lost her job.

As someone who was not well fathered, Nick is particularly alert to issues of fatherhood, whether reassuring Darren and Ainsley about how to maintain their roles as fathers despite living in the street, or conversing with a businessman about his son's drug problems, or having regular in-depth discussions with a university lecturer about how to support his severely autistic son. I have also heard him advising a father about the importance of making education playful and fun rather than expecting children to conform to restrictive codes of behaviour that might alienate them from the act of learning. To a child who asks Nick's advice about an art project on colour that she is doing for school, Nick suggests she should look at the paintings of Kandinsky and the designs of William Morris. 'Maintaining the awe we experienced as a child – that's what's important,' he told me when we first met, and it is an attitude to life that he puts into practice.

'I've seen what people can do to the next generation,' he tells me when I ask if he ever wanted children himself. 'The only time I ever imagined myself as a father was with Ryan when he used to come down here.' Ryan was a young boy with learning difficulties whose mother used to walk in Regent's Park and who would let her son run over to Nick and Pascal to play under the trees. Perhaps it was something in Ryan's vulnerability that endeared him so strongly to Nick, giving him a flickering pang of desire for fatherhood, a pang that soon passed and apparently never returned.

Once, when we are watching the clouds morph in the evening light, I ask Nick how he would define happiness. 'It's knowing your own conditioning,' he replies, adding, 'You need to experience what unhappiness is to know happiness. It's a paradox.' It is perhaps that paradox that makes Nick such an astute observer and empathetic listener.

13 Night

There is something quietly mesmerising about the bleakness of the park in December – leaf skeletons dissolving underfoot, the muted softness of the mud, the stark silhouettes of barren branches. For the first time I begin to see eyes in the trees, bald and unblinking, watching silently over the increasingly empty park. I see ancient, crinkled faces in the trunks of oak, chestnut and copper beech that emerge quite clearly in the shadows of twilight only to disappear in the full light of day. Are they accepting or disapproving of human folly, these trees who look over us and enable us to breathe? Do they enjoy the rapid patter of squirrels' feet scurrying up their branches, the grip of crows' claws, the constant tickle of unseen insects and encroaching lichens, or are they indifferent to their cohabitants?

There are no leaves, flowers or fruits to brighten or disguise the bare bones of existence now. On winter days like these, everything feels exposed.

The temperature has dropped. No matter how many clothes I put on, I find the early-morning and late-evening cold penetrating through the layers. This is a time of woollen hats, scarves and gloves, of wellies wedged too tightly on feet padded by three pairs of socks. I am living in my son's old khaki parka, several sizes too big, the weight of which presses heavily on my shoulders but offers a solid shell of protection against the wind. My gloved hands have retreated up its giant sleeves. When the wind and rain increase their tempo, my head disappears into its voluminous hood and I feel like a large shapeless form somewhere between a person and a thing.

'You look like a hobo,' Nick remarks when he sees me. 'The muted colours and the layers.' I'm not sure if his comment and tone are critical or endearing. 'Hobos always wear dark colours,' he adds matter-of-factly, ''cos they don't want to be seen.'

I look at Nick. His clothes are all in registers of grey, navy and muted greens. Even his beard has a chameleon-like quality, blending seamlessly with place and season, its frothy white edges echoing the cow parsley in spring, its auburn streaks brought out by the rusted leaves of autumn, its pale wispiness merging with the winter mists. His feet live in khaki wellies – not bargain-basement ones like mine but high-quality branded wellies with an interior lining, given to him by a well-heeled walker in the park last year. When not in wellies, his feet are buried in the depths of his sage-green sleeping bag, which has the bog-green sleeping bag I gave him on top for added protection.

Pascal always refuses to wear wellies, somewhat to the irritation of Nick, who is anxious, parent-like, that Pascal will one day catch a chill from damp feet. He dresses mainly in faded blacks, his ankle-length hair resembling a thick tail when in motion or a branch or root system when static. I remember Nick's comment: 'Pascal is rooting himself back into the ground.' Pascal's two dreadlocked beard spooks hover like antennae from his chin, though they are barely visible against his black puffer jacket. Apparently an enthusiastic dog once bit one lock off but a new one has since grown back. Collectively, the three of us blend effortlessly into the winter landscape.

My relationship to the outside has by now taken on a reverse logic. Whereas in previous winters when the weather was bleak and hostile I would huddle indoors, ignoring the icy sleet, the ever-expanding puddles and sliding mud tracks in the park, now, the worse the weather, the more compelled I feel to go outside. Nick and Pascal are in my consciousness as I close my curtains at night or open them in the morning, and even in the protracted moments in between when I sleep fitfully, half aware of the bursting clouds or sudden hail. How many hours will they have been standing up tonight? How long will my latest delivery of hot water last? Wouldn't some leek and potato soup be a good antidote to the cold, or should I tackle that stubborn squash that sits waiting to be peeled on the kitchen table? My cooking has escalated to new proportions. On the hob is a constant bubbling of curries, hotpots, stews and soups designed to combat the cold. In the oven stuffed peppers, roasting chicken thighs and cheese-and-tomato-topped aubergines compete for space.

It is not that I have lost my natural impulse and desire to huddle up inside and seal myself off from the elements. I still want to turn the heating up, linger around a candlelit kitchen table for supper, return to my computer, a book or a film, or persuade Denis to play a late-night game of Scrabble, cocooning myself against the interminable winter darkness. But the elements are no longer willing to be ignored. They have become demanding and uncontainable. The wind some-how howls louder than it ever did before; the windows rattle more obtrusively; the rain, rather than encouraging confine-ment, is now nagging me to go outside. Darkness and locked gates have ceased to be impediments. And then there is the draw of the moon – sometimes a mere splinter, at other times a perfect sphere, and everything in between.

However exhausted I feel by the tensions of a working day, I find myself padding down to my kitchen in the base-ment, putting the kettle on to boil, filling the flasks with hot water, loading up the tiffin with the latest freshly prepared meal, pulling on extra socks, scarf, hat and parka. I find my bicycle lights, then make the difficult choice between heavy, mud-clodded walking boots – better for cycling and leaping over the park railings – or wellies, better for wading through puddles in the dark but not ideal for cycling and at risk of getting caught on the railings when I leap in and out of the park, flouting official closing hours because the human need for food, warmth and conviviality feels more compelling than any regulations. As for Covid, it seems irrelevant. There is no one in the park to infect or be infected by at this hour. No visitors have crossed the threshold of my home in months, while Nick and Pascal, by living outside, seem to be beyond the grasp of the virus.

My working days at the university, though numbered, con-tinue to occupy the daylight hours, pushing my weekday visits to Nick and Pascal to the extremities. Most days I am out at dawn or sunset, in dusk or darkness. For the first time in my life the moon becomes more familiar than the sun, the sound of owls as common as those of the robin and thrush.

It's the first day of December. I have been running seminars and attending meetings on Zoom for most of the day but manage to sneak to the park just before the gates close at 4.30 p.m. It is already almost dark. I see the outline of the poster of the missing girl from Cricklewood still pinned to the oak tree and can't help wondering if she is still alive. I wheel my new bike along the secret passage, not wanting to risk locking it to the railings, and find Nick and Pascal seated in their sleeping bags, barely visible in the half-dark. They greet me warmly.

'Bachi came down today,' Nick tells me. 'He left these for us. He wanted to know if you wanted any too.' He leaps up with a characteristic 'hiyee' sound and hands me a selection of large laminated colour photos of Lizzie. It is difficult to see them without a torch so I use my bicycle light. Lizzie's dark eyes gaze innocently from the pictures. I find myself attracted to one of her looking straight into the camera, her ears flopped forward, a quizzical expression on her face. She is seated on a sofa. A rumpled velvet throw and a rich plum-coloured cushion in the background offer a sense of grandeur to the picture, giving it the air of a renaissance portrait. I recognise the image. It is the one Bachi uses as his profile picture on WhatsApp. Lizzie is still his avatar.

'I'd like this one,' I say, 'if that's OK, but not if you want it, of course.'

'Don't worry,' Nick assures me. 'He brought three of each and I don't know how we're going to store all these down here. On the face of it, it might look like an obsession, Bachi's love of Lizzie, but I think there's much more to it. She was innocence, unlike the humans he was involved with. And she was a very special dog.'

I slide the photo of Lizzie into my bag after first extracting the flasks of hot water and handing over the tiffin, which is filled with chicken and mushroom casserole. There is apple crumble for afters.

'How is Bachi?' I ask.

'He didn't stay long,' Nick replies. 'Says he's finding it hard to come to the park without Lizzie. It's only the second time he's been down. He was looking tired, I thought. What did you think, Pasc?'

'Yes, I suppose,' Pascal says almost inaudibly after clearing his throat. It is as if his vocal cords aren't used to being exercised and need warming up before articulating sound.

'I don't think he's sleeping much,' I reply, remembering my last phone conversation with Bachi, during which he explained how, without Lizzie, he had lost the daily rhythms of his existence and no longer made much distinction between day and night. 'The park seems to have become a place of pain for Bachi,' I add, 'even though Lizzie's ashes are here.'

'I think I spotted some of those on the ground this morning,' Nick comments, 'just there, under the hornbeams. They were either Lizzie's or Daisy's mother's.'

'Maybe both,' I suggest.

'Well, you won't believe this, but Barry's been down here – you don't know him, burly chap, been coming by for years. His dog is in its last phase and he said he wants to scatter his ashes here too. It seems like we're becoming the ashtray of London!'

'Perhaps we should produce a death map for dogs?' I suggest.

'Well, we used to joke with Pasc when we were down by the canal years ago and they made the new Jubilee Greenway walk that we were now a proud feature on the tourist map of London!'

We all chuckle at the idea of these alternative maps. Then Nick steps foot by foot back into his sleeping bag, jumping himself into a good position, pulling the bag up to his underarms before settling down on his tarpaulin, and I take up residence on a log. To help with decluttering their affairs in the park, my stool has finally retreated back into my study, so this damp log has become my new perch.

The sky is hypnotic tonight. A mysterious and volatile blue-black. White clouds are moving rapidly across a larger-than-life full moon, which seems to flash on and off. At times it looks to be caught in the branches of the hornbeams, which point upwards like witches' broomsticks tilted to the sky. Other times it simply hovers, casting silvery streaks of light down their trunks. Everywhere bushes and branches are gently swaying in the night breeze. It feels as if we are watching a shadow puppet show. The soft but persistent hooting of an owl nearby lends an operatic quality to the scene.

'Speaking of death,' I say, returning to our earlier subject, 'it's the anniversary of my mother's death in two days' time so I might not be down that night. One of my sisters has suggested the three of us meet up on Zoom to remember my mother and light a candle in her name. My sister's partner has told us about a Jewish ritual of remembrance on the anniversary of a person's death known as a Yahrzeit and we all like the idea of doing something equivalent.'

'That sounds like a good tradition,' Nick says.

I pause to wonder what my mother, a devout Christian, would have made of being remembered through a Jewish tradition and decide that in an odd kind of way she might have found it appealing – not because it's Jewish but because she would recognise it as a gesture of reverence and would appreciate the formal lighting of the candle. None of her three daughters has inherited her Christian faith but we have all inherited a respect for ritual and an appreciation of the other-worldliness that religions are good at evoking.

'Can I ask you something?' Nick says in a serious tone.

'Of course,' I reply.

'What did you learn from being around your mother at the time of her death?'

'I think the main thing I learned was that there was nothing to fear. Death felt as natural as life.'

I find myself transported back to her last few days, when we had installed her back in her own bedroom, reclaiming her from the machines and wires that had surrounded her in hospital. I remember the expression of peace on her face as she lay down on her own pillow, with a favourite patterned quilt from India that I had given her covering her body. And I remember the strange sight of her swollen hands, which still bore the blue bruises where nurses had tried unsuccessfully to dig into her veins to perform unnecessary but apparently obligatory blood tests. One of those tired hands was still curled around a chunky clutch cross made from olive wood given to her by a kindly hospital chaplain. Pink nail varnish shone incongruously from her fingers. It had been lovingly applied by her carer, Kinga, who was fond of bright pink. It was not a colour my mother would ever have dreamt of wearing in her pre-Alzheimer's days, but she had enjoyed the sensation of having the nail varnish applied. And what counted was the tenderness of the gesture.

Somewhere beneath these imprints left by nurse, chaplain and carer are the hands of my mother, still holding on.

I also remember how one day, after her arrival back at the house, a look of profound sadness settled over her face. Her eyes, usually half-closed, were suddenly wide open – a penetrating turquoise-blue we rarely ever saw. I wondered if this was a moment of clarity when she realised that she must be dying. I had seen her depressed on many occasions throughout her life but never with this look of utter despair. We all noticed it. I told her she'd been a lovely mother, that she mustn't worry about anything, that we'd look after it all. And then I asked her quite directly, 'Have you had enough, Mummy?' And she said very slowly, in a loud, gruff voice, with utter conviction, 'I've had enough.' I took this as my cue to tell her that we loved her and were grateful for everything she'd done. I told her she didn't need to do any more for us but could relax and let go if she wanted to. I even found myself mentioning all the significant people, including our father, whom she would meet in the afterlife. I was trying to reassure her and give her permission to leave us. Her face gradually relaxed and she fell asleep. When she awoke, that look of sadness had departed and did not return. Four days later she took her final breath.

'It was a strange time, surreal in a way,' I tell Nick and Pascal. 'We had some really weird dreams in those last few days.' Sitting in the silvery dark of the moonlit park feels like the perfect moment to recall those stories. 'It is as if death was stalking the house, not knowing who to claim,' I continue. 'One of my sisters had a nightmare in which she was being lifted up to the ceiling in my mother's hoist, which the carer used for lifting her out of bed. She was kicking her legs as she went upwards, crying out, "Stop! Stop! You've got the wrong person!"'

We all laugh mawkishly at the image of my sister being levitated in the air, confronted by the accelerated prospect of her own mortality and trying to stop death in its tracks.

'Then my niece had a horrible dream in which it was her fifteen-year-old brother who was dying. I had a death dream too. In mine, my mother was kneeling on the ground, leaning over a stone, weeping and wailing in an absurdly melodramatic tone, as if in the death scene of a Hindi film. She may even have been wearing a sari. Then all of a sudden she stopped wailing, got up and sat in a chair, as if to say, "Well, that's enough of that nonsense!" In the dream I was stupefied at my mother's sudden mobility, knowing full well that she was too weak to stand up, never mind lever herself into a chair from a kneeling position. So I turned to my sister, who in the dream was seated in an armchair nearby. "Do you realise Mum's just got up *on her own*?" I said with incredulity. "She's just levered herself into a chair!" To my irritation, my sister didn't respond. She seemed to be asleep, her face obscured by her shoulder-length curly hair. So I nudged her awake, but when she turned her head, her face had the wrinkles of a ninety-year-old woman, still framed by the same hair. It was as if old age had transferred itself directly from my mother to her!'

'Ha!' Nick laughs out loud. 'The imagination! Death roving about, everywhere and nowhere!' And I hear quieter laughter from the direction of Pascal's sleeping bag somewhere under the moon-dappled leaves. I am laughing too but I am also remembering the horror I experienced as a child when watching an episode of *Timeslip* on our old black-and-white TV. I must have been around seven at the time. My sister and I enjoyed the series but there was one episode where a woman went inside a time capsule that was malfunctioning and when the door was opened to let her out someone turned her body round and you saw her face, which was suddenly aged by several centuries and she was of course dead. The shock of the sudden sight of that withered face haunted me as a child and its imprint somehow transferred into my dream almost five decades later.

'So, I suppose the day and night were very different,' I

conclude. 'In the day, everything seemed very normal, mundane even. We were dealing with basic, down-to-earth things – keeping her company, spooning her yoghurt, offering sips of water, holding her hands. But at night our imaginations were running wild.'

'I hope to look the angel of death in the face with a smile when the time comes,' Nick remarks. It is something I have heard him say before. 'But let's hope we can avoid Alzheimer's,' he adds. 'I think my brain has always been in quite good shape and I try to keep it working. But of course you might find you collapse one day and the next thing you know someone's put you in a home and you're surrounded by a whole load of old people sitting in chairs.' He mimics people sitting around in an impaired state.

'Perhaps you'll bump into some of the people you knew from the park!' I jest.

'I'd break out quick!' Nick retorts, laughing heartily, horrified at the image of being incarcerated in a home with anyone. 'That's if I could,' he adds more quietly.

I sense – as I have sensed before – that Nick is both curious and concerned about what the end of his life will be like. As someone for whom autonomy has been so important, he does not want to find himself trapped and institutionalised at the time of death. 'I'd like to get ill once and die – do it all in one. No hanging around, no slow deterioration,' he continues, 'but that's difficult to control unless you bring it about. And that's totally against everything I hold. I want to embrace death when it comes. If someone finds one of my arms one day, broken off and desiccated amongst the leaves like an old branch, that would be fine by me. Live your life! Get to the end of it without feeling you should have done something different. Make the world a slightly better place when you leave it,' he announces decisively, as if producing a mantra for life and death.

'That makes perfect sense to me,' I say. Then I squint at my watch. Three hours have passed under the patched moonlight. 'I guess I should get going and put some supper on the table back home. They'll be wondering where I am.'

'What's it called again, that thing you'll be doing with your sisters?' Nick asks.

'A Yahrzeit,' I repeat. 'I'll tell you how it goes.'

'You'll need help with the bicycle, I suppose, unless you want to leave it here overnight. We can look after it if you want,' Nick offers.

'I'd rather cycle home,' I say, 'for speed. Also it feels safer than walking in the dark.' So, once again, Nick and Pascal leave the warmth of their sleeping bags to assist me with lifting the bike over the railings – an art we have now perfected.

I thank them for their help. They thank me for the food and we bid each other goodnight. I watch them withdraw back into the hooded darkness, then cycle home in the moonlight feeling that sense of privilege Nick often speaks of – the privilege of living in the moment and being at peace under the open sky.

That night after supper I go to my computer to complete some words to send to my sisters in preparation for the Yahrzeit. I call my piece 'Letter to dead mother'. My elder sister sends a poem about time and my younger sister a poem made up of words our mother uttered as she moved from hospital to home:*

What are you saying? What do I do
now?   I suppose I better
get up   try again. This is the
worst   place I have ever been
not too   *bad thank you*
good   who are those flowers
from   I always loved
flowers

Spontaneously all three of us have turned to writing, which feels appropriate. Our mother loved the written word. Every day, from the age of nine to eighty-six, she faithfully recorded her thoughts and experiences in her diary, until Alzheimer's robbed her of the capacity to remember what and how to write.

I don't get much sleep in those first two weeks of December. The Yahrzeit; the tying up of loose ends from four decades in academia, first as a student, then as a teacher; the knowledge that the seminars I am running are my last; the meeting with a lawyer on Zoom to clear up details of the voluntary severance agreement; the completing of various bureaucratic tasks linked to my role as director of research in the department; the

---

* Later published in *Cut Flowers* by Harriet Tarlo, Guillemot Press, 2021.

farewells to students and colleagues; the attempts to decipher the ins and outs of how to access my pension.

When my pension details finally appear in my inbox, I stare at them with incredulity. The figures are entirely at odds with what I expect and considerably lower. My heart starts pounding. Have I totally misread my statements until now? After going through the document several times, trying to find some coherence, I finally notice the name at the top of the page. I have been sent the pension details of somebody else: an electrician who has been at the university for three years, unlike me, who has been working full-time in the university sector for thirty years. While the discovery of this error is a relief, it also adds to the technical stresses of the last two weeks and requires a raft of additional telephone calls and emails.

At night I find it difficult to stop my mind from racing. There is so much to do and the college is about to reclaim the laptop on which I do everything and where all my recorded lectures, work correspondence and various research documents are stored. They have agreed to let me continue supervising three PhD students and are granting me emerita professor status but apparently still have to take back the laptop on 11 December, the day my contract ends. They are planning to send a courier to my house to collect it, given that the college is closed. What is going to happen if they cut off all my emails, I wonder? What should I be saving from the laptop and transferring to the new computer I have yet to buy since I haven't had enough time to think clearly about what model to select?

Lying in bed, fretting about these issues, I become fixated on the moon, which serves as a distraction. It seems unnaturally bright. Is it keeping me awake, I wonder? I can't resist getting up from time to time expressly to observe it, and find myself photographing it on my mobile through the bathroom window at different stages of the night as it weaves in and out of clouds, creating different effects. It seems almost impossible to believe that the light I am seeing is not emanating from the moon itself but is merely the sun's illumination of it reflected back. As the week progresses, I track its gradual waning, which echoes the passing of my final days of employment.

'The moon looks like an upturned eye tonight,' I say to Nick one evening as I'm leaving the park.

'Yes, but it's not ferocious,' he replies as we walk past the crab apple trees, whose branches look gnarled and black against a pale-charcoal sky. 'It can look hostile, but when it does it's really just your own mind. You can see the reflection of the earth if you look closely into the face of it. It changes its expression as you look.' He tells me that a few days ago the police awoke them in the night to ask if they'd seen anyone hiding in the bushes. They were searching for a missing teenager whose parents were fearful. They asked Nick and Pascal to keep an eye out.

My last seminars with students feel unreal. They are about to do their winter assignments, so I am advising them about essays and projects I will never read. They are under the implicit assumption that they are doing the work for me even though I have told them I will no longer be at the university at the start of next term in January. The undergraduate students seem to take this in more clearly than the masters students, for whom I have only ever been a shadowy figure online, apart from the single day we were allowed into college for a face-to-face seminar. That too felt surreal. The university corridors, normally bustling with life, were silent and empty and we were unfamiliar masked figures scattered widely in an oversized room. We stood around in the garden afterwards, getting to know each other's faces before retreating back into digital form for the rest of the term.

Given that my presence has been largely virtual, it is easy to see how students might not register the difference between whether I am officially there or not. Long after I leave I continue to receive emails from them, most of which I have to divert back to my colleagues.

There is a comic moment in one of my final seminars when one of my cats walks past the screen. I see my students laugh and assume they are laughing at the sight of the cat's voluminous tail wafting past. What I don't realise is that Zebedee's paw has landed on the mute button. I am talking away animatedly but have been silenced. I can't help recognising the irony of this, given that I am leaving the university partly to regain my voice. But how do you leave a place you've hardly set foot in in eighteen months? How do you say goodbye to colleagues you don't meet? How do you clear out an office you can't enter? How do you know what you feel about leaving when you're not there?

On my penultimate day I receive an electronic communication from the department administrator. It is a digital farewell card with the words 'Thank You' written across it in bright colours. I click to open it and find myself leafing through pages and pages of digital farewell wishes from colleagues and former students. Reading the comments brings tears to my eyes. The stresses of the last year have left little time for remembering the intimacy of working life and the sense of solidarity we had built up amongst both staff and students over the years. My own tendency towards self-criticism has meant that all year I have focused on my incapacity to put right various systemic problems well beyond my grasp or to ease tensions within my department that some members were intent on maintaining. But what I read here are heart-felt declarations from people who have appreciated my work both intellectually and humanly and who want to express their thanks. There is even a comment from an ex-MA student I taught ten years ago saying she cannot express how much my classes meant to her and have shaped her life. I have no idea how she could possibly have known I was leaving or who contacted her to sign the card. I feel quite overcome with emotion. The fact and finality of my leaving suddenly hit me with a jolt.

I go into Denis's study to try to share what I am going through but he is busy in a work discussion on Zoom and makes it clear he won't be free for a couple of hours. So I find Julius and together we click through the pages of my digital farewell card. I appreciate his accompanying me through this emotional journey, feeling the need to share the content with a live human being to compensate for the fact that everything is virtual.

I decide to venture out into the night to clear my head, which is whirring. I pour some home-made vegetable soup into one flask and some freshly boiled water into another, put on my winter paraphernalia and cycle out into the windy night. The moon is little more than a splinter now – a fine nail clipping in the shape of a C. In its absence the stars are visible, winking through the trees. I jump over the railings and walk with care through the undergrowth to where Nick and Pascal are sitting in their sleeping bags under the starlit sky. They both welcome me and Nick springs up to fetch my favourite log for me to sit on and offers me a jacket to put on top of it to block the cold. I share with them the news and emotions of my penultimate day at the university.

Breathing in the night air calms me and I sense the excitement of a new future. 'Will you have some rum to celebrate?' Nick asks. Someone we both know has recently returned from Jamaica and given Nick a small bottle of Jamaican rum, as yet unopened, and some sugared tamarind.

'Yes, I'd love some,' I say, holding out my tin mug. I can't think of a better way to mark the day's events than drinking rum and chewing tamarind under a starlit sky. So we clink tin mugs and make a toast to freedom, Pascal drinking tea from his flask. I talk about the strangeness of leaving a place when you are not physically there.

Two hours under the night sky is enough to clear my head and give me the strength to face my final day at work. Nick offers to accompany me to the railings. I hesitate to say yes, not wanting to unearth him from his sleeping bag, but he reads my hesitation as an affirmative and gets up anyway.

'I'm sorry to oust you from your bed,' I say.

'This isn't my bed. It's my life! It's the womb!'

'I'm sorry to rip you out of the womb, then!' I retort, to which he says, 'The womb! That's where I'm from and that's where I'm heading.'

He walks me through the undergrowth to the railings. I jump over and as I turn to say goodbye I hear him say with a warm smile, 'You're free now!'

'So are you,' I reply, to which he declares, 'I would die for freedom.'

My last day of work passes in a blur of student supervisions and farewells. At one point I receive an email asking me to enrol on a data privacy management course in January. I write back, tersely pointing out that this is my last day of employment so I am unlikely to attend the course but that they might like to invite the people who sent me someone else's pension details. At another moment the doorbell rings and one of my PhD students appears on the doorstep, delivering me a bottle of wine and a pair of knitted socks. Another PhD student turns up later in the day with a bunch of flowers. I can't ask either of them in owing to lockdown restrictions but I appreciate them taking the trouble to cycle over from their respective homes in different parts of London to wish me well. It is strange to see them in the flesh after so many months. The last event of the day is a meet-up with colleagues in a virtual pub, organised by the department administrator. There are two of us leaving on the same day and we have said we don't want a virtual leaving party but will attend the 'virtual pub' which takes place every Friday. There is a big turnout but the gathering feels strained, with no one quite knowing when to speak from their postage-stamp slots in different corners of the screen.

The virtual pub is followed by a live event – going to a restaurant with Denis and Julius to celebrate the launching of the next phase of my life. They are both enthusiastic about my decision. The restaurants in London have just reopened, so to dress up and go out for a meal is a novelty that we savour with particular delight. Five days later they will be closed again as new restrictions are put in place in the capital. Our celebratory meal in this brief moment of comparative freedom feels special in every sense, even if it passes in a confused and colourful haze of exhaustion.

I am no longer an employee of the university. In so far as I am capable of feeling anything, it feels good.

14 Frost

Before the frost and ice arrive, lacing the end of the year in whiteness, there is rain. Lots of it. On the first Sunday after leaving my job I meet up with three ex-colleagues for a drink in the park. We haven't seen each other for months. One of them left the university at the same time, so it's an opportunity for us both to celebrate our retirement, although the weather speaks more of pathos than of celebration. The huge grey clouds have a menacing quality but for now the rain is only spluttering and sporadic. We find a deserted sodden wooden table that is beginning to show signs of moss and sit on the cold, damp benches around it, enveloped in our hats and coats. The table belongs to one of the closed park cafes. On it we spread out smoked salmon, a large brioche decorated with crystallised fruits, champagne and raspberries which glow incongruously in the dank green-grey light, and we do our best to generate an atmosphere of celebration. The two of us who have just retired are presented with gifts from the department – necklaces carefully chosen to suit our tastes. Mine consists of misshapen wild pearls enveloped in chunky burnished silver, giving the impression of a string of ancient rocks, smoothed with age. We take pleasure in the materiality of these gifts and in the thought that has gone into them and we enjoy being physically present together even if we are all shivering.

On the way home I decide to deliver what is left of our champagne feast to Nick and Pascal, who are connected to my retirement in a unique way. There is half a bottle of champagne and some fruit brioche. In the process I get caught in torrential rain. By the time I arrive home I am drenched through to my underwear. The wrapping paper and elegant bag in which my necklace was presented have disintegrated, leaving the rocks wet and glistening. When I place them around my neck I see them as embodiments and deposits of my working life. There is beauty in them but they are also heavy.

On the first Monday of my retirement I am keen to do something different. I am aware of how precious and vulnerable my new freedom is, of how easily I could be sucked back into old routines and habits simply by opening my laptop, which the university has not yet collected. So instead of reaching for the computer I get onto my bicycle and cycle up to Parliament Hill to join a group who regularly meet on Monday mornings to sketch trees on Hampstead Heath.

'You'll need blankets,' I'm told, 'and a flask of hot tea. It's amazing how cold you get sitting still, drawing, in mid-December.'

I am nervous and excited at the prospect of joining this small group of amateur tree artists. I have not done any sketching since primary school, unless you count the doodle of Lizzie that I made on the back of an envelope the other evening when I caught her staring at me from the laminated photo lying on my desk. I have ordered a sketch pad online and some lead pencils and sticks of charcoal, and whilst I find myself attracted to these materials I am also intimidated by them, especially by the pristine pages of thick white textured paper in the sketch pad, which seems laden with expectations I won't be able to fulfil.

'You don't need any experience,' I've been told by the organiser, who is an artist. 'It's just for people who like trees and want to draw them.' I am hoping she will guide me and give me the courage to make some marks on the paper.

The only bit I feel confident about is the need to like trees. I have spent so much time with, beside and under trees over the past few months that I have come to love them in new ways – attentive to their changes in texture, colour and mood, to their branches, roots, leaves, fruits, catkins and lichen. When I scroll through the thousands of photos stored on my mobile I am confronted by an ever-changing forest made up of Regent's Park's trees taken in every possible season, light and weather condition. It is the winter trees, stripped of leaves, that haunt me the most and beckon me to draw. It is their bark and markings, their craggy silhouettes against the winter sky, that I see when I close my eyes at night.

The sky is tempestuous and the clouds already spitting as I pant and pedal up the vertical incline towards Parliament Hill. By the time I arrive at the cafe where we've agreed to meet, the wind is howling and the rain has set in. What begins as mere rain soon turns into a full-scale storm. As a consequence just three people turn up. Covid restrictions mean that the only seating available at the cafe is outside, so we huddle under the overhanging roof of the terrace, our hands cupped around coffees. It is far too wet to open sketch pads so we sit around chatting instead, our cheeks flushed by the wind and rain, our faces only half visible under hats. Chatting and laughing on a Monday morning with people I don't know? This feels new. It is new! And I enjoy it.

When at last the storm quietens down I cycle home, enjoying the downhill ride through the wet streets of Kentish Town, arriving home soggy and contented even though the pages of my sketch pad have retained their intimidating virginity.

Soon new Covid restrictions will be announced and the group will be forced to disband until further notice. But the idea of drawing trees has taken root, while my new materials mean that there is nothing to stop me from trying. So I decide to begin alone, working from photographs at night when it feels easier to concentrate and safer to experiment. First I make a few very tentative sketches of trunks and branches in light pencil. The results are discouraging. Then I try the opposite technique – experimenting with inks, paints, wax crayons and collage, trying to capture the atmosphere of the trees in different lights, and although the results always fall short of my mental projections and desires, I find myself compelled by the process. The more I draw and paint trees, the more intensely I look at them. And the more I look at them the more entranced I am by their details and form and the keener I become to capture these on paper. I feel I have tapped into a part of myself that has lain dormant for several decades, during which my working life has always taken precedence. What I return to is the sheer pleasure of absorption in the act of making and of venturing into the unknown. The joy of starting something without quite knowing where it will lead but nonetheless being tempted and willing to follow.

When I head to the park I share my jottings with Nick and Pascal, flicking through my latest attempts, which I have photographed on my mobile. Nick is enthusiastic, sometimes recognising particular trees, but more importantly tuning in directly to the features I am keen to evoke – their eyes, the blood-vessel-like sinews of their branches, their wisdom, gravity and poise. Living amongst the trees from dawn till dusk and through the night, he is sensitive to their shape-shifting nature and the poetry of their expressions and moods. He enjoys the imaginative journeys they invite.

'Look how those trees respect each other. See how they nearly touch but don't quite. They're giving each other space,' he says one evening of two hornbeams which grow closely together but remain forever separated by the feathered ends of their branches. A narrow rim of light passes between them. I remember how a fortnight ago I saw the moon caught within that narrow rim, as if delicately balanced between two fans. 'You have a real feel for these trees,' he says as he lingers on the images. His engaged response is enabling, perhaps more so than any advice I might have got from the now defunct sketching group.

Soon I abandon colours in favour of white chalk on black paper. Working in monochrome is both a discipline and a challenge. It enables concentration on detail, texture and form and gives the drawings an X-ray-like quality, bringing out the hidden features of the trees and their almost supernatural presence. Within a few weeks I go from being too timid to put pen to paper to revelling in getting lost in the act of drawing and feeling curiously at one with it. The first gift of my new freedom.

But how free am I? On my first Thursday evening after retirement I find myself giving a talk at the University of New Hampshire, in a seminar series organised over Zoom. It is one of ten virtual guest lectures I am committed to giving over the next few months in universities scattered around Britain, Europe, India and the US. I had accepted these invitations long before I thought about leaving my job, so now I stand committed to fulfilling them. Leaving my job soon exposes just how heavily academia relies on people's willingness to work for little or no remuneration. The invitations to deliver lectures, run guest seminars with students at other universities, write reports on grant applications, comment on manuscripts for academic journals, offer expert opinion on specialist topics, write reviews of books pre- and post-publication and the endless stream of requests for references from ex-students, some of whom I taught ten years ago, keep flowing into my inbox just as before – the daily hidden labour of academic life that accounts for why most academics feel stretched beyond their limits.

So now I am confronted with a new dilemma. How much of my time am I willing to devote to such activities now that I am no longer a salaried university employee? I soon realise that if I accept every invitation that comes my way I will end up working full-time on an unpaid basis and my sense of freedom will evaporate. So with each request that comes in I try to assess how meaningful it is to myself and to others and attempt to work out whether or not I actually want to do it. This isn't easy. In the meantime I have ten talks to prepare, an exhibition to co-curate and countless references to write, since I consider writing references for ex-students a lifelong commitment.

The rain continues relentlessly through that first week. The park has gone beyond saturation point. Huge puddles have taken on the form of small lakes where crows paddle and explore. The ground is squelchy and the area where Nick and Pascal live is approachable only in wellies. I slip and slide in and out of the park at different times of day with offerings of food and hot water, sometimes managing to catch small bursts of brilliant sunshine that occur between bouts of rain, sometimes getting caught in the downpours. Nick and Pascal are grabbing sleep when they can, between torrents. When I arrive there on Thursday afternoon they have been standing up half the night and much of the day but remain in good humour.

'The thing about pain is that you are going to have pleasure to follow,' Nick says philosophically. 'It's binary. If you keep that in mind, it helps with the pain, I find.'

What is true is that the sun after the rain feels blissful as we sit on mossy logs, lapping up its rays and enjoying the intensity of the birdsong. Pascal is busy breaking off fragments of Jacob's cream crackers and scattering them for squirrels, robins and crows, who hover expectantly around him.

'The squirrels are really fussy,' he says. 'They don't like bread but they do like biscuits.' A squirrel that has been posed beside him on its hind legs, its head to one side in a pleading posture, dives for a fragment of cracker, then darts up a tree with it. The three crows who are looking on from the branches above swoop down, trap fragments of biscuit in their beaks, then fly off into the distance with their booty. 'They'll bury that somewhere,' Pascal observes. The robins are less shy and are content to nibble crumbs right beside the skipper.

When I get home I find that the biscuit distribution has extended beyond the park. Two chocolate digestive biscuits have appeared in my pocket. They were placed there by Nick, who knows my love of chocolate. I eat them as I prepare my PowerPoint.

I am about to log on to Zoom to deliver my talk when I realise that my hair is wild and I am still wearing my muddy clothes from the park. I dash upstairs, throw a dress over the top half of my body, brush my hair and apply some lipstick in a rapid attempt to inhabit my professional role as guest speaker. Then I run downstairs and make the virtual leap to the US, where I am welcomed by a smiling bearded man sitting in front of a window. I am in the darkness of a bleak London winter evening; he is illuminated in the brightness of a snowy New Hampshire afternoon. 'It's wonderful here,' he tells me. 'It's been snowing non-stop for hours. We have twenty-seven inches of the stuff!' He picks up his laptop and gives me a virtual tour of his garden, which is padded with a gleaming mattress of thick white snow. Soon more people join us from different locations – London, New York, Italy, Jerusalem and the house next door, where my anthropologist neighbour, who is one of the co-organisers of the seminar series, is logged on. The idea that only a wall separates his study from mine feels even more strange than the thousands of miles separating me from other people on the screen. I soon find myself diving back into my expected role.

At the end of the lecture and discussion, my host in New Hampshire expresses regret that they cannot invite me for a drink as is the custom at such events. I point out that my neighbour and I could actually have a drink together in person if we did it outside! And so we arrange to meet in our street with a bottle of wine. I dash out of my front door, bottle open-er and wine glasses in hand. It is only then that I realise how odd I must look. Sticking out beneath my dress are my damp mud-splattered jeans and a pair of ancient clogs that I normal-ly wear as slippers when I remove my wellies. My park life, home life and professional life have collided.

There are other ways in which the barrier between park and home is becoming increasingly fuzzy. From time to time, when I come to the park without my bicycle because the weather is too rough, Nick offers to accompany me home, springing out of his sleeping bag and trudging across the bot-tom of Primrose Hill with me. The first time he does this I start to say goodbye when we reach the far side of the hill, but sense that he expects to accompany me further, so I lead him towards my home, knowing and regretting that I won't be able to invite him in owing to Covid restrictions. He is com-menting on the houses in the area when we see a fox stopped in its tracks. Has it followed us out of the park? We stop too and we stare at each other across the tenuous human–animal divide, before it pads off silently in the direction of the park. When we get to my house Nick peers in through the window of my study, which is on the ground floor and is illuminated. He comments on the stacks of books and the rich red colour of the walls. I tell him the paint is called Dragon's Blood, a name he savours.

'Excuse me for looking so much,' he says, 'but I'm curious.' I tell him he is welcome to look as much as he likes and that if it weren't for Covid restrictions I would invite him in. I suggest that if he doesn't mind waiting on the doorstep I can run down to the kitchen and fill up a flask of hot water for the night, but he turns down the offer. 'I don't want to put you to any trouble,' he says, then he turns heel and heads off into the night. I watch him disappear in the direction of the park until, like the fox, he becomes a mere shadow. It feels painful not to be able to invite him in, even if I am not at all sure he would want to cross the threshold.

On another occasion, after I've been joking that I wish I had a *Wallace and Gromit*-type device that could catapult food directly from my stove to the park from time to time, Nick replies, 'I've been thinking. You go to so much trouble coming to the park every day in this weather. Would you prefer it if Pasc or myself came to your door to pick the food up and save you from bringing it down?' I think about this for a while but decide I would not like it as it would tie me to specific times, and besides, I enjoy spending time in the park, even if it is often difficult trying to be in two places at once. I explain this to Nick, who seems to understand my perspective and never mentions the idea again.

As Christmas approaches, a new opportunity presents itself. My family had been intending to go to my sister's house in Yorkshire for Christmas this year, having not been able to do so last year, but a new tier system has just been introduced and Yorkshire has been classified as being in the high-risk zone, meaning travel there is prohibited. The latest rules in London suggest that people should stay within their own families for Christmas but that it is permissible for two households to join up if they are in the same bubble. It occurs to me that although Nick and Pascal have never been in any official bubble with us they have effectively been conjoined with us all along, through sharing food from our kitchen. Might Christmas be a moment to welcome them into that kitchen? Or would it feel oppressive for them to be inside and would Denis and Julius consider it an imposition? I am still ruminating over these questions when Denis says out of the blue one morning, 'Why don't you invite Nick and Pascal for Christmas?'

'You wouldn't mind?' I ask.

'No, I think it would be good to have them.' Julius has a similar response. I have no idea whether Nick and Pascal will actually want to come. I'm not even sure when they last sat around a table to eat, never mind as guests at a family Christmas. They might hate the idea or simply find it awkward. But it seems worth putting out feelers.

Next time I am in the park I tentatively invite them, making it clear that they don't need to reply straight away and that they shouldn't feel obliged to say yes.

Nick's first response is: 'Oh, family Christmas! I can't think of anything more hellish!' He laughs, remembering no doubt some of his own family Christmases. But then he changes his mind and says he is really touched to be asked. He checks that Denis and Julius won't mind and says he would love to come. He wouldn't miss it for anything. He checks with Pascal, who also seems up for the experience. The conversation soon turns to what I will cook. The atmosphere is jovial as I describe the rich combination of foods my family ritually produces every Christmas, as if the recipes are inscribed in ancient lore. Nick gets more and more enthusiastic. When I leave the park he tells me again that he is really moved by the invitation. I say they can have more time to think about it if they wish, but Nick says, 'No. We're definitely coming, as long as you feel free to change your mind.'

'I won't change my mind,' I say. 'We'd love you to come and for once I'll be able to transfer food directly from the stove to the table and we can all eat together. That will make my life so much easier. It'll be a real pleasure!'

So there it is. Finally they are coming to the house! Perhaps it is easier to bridge the gap between inside and outside, park and home, than I had previously imagined.

I fast-forward in my mind to Christmas Day. I picture Nick deep in conversation with Denis, discussing every possible topic under the sun, and imagine Pascal and Julius as quieter presences around the table while I am manically preparing food and holding things together. I also have a slightly alarming vision of Zebedee sniffing Pascal's hair and treating it as a plaything as it dangles to the floor. In preparation for the occasion I place an online order for a box of crackers containing musical whistles, thinking that playing a tune together might perhaps dissolve any potential awkwardness, although I'm aware that this idea may be met with resistance from all quarters, including my own family. I realise that I am nervous about them coming for Christmas but also excited at the prospect of sharing food together and welcoming them into our home. I picture Nick taking interest in the decorations on the tree, which include embroidered figures of William Morris and Shakespeare as well as hand-painted baubles from India and Venice, a decorated pretzel from my nephew in New York and various hand-made decorations stretching back to my son's childhood.

But reality does not catch up with my imagination. About a week before Christmas, Nick declares, 'I've decided I won't be coming for Christmas. This might be my last Christmas in the park and I want to spend it here on my own. Pascal can go but I'm staying here.'

I am taken aback by this sudden announcement, which feels so at odds with his earlier warm response. Pascal looks uncomfortable. When I catch him on his own the next day and ask him what he thinks, he says diplomatically, 'I think it's best if we come together or don't come.' I'm inclined to agree. Two days later I check to see if Nick is still intent on staying put in the park.

'Aren't I allowed to change my mind?' he snaps in an irritated tone he has never used with me before.

'Of course you can change your mind,' I say. 'I just want to understand why, because I get the impression you're angry with me.'

And then it spills out. The man who gave Nick the Jamaican rum has made some comment about how Nick could bring the rum to my place and pour it over the plum pudding on Christmas Day. Nick now suspects this man planted the rum on him to test him out and that I did the same with the champagne from my retirement picnic. He is sick and tired of people making projections. 'You'd have to live this life to know what it's like,' he adds.

I am shocked by this explanation and also extremely hurt by it. How can he possibly think I could suspect him of alcoholism and try to test him out? It feels as if all the trust we have built over the past nine months is suddenly evaporating.

'I'm sorry if it makes you angry,' Nick continues.

'I'm not angry. I'm hurt,' I reply, but the words get stuck in my throat. I can feel tears welling up in my eyes. Now I'm not just hurt but also embarrassed. We fall into a stony silence and stare at the sky.

The situation is further complicated by tensions between Nick and Pascal, who have started sleeping under different trees. I have seen this happen before for short periods. Usually, after a few days, they regroup under the same tree. But this time the unspoken tension has not abated and I am somehow caught up in the middle of it. Nick's suspicion of my intentions has become entangled with his doubting of Pascal's loyalty. I get the impression that, if Pascal agrees to come to my house, Nick will see this as proof of his disloyalty, yet he seems to be egging Pascal to go alone, as if seeking that proof.

'You're getting too involved,' I hear my mother say from her grave, to which I reply: 'Well, yes! But it's too late to say that now! Besides, I wouldn't want not to be involved!' Nonetheless I can feel hot tears rolling down my cheeks as I cycle home and I regret that Nick and Pascal have seen me tearful. It isn't the fact that they have turned down my invitation that upsets me. I never underestimated how pressured and awkward coming inside our home might feel. It is the suspicion, the lack of trust, the interpretation of my offer of hospitality as a trap. At the same time the whole thing feels so infuriatingly banal. A tiff over Christmas, for God's sake!

Round about this time I start reading the unpublished book manuscript of a friend and ex-colleague who has asked me for my comments, and in a strange kind of way it helps me process the latest developments in the park. The book is about traditional notions of house and home in Tibet and recalls her fieldwork there in the 1980s. What comes out is how offers of hospitality in this context were perceived as dangerous, coercive, threatening, paralysing even. Much social life in Tibetan villages at that time seemed to revolve around trying to avoid ingesting the potential poison of hospitality and the vulnerability and indebtedness that came with it. This reminds me that hospitality is not as straightforward as it might appear. Perhaps all hospitality is a trap of sorts?

Intellectualising this is all very well but dealing with my emotions is far more challenging. I am upset and my natural reflex is to withdraw. At the same time I don't want to spoil what we have built over the past nine months and am aware of what the relationship means to me as well as to them in terms of material things like hot food and water and immaterial things like conversation and solidarity. I remind myself that I do not have any experience of what it is to live with stigma and to be permanently exposed to the suspicious and critical gaze of others. Nor have I ever lived with a violent and alcoholic father whose explosions ruin Christmas Day. Nick has often spoken of 'hobo paranoia', which he says is born out of experience. I realise it is up to me to rise above my feelings of hurt, keep cooking and carry on. Nonetheless I sense a wary frostiness between Nick and me over the next couple of days. Pascal, meanwhile, remains as friendly as ever under a different tree, viewing the whole saga as something beyond his comprehension or concern. 'Wherever you get humans you tend to get these types of things happening,' he observes abstractly.

But soon I sense that Nick is making an effort to improve relations between us. One morning when I have come with hot buttered crumpets and coffee, he breaks off in the midst of recounting something to say, 'I trust you and I trust Bachi. It's not easy for me to trust people but I've seen your actions. You're a good woman.' I take this comment as a gesture of reconciliation and stay seated on a log chatting for an hour or two. When I get up to leave he says amicably, 'It's good to talk. We could talk all day.'

The next morning, when I arrive with coffee for Nick and myself and hot chocolate for Pascal, they produce a large Portuguese Christmas cake called Bolo Rei – covered with candied fruit – which apparently they get given every year. They offer me a fat slice and we sit breakfasting together. Their skippers are still under different trees but the air has cleared and the mood is light-hearted and convivial. Nick suggests we go for a walk if I have the time, and he takes the opportunity to show me where a flower and a mushroom have come up unexpectedly in December.

In the meantime London joins Yorkshire in Tier 4 and at home we make preparations for our first-ever Christmas where it is just the three of us. As Christmas Eve arrives, the temperature suddenly drops from twelve to four degrees. The rain of the past weeks has finally come to an end and been replaced by crisp, bright winter weather. We shiver as we queue at the local butcher's in England's Lane for a turkey. They have over 1,000 orders, 150 of which have changed at the last minute in response to the latest restrictions on movement. They have been up most of the night. In the vegetable shop I eye a pumpkin and wonder whether I should try to stuff it with a full turkey roast for Nick and Pascal, but realise that with a meal of this complexity I can't possibly serve it in two places at once. It is time to concentrate on my own family. Walking back with our supplies over Primrose Hill, Denis and I catch the sunset, which glows acid pink, orange, red and purple. The colours are fragmented by branches of hornbeam and hawthorn, creating the effect of a magnificent natural stained-glass window. I am reminded of Nick looking up at the trees and saying, 'This is our church!'

Back home, the kitchen vibrates with our usual Christmas Eve preparations. I make cranberry sauce and brandy butter, while Julius and Denis make two different types of stuffing for the turkey. In the midst of cooking, having a Zoom drink with my sisters in Yorkshire and Brighton and wrapping up presents, I prepare a few small stocking gifts for Nick and Pascal and put them in a large tote bag. I have bought them shots of lemon, ginger and turmeric in tiny slim bottles, a copy of *Down and Out in Paris and London* for Nick, who has been saying he wants to reread it for a while, a box of chocolates for Pascal and some home-made crab apple jelly. I have also bought two small hot-water bottles in knitted covers, which I fill with hot water and wrap in brown paper tied with sparkly string. I then make up large flasks of spicy butternut squash soup and freshly boiled water. I'm not sure how the gifts will be received but I'm sure that the soup and hot water will be welcome in the near-freezing conditions.

At eight in the evening I leave the warmth of my kitchen and pedal off in the direction of the park, enjoying the blast of cold and the trails of condensation left by my breath in the darkness. It feels like returning to another part of myself. When I get to Regent's Park, I hang my bags on the iron railings, check that no one is about, then leap over to the other side, stretching back to pull the goods in after me. I tread carefully through the bramble under the tree-hooded passage and then stand motionless as I arrive at the open grassland, absorbing the peace, the space without borders, the stillness of the night, the stars. Gradually my eyes begin to adjust to the darkness and I squelch my way through the mud, looking out for signs of Nick and Pascal. In a distant corner of the park I see what looks like a double groundsheet. They have moved their sleeping bags back together under the same cluster of trees.

'Well, it's Christmas!' Nick says benignly by way of an explanation. I can tell they are both smiling in the misty darkness. From where they lie it is possible to see the BT Tower in the distance, illuminated like a colourful totem pole.

There is such a feeling of peace that I wonder if I should simply leave the stuff and go. I place the flasks of soup and water on the ground. They are greeted with enthusiasm. Then, feeling slightly embarrassed, I mumble something about being Father Christmas bearing gifts.

'Catch!' I say, tentatively throwing a hot brown package containing a freshly filled hot-water bottle to Nick and another to Pascal. Fortunately they both burst out laughing, entering into the spirit of the gesture, and they stuff the hot paper packets down their sleeping bags without opening them. Then I hand over the tote bag, saying there are a few small gifts inside.

'Shall I get you a seat?' Nick asks. 'Or will you sit on the end of the skipper?'

'The skipper's fine,' I say, not wanting to unearth him from his sleeping bag. The womb. The tarpaulin on top of the skipper is wet with frosting dew. He lifts a segment of it aside and I sit down on the drier area underneath. He hands me a damp sleeping bag to put over my shoulders.

Then Nick picks up the sack of small presents. He seems slightly disconcerted by it. There is a brief moment of tension when he pulls out one of the bottles. I quickly reassure him that it is non-alcoholic and is intended to protect them from the elements.

'Should we open the other presents now?' he asks.

'It's up to you,' I say. 'You can open them in the morning if you prefer, but I've got my bicycle lights if you want to see them now.'

I get the lights out of my pocket and shine them, one red, one white, in the direction of the tote bag. Nick pulls out the first present and hands it to Pascal, who opens his chocolates. Then Nick pulls out the book.

'That's for you,' I say. It is wrapped in red-and-yellow flowery Chinese paper and Nick takes his time admiring the packaging and trying to open it without damaging the paper. 'This is beautiful. It's a present in itself,' he says. I begin to feel nervous. What do Orwell's observations about being down and out look like from the perspective of someone who's lived in the street for two decades? But when Nick sees the title his face lights up. 'I've been wanting to reread this for a long time,' he says. And then he throws open his arms. 'Can I give you a hug?'

I edge forward on the skipper and we hold each other in a warm-hearted embrace.

Next Nick hands the jar of crab apple jelly to Pascal, who unwraps it, and they take another look at the bottles of shot, Nick saying he will test it right away.

For a while we sit in silence, watching the stars and the half-moon. It is the comfortable silence of people who don't feel the need to speak, totally different from the hostile silence we experienced earlier in the week.

When I get up to leave, Nick accompanies me to the railings to make sure I get over to the other side without catching my walking boots in the bars.

'Thank you for taking the trouble,' he says, 'and thank you for the Orwell book.'

I wish him a happy Christmas.

'You'll be back sometime, I suppose?' he asks. 'You're not going anywhere?'

'No, I'm not going anywhere.' I smile. 'And I couldn't go anywhere even if I wanted to, with these latest Covid restrictions.'

He reaches across the bars and gives me another hug.

Then I pedal back through the darkness, glad as always that I took the trouble to venture into the night. That Christmas Eve on the frosted grass under the stars in the empty park with Nick and Pascal in their glistening sleeping bags will remain forever etched in my mind. Soon I am enveloped back into the warmth of my kitchen, where Julius is preparing a very welcome late supper.

Christmas Day follows the pattern of all the Christmases we spend in England – a pattern established by my parents, neither of whom celebrated Christmas as children, my father because he was Jewish and my mother because the austere Protestant sect in which she was raised eschewed such rituals. The fact that they invented their version of Christmas from scratch some-how makes it more sacred and set in stone. I lay the table with the red, white and gold Crown Derby china from my parents' house and the silver salt and pepper pots that were used only for special occasions. It is their first outing from the cardboard box in which they've been stored since my mother's death. With them comes a kaleidoscope of formal and festive family memories. We move from stockings to lunch to presents to a walk. The three of us relax into the womb-like micro-world of our decorated home like animals in hibernation.

It is two days before I return to the park. Boxing Day night brings winds of a hundred miles per hour and a storm by the name of Bella. I think of Nick and Pascal throughout the night, picturing them standing under the trees and wondering if they are exhausted or excited by the ferocity of this latest storm. Fallen branches litter the road behind the zoo and sticks float in the expanded grey puddles of the park. It is still spitting with rain when I arrive. Nick is not there and his skipper is sealed up neatly like a tomb under a blue tarpaulin, but Pascal is sitting in his sleeping bag in the drizzle, looking as if he is in a boat on the mudflats. The storm has ripped its outer layer off almost entirely and the inside layer is wet and spongey.

'It was a strange night!' he says, smiling. 'We were standing up over here. I saw a man walk past at one in the morning in the storm – just like a ghost. Then at three a.m. we heard a crash and that tree came down.'

He points to the carcass of a tree that lies like a dead body on the ground. When Nick returns he is in good spirits. He has been inspecting the fallen tree trunk, which he says is soft and half hollowed out. Nick rolls a cigarette and the three of us settle down to coffee, hot chocolate and panettone in the mud and share news of Christmas. They have received gifts of money, several panettones, a fruitcake with candied orange and cherries, some woollen socks, two new flasks, some home-made hashish chocolate and some books – all from regular walkers in the park. Nick also shows me a hand-drawn card from a child with a message for Nick and Pascal and two Mars bars stuck on top. 'It's small things like that which mean the most,' he says, noticeably moved.

'Bachi was down here on Boxing Day,' he continues, 'with a hot Christmas meal of chicken, roast potatoes, parsnips and gravy – the whole works – wrapped in layers and layers of foil to keep it warm. It was really good. And he brought us some freshly washed clothes, but we don't want those right now. In the winter you tend to stay in the same clothes. It's different if you're on the move, but we're putting down a tentative kind of root system here, in a way.'

As New Year approaches, the mud hardens, the grass turns to frost and the puddles to ice. I move between the frozen park and the Tibetan landscapes described in my colleague's manu-script. I tell Nick and Pascal about old-style Tibetan houses, with their gods lodged in the attic and the earth and water spirits lingering below, with humans inhabiting the middle layer.

On the last day of the year the whole park is immersed in a thick crust of frost. It looks empty and forbidding. The clouds are heavy and the light low. It is not difficult to imagine gods and ghosts sharing this universe where land and sky are barely distinguishable. The path to Nick and Pascal crunches underfoot. Smooth plaques of semi-opaque ice make white shapes in the puddles. I see veiled organic beings in them; Nick sees a mining landscape. Pascal's frozen gloves hang rigid from a branch above his head and crystals of frost shine from his sleeping bag. The Coca-Cola in Nick's mug has turned to ice and has to be hacked out before being replaced by the hot coffee I have brought down.

I slipped out early this morning to enjoy the frosted dawn and have been wandering around the park for a couple of hours before visiting Nick and Pascal. Now Denis has awoken and is calling me on my mobile, wondering where I am. I tell him I am with Nick and Pascal and suggest he joins us. He has only ever waved to them in passing when out walking in the park with me. He has heard much about them, of course, but has never wanted to get in the way. Usually he is in bed asleep when I set off early in the mornings, and if it is later in the day he is working. But right now he is on holiday and has more time. I am certain he and Nick will get on, and they do. When he arrives, Denis smiles and, looking at Nick and Pascal, says, 'Excuse me for asking, but how do you manage without fire? I have lived in a village in the Himalayas in extreme cold, but people there always warm themselves around fires and use fires to cook.'

Nick puts his hand to his chest. 'The fire is inside!' he says with aplomb. 'It may look mad on the face of it but it can also make sense when you're sitting here. You learn to adjust and you learn how to keep yourself warm in severe weather. It would be difficult to live without shelter if the temperature dropped to minus twenty-five, but that never happens in this country. The limitation isn't imposed by us, by the way: it's what's permitted by the park authorities. You can't make a fire or build a shelter in a Royal Park. In the past, the poor didn't even have the right to enter the park at all. It was locked and kept for the wealthy.'

'Well, I think the people of Britain are very generous to let the Queen carry on living the way she does!' Denis responds with his distinctive sense of humour.

And the two of them launch into an animated conversation which leaps from sadhus in India, Māori rituals in New Zealand and the conflicting attitudes of Newton and Leibnitz to travel, to brutalist architecture and comparisons between London and Paris, and of course references to Walter Benjamin. I always thought they would get on and that I would probably say very little once they both got talking!

'You think living outside is hard but it's going to a hostel that would be really hellish,' Nick says decisively as we bid him and Pascal farewell and wander off to watch the Egyptian geese skating on the frozen lake.

'See you next year,' Nick calls out when I return with hot food and water that evening. 'Bless your heart, Emma,' he adds as I crunch off into the frosted night.

15 Rupture

When January arrives it feels entirely different from any other I have known. I have jumped off the university timetable halfway through the academic year. There are no reading lists or courses to prepare, no essays to mark in haste, no feelings of running out of time before term starts. Everything has stopped mid-cycle. Not having to prepare for a new term makes me realise that my entire life since the age of four has been lived according to educational timetables. I have no memory of the days when Christmas and New Year weren't sandwiched like a glorious shining gift between two intimidating but familiar blocks of time known as terms. To step off the timetable after all these years is an extraordinary sensation that feels akin to leaping into space. I still have an exhibition to work on and my colleague's manuscript to finish reading, but these activities both count as pleasure now that they are not competing with other tasks on the timetable.

It is the sun, moon, wind, rain, sleet and eventually snow that now determine the morphology of my days, many of which begin with spectacular winter dawns I rarely ever saw or was even aware of in the past.

A few days into January a north-easterly wind sweeps across the country from Siberia, bringing icy sleet in its wake. It is bitterly cold outside and my only defence against it is

to cook the most warming meals I can think of. I begin with
a large tray of stuffed peppers, whose red and yellow skins
bubble and glow as I remove them from the oven. Their colour
alone seems to counter the idea of cold and you can almost
inhale warmth from the fragrant garlicky steam. I nestle the
stuffed peppers in an old earthenware pot, its lid tied on with
a shoelace.

When I arrive at the park, I wonder at first if Nick and Pascal
are asleep but I soon realise that they are simply sunk more
deeply than usual into their sleeping bags in an effort to protect themselves from the biting wind. Both have their pocket
radios to their ears and are in good humour.

'Some people suffer from depression in low-light conditions
like this,' Nick observes. 'It's the clash between chronological
and circadian time. The weather makes no difference to me,
although I do feel the cold more than I used to. I suppose that's
age.'

He looks at his hands. They are naked and I instinctively
reach out to touch them. What strikes me is not the cold but
the hardness of his palms.

'That's all the years picking fruit,' Nick explains. 'It's left
these hard calluses on my hands. I think I've got them for life
now.'

'Memories of work etched in the skin,' I mumble, then ask,
'Surely you need gloves in this cold?'

'Not when we're in our bags,' he replies. I notice that
neither of them is wearing a hat either. I offer to fill up the
hot-water bottles I gave at Christmas but get the impression

that hot-water bottles, though amusing for one night, are considered wimpish.

'Living outside, you adapt to the weather,' Nick explains. 'You must be feeling this cold, though,' he adds. My woollen hat is pulled down over my ears and my hands are gloved and buried in pockets. He passes me a sleeping bag for added warmth. I drape it over my shoulders and head, then tuck the rest of it around me, feeling like a giant snail retreating into its shell. Only my nose and cheeks are exposed to the icy wind. 'Of course we're sitting on a ball of fire, that's the extraordinary thing! And they say that when people get hypothermia they end up taking their clothes off 'cos they feel this burning sensation, which must be amazing,' he adds.

Our conversation soon turns to books. 'I've really enjoyed *Down and Out in Paris and London*,' Nick comments. 'I'm reading bits aloud to Pascal now. Darren turned up when I was reading it yesterday. He's back in the street after a month in a hotel during lockdown. He was dismissive of Orwell. "He went to Eton. What does he know?" That kind of thing. He could only see it through the class angle. But I said Orwell probably didn't have much choice about where he was sent to school as a kid. You should judge a book by what it says, not by the background of the person who wrote it, in my opinion. And this book is worth reading. Darren listened to my arguments and said he'd check it out, though I'm not sure how he'll get hold of a copy. He doesn't often come down.'

It's so long since I read the book that the only thing I can remember are the chaotic scenes in Paris hotel kitchens. I ask

Nick what elements of the book stand out most. 'It's the bit where he meets a man called Bozo at the Embankment that I wanted to reread,' he answers. Later, when he returns the book to me for safekeeping, I find myself reading the passages about Bozo with particular interest. Bozo is a street artist, stargazer, thinker and reader of books. He contradicts Orwell's general observations about London tramps of the 1930s with his intellectual curiosity, good humour and capacity to rise above his bleak physical conditions.

'It don't follow that because a man's on the road he can't think of anything but tea-and-two-slices,' Bozo tells Orwell. 'If you set yourself to it, you can live the same life, rich or poor. You can still keep on with your books and your ideas. You just got to say to yourself, "I'm a free man in *here*" . . . and you're alright.' Bozo taps his head as he speaks these words. Orwell comments that Bozo had 'neither fear, nor regret, nor shame, nor self-pity. He had faced his position, and made a philosophy for himself.' As long as he could 'read, think and watch for meteors, he was, as he said, free in his own mind . . . He was a very exceptional man.'

It is not difficult to see how or why Nick might want to reconnect with Bozo. Perhaps he has been carrying his distant memory around with him all these years. Nor is it difficult to see how or why Orwell was so impressed by this exceptional man.

That night Nick hands me a large carrier bag containing empty containers – the tiffin, the copper dome, two Tupperware tubs which I seem to have inherited. The bag is wet with condensation and spattered with mud. Strands of soggy grass cling to its base. The copper dome feels unnaturally heavy when I unearth it on my kitchen table. When I lift its lid, two small bottles of Cockburn's port peep out – secret gifts tucked inside by Nick. I laugh out loud and wonder what the person who gave them to him would think. When I thank Nick for the port the following day, he says, 'Well, it's a thank-you for all you do for us.' The champagne-and-rum incident feels far behind us.

The north-easterly wind continues for a few days and the temperature hovers close to freezing point. One evening when I am sitting under the hornbeams Bachi happens to text. I tell him I am with Nick and Pascal and we begin to message back and forth, with me acting as a go-between.

B: 'Ah, can you let them know it may well snow tomorrow night. Could you please ask them if they need anything warm from their clothes stash?'

E: 'No. They say they are fine and are prepared for every eventuality – bar one. Nick's words!'

B: 'Which one aren't they prepared for? Forest fires?'

E: 'The one no one expects – Nick's words again!'

B: 'Ah! Good point. Enjoy your evening (directed at all of you!).'

Bachi is still spending most of his time holed up indoors, restructuring his apartment, working on Lizzie's website and mourning her loss. Two months have passed since Lizzie's death and he rarely comes to the park, except to drop off food once a week, but this does not mean he is unconcerned.

My defence against the bleak east wind continues to take a culinary form. Over the next few days I cook roast aubergines topped with tomato, garlic and Parmesan breadcrumbs; green lentil curry with rice; spicy roast chicken pieces with roasted squash; and chicken soup thickened with tiny pasta stars called stellini, which I received in my Christmas stocking. I also make an apricot and lemon cake, rich with ground almonds, which feels a fitting antidote to the cold. In the mornings I continue to bring a flask of coffee, which I share with Nick, and a smaller Thermos of hot chocolate for Pascal, using one of the new good-quality flasks they received for Christmas.

'You've gone feral,' a friend tells me when I explain how much time I am spending outside. She could be right. Without a fixed agenda to my day I find myself drawn outwards by the constant changes in atmosphere and light. A sunset from the bathroom window may look fine but it cannot compare with the sensation of being outside as the sun works its way down-wards through the winter clouds, with the distant rumble of hungry lions roaring for their supper in the background.

One early evening when I arrive in the park, Nick has gone to Camden in search of tobacco and I find myself alone with Pascal. We stand side by side in silence for a long time, watching the changing light as if engrossed in a slow-motion film. The clouds are infused with muted pink, bruised purples and hints of yellow which gradually turn to grey. Can grey be warm, I wonder, as the sun slips lower behind the clouds? Then, as the light slowly drains out of the sky, the clouds linger like ghostly, semi-illuminated forms against a charcoal backdrop.

'Look!' says Pascal in a hushed voice just as the twilight gives way to almost total darkness. I follow to where his finger is pointing and there, trotting across the open field, is the silhouette of a lone fox, scarcely more than a phantom disappearing into the shadows of the crab apple trees. I know I would never have spotted it without his vigilant eye and would never have experienced this unique and magnificent nightfall were it not for my friendship with Nick and Pascal.

'It seems crazy that people are locked out of the park at the best times,' Pascal remarks.

I nod. 'But perhaps they are the best times because the space is given over to other beings.'

On another evening Nick talks enthusiastically about a Radio 4 programme he has just heard based on verbatim interviews with David Bowie. He is keen for me to check it out. 'I heard myself speaking through him,' he says, 'when he talked about being in the moment.' I say I will try to find a way of listening to it.

I get out my mobile and suggest we all watch the slam performance of a young Glaswegian poet called Sam Small. He is the nephew of a man who has been chatting with Nick about Aldous Huxley and who gave them a significant drop of money over Christmas. I have already seen the performance on YouTube and am aware that the first line could be dangerous if taken out of context but feel sure Nick and Pascal will appreciate the poem. They stand either side of me, leaning over my phone in the darkness.

Sam Small appears on my screen, bearded and wearing a

hoodie. 'If you feel worthless, you're right!' he says emphatically in a strong Glaswegian accent, then he launches into the poem, which roams exhaustively from exploring the properties of dirt, soil, ants, tables, a sandwich, the street, the city, the sun, the stars, the galaxy and the universe to reversing gear and coming back down to earth again. The key message is that we are all both nothing and everything. We are all made up of hydrogen, oxygen, nitrogen and carbon, so none of us are any more or less worthless than anything or anyone else. To listen to the poem is to travel to space and back. I can feel Nick and Pascal enjoying the outlandish imaginative leaps and following the quick-fire reasoning.

'Ah, the split! The coming together! The creativity!' Nick comments. 'He's talking about what it is to be human. It makes people think. And he does it through getting you laughing. It opens up the mind. I remember taking Pascal up Primrose Hill years ago when he first came to the area,' Nick reminisces. 'We were looking down on all the buildings and I said I looked forward to everything being destroyed. Pascal thought I meant blown up, that sort of thing, but that wasn't what I meant at all. I was talking about the ideology, the power structures, the need for a new meritocracy, breaking down social barriers, rocking the establishment in that sense.'

* * *

When the east wind dies down the temperature creeps up a few degrees and the rain returns. It is mid-January and the forecast predicts a whole week of wetness. The rain arrives as predicted at 5 a.m. and by the time I get to the park at 9 a.m. everything is waterlogged once more, having never really had time to dry out properly over the last few months. The blank grey whiteness of the sky is reflected back in the puddles. Stepping into this landscape feels like stepping into a pale-grey lake. The dank and denuded trees stare mournfully at their own reflections, which stare back at them. I find myself taking yet more photographic portraits of the twisted oaks, honing in on their expressive features, which seem enhanced and magnified in the low light. Nests break up the monotony of the skyline, hanging like densely woven baskets suspended in the air.

When I trail my wellies through the waterway that leads to the secret grove I see Pascal's distinctive figure standing alone under one of two umbrellas suspended in the hornbeam beside Nick's skipper. Pascal's skipper is once again under a different tree further off. Right now Pascal is staring intently at the ground, watching the movements of a large worm as it slowly manoeuvres through the mud. He has been standing since five in the morning. Beads of water dangle from his sideburns and beard-ends but he is bright-eyed and rosy-cheeked.

'I'm keeping my gloves in the trees so the mice can't gnaw them. They're getting into the stuffing of my sleeping bag and jacket these days,' he tells me. 'I left a packet of biscuits in a bag hanging in the tree over there this morning and when I came back they'd gone! The squirrels had taken them. You can't leave your stuff even for ten minutes!' he laughs.

Nick walks slowly towards us, his head bowed. He is reduced to a few basic forms – beard, umbrella, wellies.

After we drink our coffees and hot chocolate, I say I'd like to go for a walk to see the park in the rain.

'Do you want to walk alone?' Nick asks.

'No. I'm happy to walk with you if you'd like to come,' I say to them both.

Nick turns to Pascal. 'Do you want to go for a walk with Emma, Pasc?'

Pascal defers so Nick sets off with me around the edge of the park, each of us carrying a large umbrella. Apart from the worm, a fox, some squirrels and a variety of birds, ducks and geese, we encounter no one for the first hour. Not even dogs and joggers have come out in this. Trees, grasses, bushes, mosses, ivy and lichens are all wedded together in the slippery wetness.

'I love this weather – this misty, blurred light,' Nick comments, looking into the distance, 'although you do have to watch out for your lungs. What does Eden look like if not this? And, by the way, forgive us for blaming women!'

'We won't hold you personally responsible,' I reply.

We linger over details on our way, making time for all we see – the soft silvery pads of pussy willow that we scarcely dare touch, the vetch leaves already pushing through the grass, the untimely gorse flowers and precocious roses, a few of which are unseasonably in bloom, the fine hair-like drape of the leafless willow branches dangling into the lake, the indescribable elegance of the catkins that glow from the hazel and silver birch like silk tassels, and the faces hidden in the trees.

When I come across a tree I can't identify, I ask Nick if he knows its name.

'I'm not interested in the names of trees. Not really,' Nick says. 'They distract from their being.' While I'm keen to learn the names, I also understand his perspective. I remember one autumn going on a guided tree talk in Regent's Park and getting frustrated at how the obsessive focus on taxonomy seemed to drown out the poetry. I kept finding myself wandering off to escape the learned tone of the speaker and simply enjoy the beauty of the myriad colours on a fine autumn morning.

Birds are our main companions today. The pigeons are clustering in the treetops but the coots pad around the outside of the lake, their fantastic webbed blue feet on full display. We too have become waders in our wellies.

'Look at the head-to-feet movement. What must their brain be doing?' Nick asks as we watch them awhile. 'It's constant feeding – I suppose that's what's on their minds. But look at the shape of them, the way they glide when they enter the water. They are perfectly made.'

Near the lake we pass a half-dead tree with a huge black fungus growing up its trunk like swollen lips. One of the giant lips has fallen off and lies on the ground, a thick textured cake of digested wood, rotten and gleaming in the wet grass.

'Who says there isn't beauty in death?' Nick reflects, but to me the rotting fungus looks menacing.

From time to time Nick stands still and asks, 'Which way next?'

'Whichever you like,' I say.

'You lead,' he says, and so off we trudge in another direction which has no particular logic to it but is guided by a leaf, a bird, a tree, a reflection. In the persistent rain we are somehow suspended in dream time until suddenly jilted back to reality by the sight of a police car outside the tennis club grounds. Instinctively I lunge behind a bush, with Nick following.

'Aren't I in your bubble or something?' he asks.

'Yes, and also we have the right as two people to be out walking, which counts as "exercise",' I add, recalling the latest rules.

Nick is amused to see me dodging the police. 'I've been doing that all my life, but I wouldn't expect a respectable member of the public, so called, to do it!'

'Thanks for the "so called"!' I say, and I go on to reflect how police and customs officials can make you feel guilty simply by their uniformed presence.

By the time we get back to Pascal we have been walking for three hours and I have been outside for four. We have wandered in and out of every accessible area of the park, ending with the passage behind the zoo, where we pass the lions, camels and gibbons, all of whom are taking refuge from the rain. The forecast suggests it will carry on raining all day and night.

'Perhaps we should sleep down by the canal,' Nick suggests to Pascal, but Pascal makes it clear he has no intention of moving. I have heard that suggestion and its dismissal before.

At home I make hot dogs for lunch for me and Julius. Denis has returned to Paris, since lockdown rules have ended there and he is expected to go into his office twice a week. Quarantine regulations in both Britain and France mean that we will not see each other over the next six months, except for regular games of Scrabble over Zoom. I then implore Julius to help me tackle the two squashes that are waiting to be peeled and sliced in the kitchen. He helps willingly. I haven't warmed up since coming inside. The damp seems to have penetrated right through to my bones. I return to the park with spicy butternut squash soup just before the gates are locked and find Nick perched on a stool under an umbrella.

'Haven't I just seen you a minute ago?' he says distractedly. I tell him several hours have passed since our walk. He is surprised. With the rain and lack of sleep he has lost all sense of time.

'Would you like me to accompany you home?' he offers gallantly.

'I think you'd be better off drinking that hot soup,' I suggest, and he concurs.

When I leave the park I can't resist first cycling round the Outer Circle in the dark and rain, then walking up to the top of Primrose Hill. There is something addictive about the empty rainswept landscape. The pull of the outside is so strong that it is difficult to force myself indoors.

That night I stay up late cutting and de-pithing oranges for marmalade to the sound of David Bowie talking about isolation, the suburban curse and the satisfaction to be found in a 'desperate kind of searching' and in 'putting together the wrong pieces of information to make a third'. In all of this creative mix I recognise elements of Nick.

As predicted, it rains all night and into the next day. I am about to go to the park when the doorbell rings. On the doorstep is a heavily masked figure who turns out to be the pest control man. He visited last month and put down poison and is now here to reap the bitter harvest. As I lead him down to my kitchen I realise he has been the only person to have entered the house for months apart from we three residents.

So instead of breathing in the fresh rain air I find myself with my head inside a cupboard, sweeping out fragments of chewed-up bin liner and rat droppings. There is no sign of a dead rat. Perhaps it managed to dodge the poison and make a bid for freedom? Or perhaps it took itself outside to die. I can't help hoping that it escaped unharmed, even if I'm happy not to cohabit with it any longer. I remember how disconcerted it was when I first dislodged it from its nesting place, how it ran round and round in circles not knowing where to go.

Nick and Pascal are both asleep when I arrive with food that evening. The rain has finally stopped. Nick stirs as I put down the flasks.

'Have you managed to detach from your work now?' he asks from his near slumber.

'Yes, I'm enjoying living in the moment, tuning in to the trees and the weather in ways I didn't before,' I say. 'And today I thought it was Wednesday when it's Thursday,' I add.

'Ah, you see,' Nick says with satisfaction. 'You're losing track of chronological time. It doesn't take long. That's a good sign.' And then he settles back to sleep.

I climb over the railings and walk back across the bottom of Primrose Hill. The lamplight is muted in the misty darkness and I feel like I am walking in a 1950s film. At the bottom of the hill a huge lake has formed and several gulls are swimming, looking like ducks. The coloured houses along Regent's Park Road are reflected in the still water as if Primrose Hill has suddenly transformed into Venice. Back home, the marmalade continues to bubble and steam in my mother's old marmalade vat. It has been on the hob for three hours and its citrus fumes fill my nostrils as I enter the house.

'I slept like a baby,' Nick tells me when I arrive in the park the following morning with a pot of newly set marmalade. Sleeping like a baby is something I have yet to learn.

And so most of January passes in a mix of sleet, wind and rain, punctuated with brief moments of sunshine, and I relax into a rhythm with Nick and Pascal. Every morning I turn up at some point with coffee and hot chocolate, and most afternoons or evenings I bring a hot meal. There aren't any fixed times to these unspoken arrangements but somehow we all know they will happen.

'It's become a bit of a ritual, this,' Nick says blithely one morning in late January. 'Well, best enjoy it while it lasts!' he adds as an afterthought. The first signs of spring are in the air. A pink fluffy-clouded dawn has given way to a beam of distilled sunlight in which we bask near the hornbeam. Storm Christoph, which was predicted to hit London overnight, has passed us by. Robins and blackbirds chirp from the trees, which are swaying in the wind as we sit drinking coffee.

'Look how those hornbeam branches are dancing,' I comment. Tiny buds are already visible at their tips, bobbing up and down in the wind.

'Yes, breathing,' Nick says. 'I love the wind, even if one day it may kill me. The most amazing wind I ever saw was in a cyclone in New Zealand – trees uprooted, cars overturned, that sort of thing. But what I really remember is the sheep in the trees. The wind had picked them up and flung them into the branches, where they'd got stuck. They were dead, of course. But still, it was an amazing sight.'

'That reminds me of the Monty Python sketch about flying sheep,' I say.

'Ha, well, there's always tragedy and comedy. *Macbeth* one minute, *Monty Python's Flying Circus* the next! You know why the Pythoneers called it the circus? The circus is the city.'

Pascal wanders over. I ask him if he knows the Monty Python sketch about flying sheep. When he says he doesn't I find myself reciting it word for word, replete with the accents from the original sketch. I loved that sketch as a child and still know it by heart. We all laugh at the idea of the 'ambitious sheep' called Harold who tried to convince his fellow sheep to perch in trees and fly like birds, to inevitably disastrous effect. When I leave, I say I'll be back later with some food but need to cook it first.

It's 7.30 p.m. by the time I set back out with the tiffin stocked with a creamy pork and mushroom casserole, mashed potato and spiced red cabbage with apple. I am crossing over the canal bridge in the misty darkness when I see the silhouette of a tall figure loitering on the bridge. It appears to be heading rapidly towards me. A man with three legs. It can only be Pascal, but what would he be doing on the bridge at this hour? Tentatively

I call out his name. He raises a hand in a friendly waving gesture and comes right up to me.

'We've been evicted. The police came with the deputy park manager and threw us out of the park.'

'*What?*' I say, scarcely able to register what he is saying.

'They evicted us. We had to leave. There was no choice.' He speaks in short staccato sentences, but I find them difficult to digest. 'We knew you'd come down. We didn't want you going to the park, finding it empty and worrying, so I've been waiting here for you,' he adds.

'How long have you been here?' I ask incredulously.

'Two hours, maybe,' Pascal replies. 'We're down by Bridge Nine. Shall I take you there?'

'Yes,' I say. My head is spinning and my heart pounding. Why would anyone choose to evict them now? In the darkness? In midwinter? Midway through a lockdown? Why bring the police?

Pascal leads the way with long strides and I follow, watching his giant locks of hair swing from side to side. He takes me along the dark, narrow, hooded upper path that runs parallel to the towpath below. The way is obscured by shadows from the overhanging trees. It feels like a set for a murder scene. I'm relieved to have Pascal with me but even so I can't help feeling scared – of both the dark passage and what I will find at the end of it. Years ago a colleague of mine was pushed off his bicycle into the canal and was dragged out unconscious near Camden Lock.

Eventually we get to Bridge 9 – officially known as Macclesfield Bridge but colloquially known as the Blow-Up Bridge, owing to the fact that it was destroyed in an explosion and rebuilt in the 1870s. It is a huge Victorian brick structure with hefty iron pillars. I recognise it as a bridge I normally pass under as quickly as possible. I see that the words 'Zombie Punk' are sprayed on the walls as I approach.

'Welcome to our new home!' Nick calls out from the darkness. 'I'm sorry I can't offer you anywhere to sit!' There is laughter in his voice but also quivering emotion.

Nick has neatly installed a groundsheet, sleeping bag, radio and a few possessions under the brick arch in an orderly fashion and is sitting up in his sleeping bag in the dark. It is a shock to see him plucked away from the grass and trees and transplanted to this grim urban backdrop of graffiti-sprayed bricks.

'Well, we've been here before,' he says. 'I've been expecting it for years. This is my life, after all, so I tend to have a vested interest. And this is exactly what happens. Just read George Orwell. You get shifted from spike to spike so that you can't put roots down.'

I notice a dark stain on the wall behind him and think I catch a whiff of urine. The bridge vibrates with alien sounds – cars driving overhead, cyclists rattling past along the towpath, conversations of passers-by on the pavement above. We are in pitch darkness most of the time but when cars turn to drive over the bridge above us their headlights cast sudden beams of light, throwing tree shadows across the curved brick roof, illuminating the graffiti on the walls and enabling me to see Nick's tired expression. I feel I have entered a scene from a post-apocalyptic film. After the peaceful latticework of the hornbeams and the beauty of the moonlit open sky, the bridge feels like a prison in which the doors are perversely left open so that silence and privacy are impossible.

I linger awkwardly against the railings under the bridge. I was looking forward to offering what I thought was a particularly enticing meal but the idea of creamy pork and mushroom casserole with spiced red cabbage and mash feels pretentious, jarring and irrelevant now.

Pascal remains standing all the while, hovering indecisively. He asks me if I have any bin liners. Nick explains that he is worried about how he will shift his sleeping bag, which has become too swollen to roll up small. Many of his possessions are still in the park. I say I'll take a look when I get home.

'One thing about having been considered a loser from the beginning is that it doesn't matter,' Nick says. But of course it matters. And it feels like it matters more than ever. I try to ask about what happened in the park but catch only fragments.

'It was dark. Some guy was shining a torch in my face, saying, "Oh, sorry, is my torch shining in your face?" He asked why we were there and I said, "We had a bit of trouble down by the canal," which was true, only it might have happened ten years ago . . .'

I remember Nick recounting to me that episode from the past, how he and Pascal were pelted with stones and bottles at night by some youths under one of the canal bridges and took shelter in All Souls Church – the more brutal side of life in the street, from which they were protected in the park.

'What did they say after that?' I ask.

'What could they say? They always ask the same things in the same order 'cos that's the way they've been trained. Pascal saw them clearer than me. What could I see with a torch in my eyes? He said there was a woman, a black guy and a white gee-zer – all police – and of course the deputy park manager.' This was the man who'd issued them the eviction notice in August but had left them alone ever since. Why had he called in the police now? Didn't they all have better things to do?

'This is what they've been doing ever since Thatcher,' Nick goes on. 'You push people into the street through lack of jobs with a decent wage and then you chase them off the street. And that's how they push people over the edge. "You can't stand on that patch. But you can't stand on that one either!" And then you're surprised there are mental health problems. And best watch out for the social workers. They'll be patrolling this area bright and early at seven a.m. They'll want to shove us into a hostel, so we need to get up early.'

I'm not sure if Nick is addressing me or Pascal. His mind is roving. He begins to wonder if the man who gave the rum is somehow in cahoots with the park authorities. The hobo para-noia he has mentioned from time to time suddenly feels more understandable. It isn't difficult to see how precarity breeds suspicion and mistrust.

'They never resolve the issues. They put people who are vulnerable in shelters, then shut the door. They used to sep-arate out the drug addicts and mental health problems. Now they just bung everyone together. So you get people caught in cycles – drifting into hostels, getting a sense of freedom when they leave, but then there's the inevitability of return, the lack of provision, the horror of finding yourself face to face with a bunch of losers. It's not the right atmosphere for anyone to thrive in. I could never live in one.'

I remember how Nick once told me, 'The world is my home,' and talked of putting down a 'tentative kind of root system' in the park. Now, all of a sudden, he has been brutally uprooted and made homeless in a way he never was before.

I linger a long time under the bridge that night, shifting uncomfortably from foot to foot in the darkness, reluctant to leave Nick and Pascal in this new environment which feels threatening and hostile. Eventually I remind them that there is some hot food in the tiffin and take my leave as Nick begins to eat. I say I'll bring coffee and flasks of water in the morning, then plod home heavy-hearted. The first thing I do on arrival is phone Bachi. The second thing I do is find some bin liners and strong bags and cycle them to Pascal.

In the morning I prepare coffee, hot chocolate and crumpets with butter and marmalade and lug them to the Blow-Up Bridge. Nick and Pascal's things are there, but not them. I try the park instead and to my surprise find them lying side by side in the open in the winter sun.

'It's gorgeous!' Nick says, smiling.

I'm exhausted, having had a sleepless night, haunted by images of their eviction and the hostile environment of the dank, smelly bridge. They, by contrast, say they both slept well. They apparently rose at six o'clock and came back into the park at seven, with just a few belongings for the day. I am pleased to see them back here but can't help still feeling a deep sense of unease. They have a right to sit in the park like anyone else but will the deputy park manager and the police see it that way now that they have got involved?

'You seem a bit preoccupied,' Nick comments when he sees my face, 'not your usual smiley, bouncy self.'

'I'm disturbed by what happened last night,' I say as I sit on a log.

'Oh, I wouldn't bother about that,' Nick says, offering me one of the crumpets I have brought. 'I've been chucked out of better places than this, I'll have you know. I was chucked out of a five-star hotel in Sydney one time because I had flip-flops on and my mate was in work boots and shorts. We looked like a couple of Aussie yackers!'

I talk about how I am used to security in life so am horrified that someone can just uproot them like that.

'Well, you wouldn't last long on the street,' Nick says. 'But then, why would you? Who in their right mind would take a nosedive into the abyss and then find one of the nicest men he has ever met and the loveliest woman? I'm not just saying that. If I thought you were an arsehole, I'd say it. And I'd expect the same from you if I was being an arsehole. This life has been a wonderful experience,' he continues, 'and I may get another ten or twenty years. Who knows? These experiences are priceless. And I think as a society we're maturing. We're going round and round in a washing machine, backwards and forwards, until we will wake up one day without disturbing the fabric.'

And so, on that first morning after the eviction, there is a curious atmosphere of normality and even bravado as they continue to sit in the park in their sleeping bags, lapping up the rare winter sun. But the deputy park manager returns that afternoon, saying they don't have a right to sit in their sleeping bags. By 5 p.m. the police have turned up with three vans, saying any stuff they leave in the park will be destroyed.

When Bachi and I arrive together at the bridge that evening, the atmosphere is sombre. Nick sounds angry, frustrated and confused. But when we offer to contact the park authorities he is adamant that he doesn't want us getting involved. Bachi tries to concentrate on practical details. Do they need any spare socks or hats? Do they want to store any more stuff at his place?

Next morning when I arrive at the park I find Nick pacing around near the hornbeam, picking up litter with his metal pincer. He looks weary and desolate. His affairs have been neatly packed and sorted into three piles: a groundsheet, bag and backpack for taking to the canal, three bags for Bachi to store, and one for me, consisting of books, papers and gifts he received for Christmas.

Nick is furious with Pascal, who is lying further off in his sleeping bag as if nothing has changed, and tells me he never wants to speak to 'that man' again. He says that ever since the eviction notice in August, and even before that, he has wanted them to shift to sleeping under the bridge at night so as not to flout the authorities, but that Pascal always refused, so they stayed in the park. Now Nick is plagued with guilt in relation to Michael Wood, the park manager with whom he has maintained a good relationship for five years. He worries that he has let him down. But above everything else he is discombobulated, and it is painful to see him in such a stressed state. At one point he stares directly at me and says pleadingly, 'I'm a good man.' I move towards him and give him a big hug, and as I pat his back I can feel him sobbing.

'Of course you are. I know that,' I say.

When we separate, he says, 'Damn it,' and apologises for crying, but later he says it helped clear things up. 'All I want is for Bachi to come and take this stuff away,' he says bleakly. I phone Bachi, who arrives within half an hour and takes the stuff off in his Jeep.

That night I wonder if they will be under different bridges, given Nick's outburst against Pascal, but I find them camped out together under the same one. The atmosphere feels calmer, even though the police have been back a third time to check up on them. I have printed out an engraving made in 1874, depicting the original bridge that stood in this place exploding when a barge passed under it carrying sugar, nuts, petroleum and five tons of gunpowder. The dramatic black-and-white engraving shows debris flying everywhere and a man being blown overboard by the force of the explosion. 'That's me!' Nick says when he sees it. The explosion caused pandemonium at the time, killing the crew, blowing glass out of the windows of houses within a one-mile radius and causing havoc amongst the animals in the zoo. 'Poor animals. Did they escape?' Nick asks hopefully. The bridge was rebuilt in 1876 using the original iron pillars, which continue to bear witness to its violent past.

At night I lie in bed, ruminating. Should I write an out-raged letter to the *Guardian* about two innocent, much-loved local men getting kicked out of the park in midwinter during a global pandemic? Should Bachi and I try to kickstart a cam-paign on their behalf? To do nothing feels terrible but Nick has made it clear he doesn't want us intervening, and we certainly wouldn't want to make things worse inadvertently or trigger their being carted off to a hostel against their will. I am also aware that Nick and Pascal have been navigating the streets for seventeen years. If anyone knows how to survive, they do, and to try to act on their behalf would be undermining their autonomy. So I have to content myself with writing outraged letters in my head only, and conclude that the best support I can offer is to simply carry on bringing home-cooked food, flasks of hot water and hot drinks as before.

Three days have passed since the eviction. On the fourth morning I catch a spectacular pink dawn sky through my bathroom window, but I'm tired so go back to bed. When I awake I sense the light has dropped and there is an unnatural silence. When I get up and draw the curtains I am greeted by snow tumbling rapidly and magnificently from the sky and settling on everything it touches.

I fly into my clothes, fill two flasks with hot drinks, buy a packet of madeleines from the corner shop and set off along the snowy path towards the Blow-Up Bridge. The snow is untouched underfoot and the overhanging trees look magical. They have taken on new, softened shapes – the willow branches creating vertical trails of whiteness; the round fruits of the plane trees looking like Christmas puddings topped with icing; the catkins offering a glorious frozen drapery. The passage I found so sinister at night now feels like a place of unimaginable beauty.

When I get to the bridge I see Nick and Pascal's sleeping bags and tarpaulins, but no sign of them, so I head to the park. When I traverse the secret passage I see white-capped umbrellas suspended in the hornbeam trees, which are sugared with snow. With nobody beneath them, the umbrellas look like something out of a Magritte painting.

Soon Nick appears, carrying another umbrella.

'How are you?' he asks, beaming.

'Very happy to see the snow!' I say, beaming back.

'It's a chance to see the same world differently,' Nick says with delight. 'And did you see the sunrise? Liquid raspberry, shining like sauce. I thought of you. You'd have loved it.'

He is in high spirits. When a passer-by asks, 'How do you manage in the snow?' he replies, 'We do what we've always done,' and then cheekily challenges him to a snowball fight. When someone else asks if he can interview him about homelessness, Nick says dismissively, 'I've never considered myself homeless.'

'See the smile on everyone's faces?' he says, delighted, when he returns from throwing snowballs. His mood, like mine, is soaring in the snow.

Pascal is dressed in two gifted jackets and wearing a hat and gloves. Snow clings to his beard locks and his cheeks are glowing red. The feathery branches of the hornbeam look otherworldly in the snow and we stand around for a while eating madeleines and drinking coffee and hot chocolate.

After a while I say my feet are freezing and suggest going for a walk. To my surprise they both say they'd like to come, so the three of us set off around the park in the tumbling snow. At one point, when Nick is occupied with conversation elsewhere, I find myself alone with Pascal, and take the opportunity to ask him if he is feeling anxious about the recent events.

'I'm not prone to anxiety,' he replies with a gentle but convincing air. 'It's not my thing at all. Anxiety is a modern condition. A lot of people these days seem to be swimming in anxiety. They are drowning in it, but it's not for me.'

I ask him if they'll carry on sleeping under the bridge.

'It seems we don't have any choice at the moment in this madness.'

Later we get onto the subject of Algeria and the landscapes he was fond of there as a child. I ask him how often he used to go.

'Algeria was holidays,' he says. 'Paris was school.'

'And what is London?' I ask.

'London is hobo!' he says with a gentle laugh.

I can't resist asking him that ghastly question I have never known how to answer: 'What do you imagine yourself doing in ten years' time?'

'Who knows?' he says with a shrug. 'I don't think years ahead. I don't think more than a few hours ahead!'

When I next meet up with Bachi we agree that we could all do with taking lessons in relaxation from Pascal.

As we trudge around the park and circle the lake we enjoy watching children, dogs, ducks, coots and Egyptian geese in the snow. We pass a freshly made snowman wearing a face mask and another wearing a wig made out of grass. By the time we get back to the hornbeams we have been walking for over two hours and are cold and tired. I suggest that if they accompany me to my house I can offer them some hot food to take back with them. When they get to my doorstep I ask them if they want to come inside, given that they are in my bubble, but they prefer to linger outside in the cold while I heat up the food and fill some flasks with hot water.

That night the temperature drops to minus four.

* * *

When I head to the park in heavy rain on the penultimate day of January there is no sign of Nick and Pascal, nor of their umbrellas in the trees nor any of their affairs. It is the first time I have come to their home under the hornbeams and found it completely deserted like this. It is like stepping onto the stage of a theatre and finding that I am the only actor left. It feels unutterably wrong. Our three logs stand forlorn and desolate in the rain – the only traces left of their five years living in the park.

'You have to get the balance right between the bridge and the park,' Nick told me two days ago. But the balance has now tipped. The park no longer feels like a place of freedom.

From this day on I never again see them sitting or lying in their sleeping bags under the hornbeams. The Blow-Up Bridge has become their new home.

16 Adaptation

'It doesn't really matter where you live – under here or in an enclosed box somewhere – it's all the same if you've found your balance, the mustard seed, the kernel,' Nick explains. 'It's metaphoric but it's real. Out of the seed new shoots grow.'

We are now in February and the temperature has dropped below freezing again. We are sitting in pitch darkness under the bridge. The only new shoots I can see are the beginnings of icicles lacing either side of the brick arch like teeth in the early stages of formation. Nick and Pascal are sitting in their sleeping bags facing the canal. I am crouched uncomfortably on a downwards slope on the end of Nick's skipper, facing the dank graffiti-covered wall behind them. My back and legs are aching from the uphill angle and there is a biting wind funnelling under the bridge. I admire the principle of what Nick is saying but personally I am pining for the openness of the star-studded sky and the beauty of the frosted fringes of the hornbeams.

'When they roasted St Lawrence on a griddle, you know what he said?' Nick continues in jovial mood. 'He said, "My flesh is well done on this side – please turn me over so that you can roast the other side!" It's like that here – only with the cold, not the heat. And it's a bit like that with the police and the park authorities. They were threatening us with the

Vagrancy Act the other day. Let's see how long we last under here before the Old Bill comes down and moves us on. It's only a matter of time.'

There are some decrepit muddy steps leading from the street down to the canal right beside the Blow-Up Bridge. I have taken to cycling along the road as far as the bridge, then climbing down these steps to avoid walking along the canal path at night. Even so, every time I turn my back on the street lights and plunge downwards towards the darkness of the canal, I find myself expecting to be knifed from behind. The memory of being followed and mugged in the darkness when crossing one of the canal bridges twenty years ago feels as fresh as if it had happened only yesterday. What I most resent about that attack is not having my bag ripped off my shoulder, nor being thrown to the ground, but the imprint of fear it created, leaving me reacting like a startled cat whenever I hear footsteps coming up behind me in the dark.

I never do hear anyone behind me as I squint to see the steps and descend towards the oil-black water of the canal, but I am never able to dispel the sense of dread creeping up my spine. Unlike the park, where the sky offers a glimmer of reassuring light, here there is nothing but ominous water, the depth of which is indeterminate in the dark. As soon as I hear the voices of Nick and Pascal or the scratchy muffled sound of their pocket radios I feel a sense of relief. I know I am safe.

'I think there used to be seats between the pillars in the old days but they took them away. That was to stop people sleeping there, I suppose,' Nick tells me.

'Possibly,' I reply. 'Removing seating is part of a deliberate urban-design strategy known as hostile architecture. That's why those seats at bus stops all slope downwards and why they introduced those notorious weirdly shaped solid concrete benches in Camden. They were specially designed to prevent people from sleeping or skateboarding. It's all part of making public space less accessible.'

'Like those spikes,' Nick says, pointing upwards at a row of thin iron spikes suspended between the pillars of the bridge. 'Even the birds aren't allowed to sit, it seems.'

'There used to be regular raves under there!' he continues, pointing between the graffiti-splattered pillars towards the opposite bank, which stretches right down to the water level and is littered with debris – some wooden pallets, a couple of torn bar stools, a ripped armchair, the rigging where lighting once was and other unidentifiable stuff that has been abandoned. 'You used to get ten to twenty people under there on a Friday night at one time.'

I remember how in the past I used to take a nervous glance in that direction, then look straight ahead when walking under the Blow-Up Bridge, uncomfortable at the sight of people dwelling in the murky darkness on the other side. More recently, under 'our side' of the bridge, there was for some months a man camped out with a small tent. I tell Nick I used to say hello to him from time to time but that he never replied. He usually had a beer can in his hand and seemed lost in his own world. 'He was Hungarian,' Nick informs me. 'I don't know what happened to him. I think he might have gone back to his country.' I wonder what this man must have observed of life on the edge of the canal and whether he is now living in better circumstances.

'I'm very good at adapting,' Nick asserts. 'I've been doing it all my life. But to the wrong things, seemingly!' He then tells me that he is sleeping better since he moved under the bridge because he doesn't feel he is breaching his unwritten agreement with Michael Wood, whom he has always respected. 'And when you're staring at the bridge all night, it's quite interesting,' he continues. 'You've got the total blackness in the middle, so you're looking into infinity. Then you've got the two sides lighting up as traffic passes, so you're back to the finite. Those are your two planets.'

Later, when I am alone with Pascal, I ask him how he feels about sleeping under the bridge. 'It's strange having a roof over my head,' he says. 'It's not a roof, really – more like a brick tent. But I'm not used to sleeping with any kind of structure over me. Haven't done that for years.'

Both Nick and Pascal say the canal feels much safer than it did a decade ago, when they often slept in the undergrowth beneath a nearby bridge.

'You don't get the drunks and psychos any more,' Pascal comments. 'I don't know why. Maybe it's the lockdown. And at least under here we get some shelter when it rains, so there's some advantage. But I prefer to be under the open sky.'

One misty evening while we are sitting under the bridge, our conversation is interrupted by the persistent hooting of an owl coming from the corner of the park that used to be their home. 'I think that owl is trying to call you back into the park,' I suggest hopefully.

There is some comfort in the fact that birds and wild animals are not confined by park regulations in spite of the metal spikes on the bridge. They can move between the park and canal with impunity, keeping the connection between the two spaces alive. Within a few days Nick and Pascal have two or three robins gathered around them like familiar companions. Could they be the same ones that hovered around them in the park? Sometimes you see a robin sitting on one of their boots or on Pascal's sleeping bag or even his head. Pigeons are also relaxed in their presence and two jays have appeared in a nearby plane tree. From time to time they swoop down to peck up some cornflakes or bread, then fly back into the tree, giving us a view of their spectacular blue feathers in motion.

Before long, Nick and Pascal have inadvertently acquired a young fox who takes up residence with them under the bridge most nights and patrols the area quite uninhibitedly during the day.

'I think it wants to be domesticated,' Nick says, 'but then it will bite your nose off later!

'You should give it a name,' Bachi suggests enthusiastically during one of his now irregular evening visits. 'I'm sure you could train it. It's not much different from a dog. I could give you some techniques.'

But Nick is against the idea. 'We don't know how long we'll be under here and we don't want it getting dependent. What would happen when we move on? I know,' he says cheekily, as an afterthought, 'we could hand it on to you, Emma. You could take it out for walks on a lead on Primrose Hill!'

'Thanks a lot!' I say. 'I've never wanted to be tied down by a dog, never mind a fox. I'll stick with cats, thank you.'

'Yes, I've always liked the independence of cats,' Nick says.

Given that we're on the topic of human–animal relations, I mention an episode of the late-night Radio 3 programme *Free Thinking* in which my sister, who is a poet, and other literary specialists participated earlier in the week. It was on the topic of ecocriticism. Nick was intending to listen but fell asleep before it started.

'They were talking about decentring the human, focusing on writers who try to imagine life from the perspective of other species – animals, plants, that sort of thing,' I summarise somewhat inadequately.

'Ah, decentring the human!' Nick retorts. 'But then it's the humans doing the writing and the decentring! There's the contradiction. But I suppose at least it's an attempt to stop centring everything on ourselves.'

I am reminded that Nick and Pascal hardly need literary critics to tell them about something they have instinctively been doing for years.

* * *

In the daytime I often approach the bridge along the canal path. I can't help noticing the rats that weave their way in and out of the undergrowth and wonder if 'our rat' has perhaps made it down to the canal. The closure of all the restaurants during lockdown has apparently drawn many London rats indoors in search of new sources of food. But these bankside rats seem content in the wild and certainly look less disturbing in the undergrowth than in a kitchen. I also notice a pair of burnt-out Nike trainers, their logo still just about decipherable amongst the ashes. A few metres away is an electric box sprayed with the words 'MASS WASTE CULTURE DESPAIR'. I wonder if the shoes and message are connected and whether they are linked to the 'Zombie Punk' tag sprayed on the side of the Blow-Up Bridge.

Despite these dystopian elements, the surroundings of the canal look much better in the daytime, not least because the trees and plants soften the landscape of the towpath and the water of the canal ripples with their reflections. It is not uncommon to see a lone heron flying overhead or the occasional cormorant disappearing into the water, then shaking the droplets from its oily neck as it resurfaces. Coots, moorhens and Canada geese are more regular passers-by and the trees vibrate with the song of blackbirds and thrushes. But much as I enjoy walking along the canal path I never feel like settling under the bridge for my morning coffee as it feels enclosed and cuts off access to the sky.

So most mornings I continue to head to the park first thing to savour the winter dawn skies, enjoy the sounds of the gibbons and watch out for small signs of the encroaching spring – snowdrops, crocuses and even, to my surprise, frosted daisies. Sometimes I take my flask of coffee to the Secret Garden, perching on a bench which I share with a robin; other times I settle on a log under the hornbeams in Nick and Pascal's old dwelling place, always hoping that they might have changed their minds and come back into the park for the day, but they never do. Recent experiences have left a negative taste. The ban on sitting in sleeping bags and the challenge of what to do with their stuff during the day have made spending time in the park impracticable, especially in this freezing weather. Sometimes when I arrive I spot small offerings people have left for them – two tangerines, a pack of biscuits, a roll of loo paper propped in a tree. Clearly people still expect to find them there.

The joy of sitting under the hornbeams again feels tainted by Nick and Pascal's absence. I feel almost guilty sitting there without them, even though they were never possessive about the space.

'You have all of this!' a man once told Nick, gesturing to the trees and open grassland before them. 'So do you!' Nick replied. I remember how he was surprised by the man saying, 'Thank you!' as if Nick were making a generous concession. 'It's never been about ownership,' Nick specified. 'The park is for everyone.'

Everyone except them, it now seems.

It is only after I have imbibed the beauty of pink dawn clouds and the lightly frosted landscape of the park that I head under the bridge with breakfast supplies for Nick and Pascal, including the remaining half of my flask of hot coffee, which I reserve for Nick. Seeing how uncomfortable I am sitting on the edge of his skipper, Nick climbs down the bank on the other side of the bridge and finds a large old black plastic flowerpot for me to sit on. It is badly cracked, but with a strategically placed jacket on top I can sit on it without it collapsing under me.

I am not alone in wishing Nick and Pascal were still in the park. Sandy, a retired American film producer who brings gifts of home-made banana cake, CBD oil and carefully chosen second-hand books (most recently Aldous Huxley's *After Many a Summer*), tells them quite frankly that he thinks they should pack up their stuff and return to the park. 'But you can't see the sky from under here,' he remonstrates when they say they are fine under the bridge.

'Oh, there you are!' I hear a woman cry from the towpath below when she spots them in their new location. 'I was worried about you. I miss seeing you in the park.'

'You're not the first person to say that,' Nick replies.

'Did you get kicked out?' she asks directly.

'Well, we sometimes used to sleep in there. Apparently we weren't supposed to, so now we're sleeping here,' Nick says diplomatically.

'Can I bring you anything?' she asks.

'Only your smile!' Nick replies.

To others, I hear him say, 'We just decided to take a little holiday by the canal!'

'I feel something is missing when I walk this way,' a dog walker tells me when passing the hornbeams in the park. 'My dog would always head straight for Nick and Pascal. They'd often give her a treat and she'd drink water under the tree. It was part of her daily routine.'

For Bachi there is the added pain of knowing that Lizzie's ashes are no longer in the company of her old friends. 'The whole point of scattering her ashes there was so that she could be close to Nick and Pascal, with whom she'd spent some of her happiest moments, and now they're no longer there,' he says with a mixture of sadness and anger against the park authorities.

One day, when I am sitting on my cracked flowerpot under the bridge, two young girls appear with their parents.

'I thought you lived over there!' the youngest one says, pointing in the direction of the park.

'We did, but now we're here,' Nick replies.

'She means we thought that was where you lived permanently,' her father specifies.

'Nothing's permanent,' Nick says simply.

'Too true,' the father replies. 'That's Buddhist.'

Nick goes on to tell the little girl that the card she made them for Christmas is now with me for safekeeping.

'Do you live here too?' the girl asks earnestly, turning to me.

'No, but I live nearby,' I say.

'Do you sleep in a house?' she asks, trying to make sense of the situation.

'Yes,' I say, 'but sometimes it can be nice to sleep outside.'

'What do you see when you look up when you lie in bed?' Nick asks.

'The ceiling,' the girl replies.

'And what do you see if you look up when you're outside at night?'

The girl is confused about what to answer. 'You see the stars, don't you?' her father encourages, and Nick nods.

'Exactly,' he says with a smile.

But you can't see the stars from under the bridge, I'm thinking, although of course I restrain myself from saying it. Even I have to concede that, when the rain and snow come, being under the bridge is not such a bad option.

And very soon the snow does come again. The official temperature in London is minus one but the forecast states that the bitter easterly winds make it feel more like minus twelve. When I arrive at the bridge one morning I find that the icicles have grown into magnificent dangling structures several feet long that glisten like chandeliers at a winter ball.

'Don't walk under those!' Nick calls out. 'If they drop they could kill you!' But with the snow still drifting from the sky, there is more likelihood of them expanding than falling. Seeing the weather, I have come with flasks of hot water, coffee, hot chocolate and soup.

'Keep my place warm for me, will you?' Nick says as he vacates his sleeping bag and heads off to use the toilets at the bottom of Primrose Hill. I don't climb into the bag but I do sit on top of it, and for the first time I see the view from under the bridge from Nick and Pascal's perspective. Instead of staring at a dirty wall, they look out onto the rippling water, with a vista of trees on either side of the bridge and the bank opposite.

Willows, hawthorn, plane trees and assorted bushes. Today the view has a fairy-tale quality, what with the pelmet of icicles and the confusion of the whirling snow.

When Nick returns I say I'm keen to go for a walk along the towpath and ask if either of them wants to join me. 'I'll come,' Nick says. 'It's good to keep the blood moving in this cold.' And so we set off in the direction of Little Venice, with snowflakes gently settling on our shoulders. I am wearing a woolly hat, hooded parka and snow boots. Nick refuses to wear a hat, so within a few minutes his beard and hair are white with fine flakes of snow that refuse to melt.

On the way we pass great piles of rusty metal that have been dredged out of the canal. Nick points out the number of busted safes, telling me that he and Pascal saw two men on a motorbike tipping a safe into the canal one night.

There is hardly anyone about in the snow so we don't have to walk in single file, maintaining social distance against nervous passers-by, and we soon fall into an easy rhythm walking alongside each other. Nick says he hasn't been to Little Venice for many years but soon it is far behind us as we carry on heading westwards along the towpath. We have been walking for two hours but neither of us feels like turning back, so I suggest we pop up into the Harrow Road in search of something hot to keep us going. To our delight we find a fish and chip shop and I buy us each enormous parcels of chips, which feel made for the occasion, warming both our hands and our insides. Nick hesitates to finish his, saying he should save some for Pascal, but I point out that they won't have the same appeal when cold and soggy. He agrees and finishes his packet as we head back to the canal path, where I give the remains of my chips to some hungry moorhens and Canada geese. We could head back at this point but neither of us feels like it, so we carry on trudging through the snow, which never becomes heavy but never stops falling either.

We enjoy the curious in-between landscape of the canal – neither rural nor urban – noting how the atmosphere changes along the way. Sometimes our view is of the jumbled backs of terraced houses, sometimes industrial warehouses, large expanses of open railway track, wasteland or cemetery. And moored the whole way along the canal are customised boats – some large and well equipped, others small, improvised and eccentric, some made from converted rescue boats. There is much humour and individuality in these alternative semi-mobile homes that inhabit the marginal watery seams of the city. We see the Hindu goddess Kali triumphantly astride a tiger, Buddhist sculptures, Tibetan masks, teddy bears, mannequins in extravagant hats, a stuffed toy lion, skeletons, improvised book stalls, pots of plants and sofas, all of which look surreal in the snow.

'I did once contemplate getting a boat when I was in the financial position to do so,' Nick tells me. 'But I didn't want the responsibility of the upkeep and I wanted to be able to go where I wished, not where the boat wanted to take me.'

I mention that one of our MA students lived on a barge and wrote her thesis about life on the canal. We talk about how people seem to be able to design their own lives with a certain freedom in such spaces.

'You too seem to have mastered the art of living, which many people haven't,' I suggest.

'Well, if I have bleak moments I always know there's a new day coming,' Nick says reflectively.

I don't know what we talk about most of the time but there is pleasure in just wandering, and whenever one of us asks the other if they want to turn back, the answer is always no – until I suddenly realise that if we don't turn back now I'm going to miss the six-thirty Zoom meeting I've arranged with my sisters to commemorate our mother's birthday. And so reluctantly we turn back. I suggest we might try to catch a bus, but Nick tells me he hasn't taken public transport for twenty years and I'm not sure the buses are even running on a snowy lockdown afternoon. What we haven't anticipated is that on the way home we will be walking against the wind, with the snow flying directly into our faces, making progress difficult. From time to time I am desperate for a pee and Nick stands guard as I head behind a bush or shrub, not that there is anyone to be guarded from in such weather. By the time we approach Little Venice I am so cold and stiff that I can scarcely put one leg in front of the other. Nick jokes that if I collapse in the icy water he certainly won't be diving in to rescue me. The sight of a cormorant darting in and out of the water with agility offers some inspiration.

It is 6 p.m. and dark by the time we reach the Blow-Up Bridge, where Pascal has been lying peacefully in his sleeping bag all day. I am struck by how my feelings towards the bridge are beginning to change. After a seven-hour walk in

persistent snow, it now seems to represent comfort, famil-
iarity and even homeliness. In our absence a woman from
Islington has come with hot food and a new sleeping bag for
Pascal. Last week she brought him a leaf-and-dung-powered
stove known as a Kelly Kettle, which they tried to give to
me, but I refused to take it. 'We can't leave you alone for one
minute!' Nick quips to Pascal.

Nick accompanies me on the final stretch to my house so
that I can give him some hot water for the night.

'Would you like to come in?' I ask.

For the first time, instead of waiting on the doorstep he
agrees to follow me inside. Perhaps it is because we have
just spent the whole day together so maintaining distance
no longer seems to make sense. Or perhaps it is just that it
is snowing. Whatever the reason, it feels good to know the
threshold has been crossed.

'It's like a labyrinth,' he says as I lead him along the narrow
corridor and down the stairs to our cluttered, old-fashioned
kitchen. 'There's a good atmosphere in this place,' he goes on,
looking around. 'It's not just the things but the feeling of the
place. It's good.'

I show him a large old copper cooking pot in which I've made
so many of the soups we've shared, and the old hand-beaten
ladles from Gujarat, which I sense he will appreciate. I notice
his gentle way of interacting with the more nervous of our
two cats. He offers her the back of his hand to explore and,
when she feels confident, gives her some gentle strokes. When
we go upstairs he catches a glimpse of my study on the ground

floor and spots a painting I made of a plane tree at twilight before I turned to monochrome drawings. The fruits of the tree are gold and the sky mauve-blue.

'You've really captured the feeling of that tree,' he says, staring at it for a long time.

After a few minutes Nick opens the front door and disappears back into the snowy night, carrying a flask of freshly boiled water.

I dive straight onto Zoom, where my sisters tell me I look like a ghost, then stagger upstairs for a hot bath and early night. But once in bed I find myself completely unable to warm up. My skin is burning on the outside but my blood feels cold and my limbs are heavy and aching. At 2 a.m. I hobble downstairs, make myself a hot-water bottle and boil up a mixture of ginger, turmeric, lime and honey. I wonder how on earth Nick is managing, sleeping under the icy bridge.

When I greet him in the morning he tells me that he slept like a baby after the long walk and only felt a slight twinge in one leg this morning. I, despite being eight years younger, am aching all over, from my neck, shoulders, thighs and hips right down to the soles of my feet.

The freezing weather persists for several days. And the sight of Nick and Pascal sitting surrounded by icicles has a curious effect on passers-by. An Italian woman looks at their situation with horror. 'But where do you actually sleep?' she asks.

'Here!' Nick replies.

'But there must be warmer places,' she remonstrates. She can't bear to see them sitting under the frozen bridge and immediately hands Nick a ten-pound note. Later in the day, she is back with a bag of clothes.

'You just can't stop people giving stuff today!' Nick says blithely. 'First there were two geezers from the East End. They asked if we were alright and handed us twenty quid. One of them asked, "Are you together?" – pointing at Pascal. I said, "No, I don't know that bloke," and we had a good laugh! I explained that we share.'

No sooner has Nick recounted this than a woman called Nell, who knows them from the park, pops up from the tow-path below.

'Don't tell me – you're about to give me money!' Nick says.

'I am,' she says, laughing and handing over ten pounds, ask-ing him to share it with Pascal as she doesn't have change.

When she leaves, Nick says to me, 'Here, have some of this!', thrusting a ten-pound note in my direction. I refuse to take it.

'Can I offer you a hot chocolate, then?' To that, I say yes. 'Well, it's a pleasure to share,' Nick says, 'especially when we are so often taking from you.'

The next thing I know they are offering me fresh cherries that Bachi brought down last night and some home-made gin-ger biscuits made by a friend of mine.

'Stop!' I say as Pascal tries to get me to take a madeleine. 'I had breakfast before I came and you've given me enough!'

'It fascinates me, giving,' Nick concludes, ''cos I've been on both sides of it.'

Meanwhile the towpath continues to throw up a mixture of strangers and familiars.

'What, still having a lie-in, are we!' one man asks with a grin as he cycles past. He is someone they have known from the street for many years who shares their capacity for humour in adversity. 'Keeping OK?' he adds more seriously, and Nick replies that it isn't really cold, not when you think that it goes down to minus thirty in some countries.

That day, when I say I want to go for a wander, Nick says to Pascal, 'You go! You'll enjoy it and it'll do you good to get some exercise.' To my surprise Pascal rises up from his sleeping bag, puts on his walking boots and prepares to accompany me along the towpath.

'Are you sure you don't want your hat?' I ask, knowing that the temperature is minus five.

'I don't like hats,' he replies. 'I only wear a hat when it's raining.'

The canal is partially frozen. A thick lip of ice projects out from our side of the bank and we see a perfectly formed fox trapped and entombed within it.

'They fall in from time to time,' Pascal comments matter-of-factly. 'Jim tells us he sometimes has to fish them out.' Jim is the cleaner who has been supplying them with flasks of water for years.

I realise that Pascal has never strayed far along the towpath even though he has been living in and around Camden and Regent's Park for well over a decade. His geography of London is limited and, unlike Nick, he is not particularly curious about architectural nuances, although he does ask about the homes in Little Venice.

'What do people pay for such houses?'

'Several million pounds,' I say.

At this he laughs. 'All of that just for a few bricks!'

I ask him if he thinks he will ever live inside a house again.

He raises his eyebrows. 'Who knows! Never say never,' he replies, then adds, 'I've always thought being indoors was overrated.'

I ask him if he ever misses speaking French.

'Not at all,' he says. 'We didn't really speak French at home anyway. We spoke a mixture of French, Berber and Algerian. I think that's good. You learn how to mix things up.'

I ask if he has had any news of his family during the pandemic.

'They're all OK,' he says. 'But I do have one relative who died. An uncle. He was old but fit till he got Covid. He was quite well known in Algeria but they wouldn't let him be taken to his home town for burial. He had to be buried in Algiers with very few people present.'

I'm interested to hear that Pascal has somehow managed to obtain news of his family.

'When did you last speak to your parents?' I ask.

'About ten years ago.'

'Do you think your mother worries about you?'

'Probably,' he replies, and I sense that he has had enough of such questioning. But I remember Nick once telling me that years ago when they were queuing for handouts in central London, one of Pascal's relatives spotted him from a bus. An uncle, Nick thought. He got off the bus and spoke to

Pascal for some time. 'He was well dressed and looked like a well-educated person, maybe an academic,' Nick recalls. 'I get the impression Pascal is from what you'd call a good family, but they were speaking French so I have no idea what they said.'

Pascal is interested in how few hobos we spot along the towpath. 'They must have taken them all into hotels. Perhaps they are giving them a tour of all the hotels of London!' he says, amused. He tells me that their friend Darren didn't last more than one month in a hotel. 'It was too noisy. And you have to put up with all the other hobos. It's too much! Most hobos just want quiet.'

Walking with Pascal feels fundamentally different from walking with Nick. Not only is he often silent but he also has a very different presence and gait, bounding from foot to foot with his matted hair swinging out behind him. I notice, when we pass a man cycling along the towpath with wood he has gathered, that he gives Pascal a hobo-to-hobo look. The next day he turns up under the bridge with some food. I remember how, when I walked with Pascal in the park, there was a man behind us secretly photographing his hair. On another occasion I see two blokes stop their exercises and stare when they see Pascal passing along the bottom of Primrose Hill on his way back from the washing facilities. There is an almost unworldly aura to his appearance, as if he has just stepped out of a forest, and people find this difficult to ignore.

Today, on our icy walk along the towpath, we stop off at the same chip shop I visited with Nick. On our way home I check the date of Nick's sixty-fifth birthday. It is, as I thought, in two days' time. In our absence Nick has received a number of fresh donations.

'You know where this stuff is going?!' he says to me. 'I've prepared two bags of clothes for you!'

'No, thanks,' I say. 'I'm still trying to get rid of stuff, as you know. Perhaps you should open up a stall under the bridge!'

Back home, I phone Bachi and we decide to make a joint visit to celebrate Nick's birthday and to tell Pascal to keep the idea a surprise. I make a lemon cake with home-made lemon curd inside and white lemon icing on top. I decorate it with small shavings of peel. A white cake for an iced environment. I fill the copper dome with Tunnock's marshmallow teacakes in their bright-red and silver foil and wrap two very small gifts, conscious that the last thing Nick wants in life is more stuff. One gift is a bulb of smoked garlic, which won't pose problems of accumulation. The other is a tiny sandalwood elephant covered in pure gold leaf that I purchased from its maker in Mandalay and gave to my mother. I recuperated it from her mantelpiece when clearing the house after her death. It is so small and light that you could carry it in a pocket without even noticing. Perhaps it could function as a mascot if Nick ever decides to go travelling? I feel he may not want it but I'm certain that he'll like it, and if he doesn't want to keep it I'll be only too happy to have it back. Lastly I make a card out of the painting of the plane tree he so liked when he came to the house. I select a few verses from Sylvia Plath, which I copy inside.

At 3 p.m. on 13 February, Bachi and I meet on the towpath in sub-zero temperatures and arrive under the bridge singing 'Happy Birthday'. Pascal laughs conspiratorially and Nick, at first, looks almost disturbed.

'I've made you a cake,' I say, pulling the broken plastic flowerpot over. I get the cake out of the tin, arrange it on a china plate on the flowerpot and stick a candle and sparkler in it.

'Over to you to light it,' I say. Nick gets out his lighter.

'Well, I never thought I'd be celebrating my birthday under the bridge!' he declares. Now it is me thinking of that mustard seed. It really doesn't seem to matter at this moment where we are.

'Did you say you made this?' Nick asks of the cake, and when I say yes he springs up and gives me a hug. He may have been disconcerted at first but now he has entered into the spirit of celebration and greets his gifts and card with enthusiasm. He uses his penknife to cut the cake and the four of us enjoy eating it, as does a robin who hovers around Pascal's piece, hoovering up the crumbs.

'Thank you, thank you,' Nick says, and soon he is playing with the tiny golden elephant. 'It's a treasure,' he says, and I feel happy that this object which my mother treasured will now be treasured by him. Soon he is balancing it on top of the copper dome and arranging the teacakes into patterns whilst making references to Rudyard Kipling. I am reminded of how much I admire Nick's capacity for playfulness.

'Please take a piece of cake for Julius,' he says as I leave. And I do.

The celebration of Nick's birthday under the bridge marks the moment of my acceptance that he and Pascal are no longer in the park. A few days later I find a large flat log in the undergrowth and Nick lugs it over and places it under the bridge.

'This can be your seat now,' he says. 'Perhaps we should inscribe it with the names of everyone who sits on it, with your name at the top. You are part of the fabric of this place.'

The log becomes a welcome resting place, used by both me and others who stop by to chat with them under the bridge. It is sitting on this log that I get daily news of happenings along the canal. One day in early March, Nick tells me that a woman asked him for help retrieving her mobile out of the water. Nick didn't want to enter the canal as he didn't have any means of getting dry but he offered his arm for her to lean on and she managed to dive in and find her phone. She came back later with some tobacco to thank him.

On another occasion, I comment on how peaceful it is down by the canal. 'It wasn't peaceful earlier,' Nick says earnestly. Then he proceeds to tell me how a young woman, who had been staring blankly into the canal for a long time, slid into the icy water in what seemed to be a suicide attempt. Some passers-by dragged her out and called the police. But when the police arrived, the girl was terrified and slipped back into the water, crossing over to the opposite bank.

'I could see she was really scared of the police so I crossed over the bridge and sat down beside her and just talked to her.'

'What did you say?' I ask.

'I said, "You've got to look beyond the police uniform. There's a person in there who's trying to help you." She didn't say anything but I could tell she was listening. Then I said, "Forget about the past and forget the future. The only thing that matters is the here and now. Look at me! I'm a tramp living under a bridge. I could decide to disappear into the water in despair or I could get up, dust myself down and carry on." You know me, I just went on talking, and the police were good, they held back, and eventually the ambulance came and took her away.'

And so the relationships of giving and caring that were so palpable in the park seem to be reconstituting themselves under the bridge. But Nick and Pascal's relationship to their new dwelling place feels different, not least because their new home is so much more public.

'It's like a motorway here at weekends,' Nick declares. 'There's the fast lane – that's the canal; the middle lane – that's the towpath; the slow lane – that's the upper path; and then the hard shoulder. We're stuck here on the hard shoulder.'

When they were in the park, they could retreat into the undergrowth and hardly ever moved far from the hornbeams. Now that they are out of it, both they and I seem to have become more mobile, and as Bachi slowly emerges from his grief he too is walking around the park once more. One day we bump into each other and decide to walk together. My eyes are pinned to the bark and lichens; his are darting from dog to dog. 'There's Rex!' he exclaims, pointing to a Dobermann. 'Oh, and Gus – he's half Alsatian – and that's Juliette,' he says as a German shepherd dog comes bounding towards him. Soon a small bulldog called Wu is circling Bachi excitedly and refusing to go off with its owner, whilst a bouncy mixed terrier called Nigel joins in. Jasper, Bobby, Nelson, Loki, Maisy, Barnie, Dulcie, Oscar and Dexter all make appearances. 'They're all Lizzie's friends,' Bachi reminisces.

'You should get a new dog,' I suggest.

'I will, but only when I'm doing it for the dog and not for myself,' he answers.

Later I text him with the argument that Lizzie, being a generous soul, would surely have wanted him to be happy with another dog. He agrees but says he is not ready.

As winter morphs into spring, my walks have become more and more extensive and many of them are with Nick. 'You've gone a bit bush!' he tells me, referring to the fact that I am outside so much of the time. On another occasion he announces, 'We've decided we're going to give you a hobo certificate for life. You can put it amongst your university qualifications!'

'Well, I like to wander,' I say.

'I've been wandering all my life,' he replies. 'Even when I'm sitting down I'm wandering in the mind, but this is a different type of wandering. Thank you for getting me walking again. It reminds me how much I enjoy it. I never intended to put down roots in the park in the way we did, even if, when I go back, it feels like a part of me has been taken away. By this time next year I plan to be off . . . I'd like to walk along the canal paths of Britain – perhaps down to Cornwall or up to

Scotland. Pascal is welcome to join me if he wishes. This is a rehearsal in a way.'

While most of our walks are along the towpath or in the back streets of Maida Vale, occasionally we stray back into the park and visit their old dwelling place.

'It feels like returning home,' Nick says as we approach the hornbeams one spring evening, passing the bramble, hawthorn and nettles that edge the secret passage. It is late April, exactly a year since I first met Nick and Pascal. The cow parsley is burgeoning once more and the crab apple trees are back in blossom. 'I'd like to sleep here one last night before I go away,' he says quietly, 'but I'm ready to move on.'

I tell Nick that I want to write about the magic of this place and the time that he, Pascal, Bachi, Lizzie and myself shared here. He approves and tells me to feel free to write exactly what I want.

'It will be an archive of our time here,' he adds. 'It's about relationships. What matters is relationships.'

A few days later I settle under one of the hornbeams in a patch of sun. I have spotted two speckled mistle thrushes in the long grass and am watching a flock of starlings circle overhead. The parakeets are back in the high branches of the chestnut and the crows don't seem to have ever been away. The hornbeam is atwitter with the sound of goldfinches and in the background I catch the plaintive cry of the gibbons. I am just pouring some coffee into my old tin mug when a woman walks past.

'What a perfect place to start the day,' she comments brightly. 'There even used to be people living here, you know.'

'Really?' I say, and I watch her wander off, smiling in the knowledge that while Nick and Pascal may no longer be here physically, this place will forever be imbued with their presence.

Thank-Yous from
Nick and Pascal

Abdulla – Salaam and thank you.

Adam and family – As Van Morrison reminds us: no guru, teacher or method needed.

Alice and Fracescu – For your gifts of food and kindness itself.

Ajuna, Gloria, Amelia, Julia and Dan – Brazil 3–Italia 3. That's the best of all score draws x

Anais – Deus Ex Machina plus hot water. Perfect!

Andrea of Angola – Warm heart, warm smiles, warm spirit!

Andrew and Nicky – Thank you for your gifts – gentle of mind and warm of heart.

Andrew M – Thank you for your article in the *Spectator* and the chat.

Andrew and crew (London Waterbus Company, Regent's Canal) – Thanks for your wave and smile and hard-boiled eggs.

Angie of Islington – Your angelophany + eternal logos = cottage pie!

Anne, Bandit and Alice Cooper – Our love to you.

Antonia – The weather may have spoilt the notes but whatever you wrote, thank you.

Arie – Who wished us joy and happiness – straight back to you, Arie!

Audrey – Warming food, conversations and jackets in mid-winter – thank you.

Bachi and Lizzie – Never separated, not by death. A lovely man and memorable dog.

Barnaby – Enjoyed your Tokyo stories of guitars, memories and S&M!

Barry, Nicole, John and Laura – Argentos, chimps, bananas plus your love.

Briel – Thank you, Gabriel, for E. L. Doctorow's *Ragtime*, money and warming hearts.

Bruce and Rosie, Catherine and Baxter – Sunday-morning conversations from devilled kidneys to sweet biscuits and Walter Benjamin's *One Way Street*. Forgive me, guys – 'It is better to have loved and lost than never to have loved at all.'

Carlos – 'In order to truly live, we must first die.' You seem to have transcended that paradox. Thank you for your companionship. Hari Rama.

Cathy and Alex plus dog – Your home-made cooking and baking has been good for our health but the best recipe is your love, Cathy.

Cathy – Running past with your T-shirt which says 'Yes! Yes! Yes!'

Cecelia – Still telling truth to power through the arts. Thank you for the Herman Melville book and enriching conversations.

Charlotte – A Christmas box of love. Clearly naturals such as you don't do panettones by halves, thankfully!

Christian, Shaun and Drew (police) – Fair men and women who navigate daily our often unfair streets. No greater love than to lay down your life so that others can remain safe.

Cornelius – Kind and generous man whose words match his deeds and so 'fulfil the book'.

Costa plus Alsatians – Peace of mind is a constant.

Cowshift – A rescuer of abandoned dogs. A gentle soul with his four-legged alter ego found in Mumbai.

Clare and Dave – Thank you for your generosity of heart and mind.

Danish men × 3 – Thank you for Isaac Babel's *You Must Know Everything* and the astonishing gift that came with it.

Donna – You've 'loved thy neighbour as thyself' and the rest is just commentary.

Donovan and family – Warm winds hail you homewards to the sound of Caribbean church bells. Best wishes for your marriage.

Elana and family – An Anglo–Russian partnership coping very well with the curse of living in interesting times. Love.

Elisabeth the jogger – Silence is golden.

Emma, Denis and Julius – Together with little Alice we will slip past the smooth, cold surface of the looking glass and find ourselves in Wonderland, where everything is at once so familiar and recognisable, yet so strange and uncommon. (Inspiration from Lewis Carroll, *Through the Looking-Glass*.)

Frances – Might take you up on that offer to camp in your garden in Somerset!

Gary and family – Wonderful gifts at Christmas, the very best being the awe on your five-year-old's face when he realised that grey squirrels climb, run and jump and that red squirrels can glide between trees too! Simple pleasures. Our privilege. Thank you.

Gary of Canada – Discussing birdwatching and the law.

Godfrey – Kosher bread, potatoes and leeks = your kindness. Shalom aleichem!

Gordon and Fiona from Aberdeen – In London for superspread Christmas. A Christmas lunch given with love!

Graham and family – Body warmers, boots and a peaceful countenance of the anima mundi.

Graham of Glasgow – Thank you and shalom.

Hasan I – Building a home here in dear Blighty. 'Cooked too much chicken for myself,' you said. Thank you.

Hassan II – Once you built dams around our world. Nowadays you leave your work where all people can meet in peace, the United Nations.

Heidi, Tanya and Titan the dog – Thank you for your warm souls, gifts of food and the dog-hunts for Titan!

Helen – 'Lover of books' – thank you for John Wyndham's *Seeds of Time*.

Henry (in memoriam) – A gifted artist and human being. A privilege to have met you.

Horatio and mother – We met under the hornbeams when Horatio was five years old. 'Love evolves.'

Hugo, Jack and family – You spoke of a Caribbean paradise, the importation of fine wines, the elixir of family life and an investigation into Elysian fields. Glad to hear you are now pain-free, Hugo, at last. We try to pass on the love your family has given us over the years.

James (Jim) – Who works on the Regent's Canal and brought us a flask of hot water every day for years. Thank you, Jim, for the aqua caelestis.

Jan and son – Chocolate cake and warm hearts.

Jita and Blake the dog – 'I conversed with the spiritual sun and saw HER on Primrose Hill' (William Blake). Maybe one of us will wait along the way for the other.

John and Laura, Violet and Yogi – You helped keep us healthy. The very best to you guys today and always.

Joseph – 'The bad news is: time flies. The good news is: you're the pilot!' Many congratulations on the gorgeous Louisa! A new baby for a new age.

Karl Drake – Park policeman in the early years. Thank you, Karl. Hope your family and the 'Kray Twins' are well and happy.

Katie: *On the Road*. You could say we met because of Jack Kerouac's book! Thank you for that.

Kennedy, Elizabeth and Peter – Vi Veri Universum Vivus Vici.

Lynette – We remember the kindness of you and your lovely brother, Henry.

Marek – Loved our conversations and the cheese too.

Mariam and Monk: Salamati, M&M!

> *The breeze at dawn has secrets to tell you.*
> *Don't go back to sleep.*
> *You must ask for what you really want.*
> *Don't go back to sleep.*
> *People are going back and forth across the doorsill*

where the two worlds touch.
The door is round and open.
Don't go back to sleep.

(Jalal al-Din Rumi, 'The Breeze at Dawn')

Martin – Thank you for the Christmas present of your book on Regent's Park.

Maryam – '"The time has come," the walrus said, "to talk of many things."' (Lewis Carroll, *Through the Looking-Glass*)

Michael – Thanks for your copies of the *Spectator*. Lechayim.

Mohammed – Ramadan bread from your mum. Salaam.

Monica and Brian – Hot food and conversation after dark. Thank you.

Neal and Carolina plus hounds: Your warm clothes still keep us warm even today. Thank you both very much indeed.

Nell B and family – 'For me, beauty is physical, so fixed in Time. Elegance is found in those diamonds of the mind's eye, so out of Time.' You seem to manage to possess both at the same moment! Love to you from us.

Nial – Waterproofs, pizza, hot tea and conversation. A gentle and very kind person. Thank you.

Nicholas – Loved your book, *You Are Here*, and our conversations over the years.

Nicholas of Warwickshire – Shalom aleichem to you, your sons and partner.

Nicholas B – No 'N', then no 'N and P'.

Nicky and Peter – Hot coffee and chocolate. Loved our tea and conversations over the years.

Oliver and Ross – Babies, batteries and Ozzy banter. The best of days to you.

Paddy and brother – Hope you and your business still stand ever stronger.

Patina – Caring and standing by her old and infirm dad. Patina is to Sterling what character is to a fine face (Sarah T. Lee).

Paula and partner – We remember your many kindnesses and that of Andrew the golfer and your friends from Greece whose names have flown away.

Penny – Variation and adaptation, as you well know, is what makes us a wonderful species of earth dweller. Love to you.

Raoul and family – Thank you for the batteries and radios. 'Do not disturb!'

Roger of Eye – Your holistic solution to my injury was wonderful. Many thanks for that and our conversations.

Ronnie and family – You've never forgotten us. We wish you peace of mind forever.

Rory – Enjoyed our conversations and hope you are well.

Rumbi and Damien – Many thanks to you, Rumbi, for your pragmatic help. You and Damien are St Mungo's Übermensch.

Sandford (Sandy), partner and Muttley – Rat-catching, cheese and maker of movies. God Bless America!

Scarlett – Hot chocolate and cake. 'I AM.' Just you and I sitting in the Garden, wet with rain.

Shaun and Cathy – Books and pralines. Yep!

Shaun and Elizabeth with Zavia, Theo and Shanti – Congratulations on your marriage and your kind-heartedness to us.

Sheila – Conversations on adults, children, walking and Being.

Shirley, Julia, Bren and the posse – Thanks for *Animal Farm*, home-made jam and wonderful conversations.

Sima and Abdulla – Thank you for R. L. Stevenson's *An Inland Voyage* box set. Long life to you both.

Song – Many thanks for the *Tao Te Ching*.

Stella and John – Best figs in the world. Thank you.

Steve – Thanks for the conversations we've had over many years. Good to see you fit and well. Wishing you peace of mind.

Steve, Lynette, their son and dog – Thanks for the hot-water bottles, home-made food and limitless kindness.

Sue ('The Hat') – It was the best of times, it was the worst of times, as Dickens would say.

Taybah – Many thanks for your wholesome food and nature.

Tim and Kate – Still holding hands after many a step together.

Victoria – Hope you get to see your family in Argentina.

Vivian and Redman – Whistle! I know you know how!

Wan-Hue Park – Whose smile does just as much good as her gifts of food! Wishing you a full recovery after your operation.

William – Beautiful man with a tattoo of the Sistine Chapel on his chest. Love to you.

Thanks also to all the nameless people who have brought us food, clothing and equipment over the years. Your kindness is not forgotten.

Acknowledgements

This book would not exist were it not for the openness with which Nick, Pascal and Bachi welcomed me into their lives, shared their stories and trusted me to render our collective experience into writing. The time we spent together under the hornbeams has left an indelible imprint on my life. Thanks also to Lizzie for her memorable and endearing doggish ways.

Heartfelt thanks to Denis and Julius who accompanied me through the living and writing of the book and adapted to the unusual eating schedules that this entailed.

Thank you also to all those who commented on drafts, especially Frances Pine, Rebecca Cassidy, Pierre Hodgson, Harriet Tarlo, Laura Tarlo-Ross, Bachi Harsh Mehta, Denis Vidal, Julius Tarlo Vidal and my agent, Emily Sweet. Emily believed in this book from the start and has been an invaluable source of encouragement, wisdom and support at every stage of the writing process. Thank you also to my editor, Fiona Crosby, for tuning into the book with such care and my copy-editor, Silvia Crompton, and the wider team at Faber for bringing the book to fruition.

Finally, I would like to acknowledge the role of Regents Park in this story and thank all those who make it the extraordinary place it is, from its gardeners, litter-pickers, volunteers and other staff to the birds, animals, trees, flowers and people passing through. Where else in London can you hear the haunting call of the gibbons over breakfast?